NEW HORIZONS
IN FORENSIC PSYCHOTHERAPY

FORENSIC PSYCHOTHERAPY MONOGRAPH SERIES
Series Editor: Professor Brett Kahr
Honorary Consultant: Dr Estela V. Welldon

Other titles in the Series

NEW HORIZONS IN FORENSIC PSYCHOTHERAPY

Exploring the Work of Estela V. Welldon

Edited by

Brett Kahr

Routledge
Taylor & Francis Group

LONDON AND NEW YORK

First published 2018 by Karnac Books Ltd.

Published 2018 by Routledge
2 Park Square, Milton Park, Abingdon, Oxon OX14 4RN
711 Third Avenue, New York, NY 10017, USA

Routledge is an imprint of the Taylor & Francis Group, an informa business

British Library Cataloguing in Publication Data

A C.I.P. for this book is available from the British Library

ISBN: 9781782205050 (pbk)

Edited, designed, and produced by Communication Crafts

In loving memory of
two brilliant and much cherished comrades:

Professor Gill McGauley, who died on 13 July 2016,
and
Dr Alan Corbett, who died on 22 December 2016.

Each contributed a chapter to this book.

Each left us far too soon.

"You do not need medicines to make people better . . .
You can heal them with your personality. Please remember this."

A South African patient to Dr Ismond Rosen, circa mid-1940s,
quoted in his unpublished autobiography, Along the Way

CONTENTS

SERIES EDITOR'S FOREWORD

The Karnac Books "Forensic Psychotherapy Monograph Series" owes its inspiration entirely to Dr Estela V. Welldon.

I first became Dr Welldon's student in 1987—fully thirty years ago—and I remain a student to this day.

Estela opened up enormous new horizons for me and for so many of my colleagues in the mental health field by having championed, if not created, the discipline of forensic psychotherapy. I shall never forget Estela's uplifting teaching, and her impassioned clarion call that we must endeavour to offer *treatment* for criminals, not *punishment*. Estela inspired us not only by her clinical brilliance but, above all, by her humanitarian posture.

In previous centuries, physicians referred to such violent patients as "Criminal Lunatics" (Anonymous, 1861, p. 31), many of whom would be incarcerated for life or even executed for their crimes. Dr Welldon never denied either the criminality or the lunacy of the forensic patient, but, by contrast, she championed the right of such offenders to be treated with respect, in spite of the fact that they had never treated their victims in such a manner.

Ten years after first having met Estela, I received a most kind invitation from Karnac Books to edit a monograph series devoted entirely to the field of forensic psychotherapy. I accepted this unique opportunity with gratitude, but I insisted that I would do so only if Dr Welldon could be appointed as Honorary Consultant to the series. This request met with no resistance whatsoever, and to my good fortune, Estela offered her benign and helpful support across the next twenty years, as we published titles on such diverse topics as murder, paedophilia, psychotherapy in prisons, violence as a public health epidemic, dangerous children, dangerous adolescents, and so much more.

As Estela has had to navigate a busy professional life of patients, lectures, conferences, organisational leadership, media appearances, and book projects of her own, I turned to her for guidance about the monograph series only sparingly. But whenever I required her counsel, she offered it with graciousness and with generosity. Somehow, since the publication of our first forensic monograph in 2001, we have now produced eighteen rather choice titles that have, I hope, helped the field of forensic psychoanalysis and forensic psychotherapy to grow just that bit bigger.

One editorial moment stands out above all others, and it conveys, I believe, something about the loving, embracing, independent mind and disposition of Estela Welldon.

Several years ago, we received a proposal from the very eminent American psychiatrist Dr Barry Maletzky, a long-standing leader in the treatment of serious sexual perversions, for a book about the understanding of paedophilia and other sexual offences. Although sympathetic to psychodynamic ideas, Dr Maletzky draws upon a very wide range of methods in his efforts to help those dangerous people who have perpetrated acts of gross abuse. As Karnac Books occupies a unique position as the world's most noted publisher of *psychoanalytic* books, and as we conceived our "Forensic Psychotherapy Monograph Series" as an exclusively *psychoanalytically* orientated venture, I became quite uncertain as to whether we should recommend Dr Maletzky's excellent book, in spite of my multi-decade admiration for his work.

I discussed the matter with Estela, who replied in straightforward Welldonian tones: "Don't be so ridiculous. Serious sexual offences are such difficult illnesses to treat. We must learn from *everybody*, whether they are psychoanalysts or not." The tremendous wisdom of Estela's immediate response encouraged me to recommend Dr Maletzky's (2016) book for publication, and I remain extremely pleased to have done so.

All of the chapters in this volume and, indeed, all of the books in this monograph series, endeavour to shed light on some of the ugliest aspects of human nature. And we trust that the current collection—a Festschrift for Dr Welldon—will be of use and of inspiration to forensic mental health professionals, irrespective of theoretical background, training, or accent.

Dr Welldon has not only inspired an entire book series and a professional training but, of greatest importance, a new branch of specialisation within world mental health. We hope that the volume under consideration, *New Horizons in Forensic Psychotherapy: Exploring the Work of Estela V. Welldon*, will pay fitting tribute to the contributions of our unparalleled leader and muse, in the hope that future generations will benefit from her warmth and genius, as we have done.

REFERENCES

Anonymous (1861). Criminal Lunatics. *Medical Critic and Psychological Journal*, 1, 31–37.

Maletzky, Barry (2016). *Sexual Abuse and the Sexual Offender: Common Man or Monster?* London: Karnac Books.

Professor Brett Kahr
Series Editor
London

ACKNOWLEDGEMENTS

I wish to express my deepest thanks to Dan Welldon, son of Dr Estela Welldon, and to his wonderful partner Joanna Hall, and to their beautiful daughter Isabella Maria Welldon, for their long-standing support of this project. Dan not only approved the plan to organise a surprise Festschrift in his mother's honour and offered warm encouragement throughout the process, he also created the magnificent portrait for the front cover: one of the many precious moments captured by this masterful photographer. I thank Dan and Jo for years of much valued friendship and camaraderie.

Naturally, I extend my huge appreciation to the accomplished contributors to this volume. We have all grown up professionally in the Welldonian orbit, and our paths have overlapped pleasantly at so many conferences and meetings and social functions across the decades. As someone who has only ever worked part-time in forensic mental health, I have the utmost admiration for these consummate colleagues who, daily, make Great Britain a safer and saner country. I salute you all: Alan, Anna, Carine, David, Gill, Gwen, Paul, Richard, and Ronnie.

No author could function without the wonderful support of Karnac Books, who commissioned the "Forensic Psychotherapy Monograph Series" in 1997 and who have supported this library so lovingly since the appearance of the first volumes in 2001. Mr Oliver Rathbone—the very best of publishers—has long championed this monograph series, and with graciousness, he even agreed to keep this particular volume secret, so that we could all club together to give Estela Welldon a birthday surprise. I offer my deepest appreciation to Oliver for all that he has done to foster psychological publishing worldwide, and to his wonderful team, especially Ms Cecily Blench, Ms Constance Govindin, Mr Fernando Marques,

Mr Alex Massey, Ms Siobhan Mulcahy, Ms Kate Pearce, Mrs Rachel Rathbone, Ms Taneisha Smith, Mr Richard Szymczak, and Dr Rod Tweedy. It also gives me the greatest pleasure to convey my deepest thanks to Mr Eric King and Mrs Klara Majthényi King of Communication Crafts for their spectacular work as the most skilled and convivial of copy-editors.

As ever, I thank my family and, in particular, my wife Kim. I shall never forget the first time that she and Estela and I met for supper many years ago. Kim struggled, at first, to decipher Estela's wonderfully resonant Argentinean accent, but after the dinner, she whispered to me, "I could barely understand a word she said, but I had one of the very best evenings in my entire life!"

ABOUT THE EDITOR AND CONTRIBUTORS

Gwen Adshead is a forensic psychiatrist and psychotherapist. She trained at St George's Hospital Medical School in the University of London, at the Institute of Psychiatry, and also at the Institute of Group Analysis. She is trained as a group therapist and as a mindfulness-based cognitive therapist, and she has also been trained in mentalization-based therapy. For nearly twenty years she worked as a Consultant Forensic Psychotherapist at Broadmoor Hospital, running psychotherapeutic groups for offenders and working with staff around relational security and organisational dynamics. She now works in a medium secure unit in Hampshire. She also holds a master's degree in Medical Law and Ethics, and she maintains a research interest in moral reasoning and how this links with "bad" behaviour. Gwen Adshead has published a number of books, including *Ethical Issues in Forensic Mental Health Research* (with Dr Chris Brown) and *A Matter of Security: The Application of Attachment Theory to Forensic Psychiatry and Psychotherapy* (with Professor Friedemann Pfäfflin), as well as over one hundred papers, book chapters, and commissioned articles on forensic psychotherapy, ethics in psychiatry, and attachment theory as applied to medicine and to forensic psychiatry. She was honoured with the President's Medal from the Royal College of Psychiatrists in July 2013, for services to psychiatry. And she is the Visiting Gresham Professor of Psychiatry for 2014–2017.

Alan Corbett began his career in social work and then trained in psychoanalytic psychotherapy with adults at the Guild of Psychotherapists, and in forensic psychotherapy at the Portman Clinic in London. He received his doctoral degree in clinical science from the University of Kent. Corbett co-founded the unique charity Respond, which became the first organisation in Great Britain devoted exclusively to the provision of psychotherapeutic treatment for men, women, and children who struggle with learning disabilities and intellectual disabilities. His many publications include *Witnessing Nurturing Protesting: Therapeutic Responses to Sexual Abuse of People with Learning Disabilities*, co-authored by Tamsin Cottis and Stephen Morris, followed by two solo-authored books, *Disabling Perversions: Forensic Psychotherapy with People with Intellectual Disabilities* and, ultimately, *Psychotherapy with Male Survivors of Sexual Abuse: The Invisible Men*. Corbett devoted a great deal of creative energy to many psychotherapeutic institutions in Great Britain and Ireland and served, *inter alia*, as a member of the Board of the International Association for Forensic Psychotherapy and as a Trustee of the Institute of Psychotherapy and Disability. Shortly before his death, Respond established an Alan Corbett award in his honour, and the Institute of Psychotherapy and Disability appointed him a Fellow. Sadly, Dr Corbett died in 2016 after a long illness. He will be much mourned by his many friends and colleagues.

Richard Curen is Consultant Forensic Psychotherapist at Respond in London, where he has worked since 2002. At Respond, he leads the forensic service for young people and adults with intellectual disabilities or autism, providing risk analysis and risk assessment, forensic psychotherapy treatment, as well as training, supervision, and consultancy. He trained at the Gestalt Centre in London and at the Portman Clinic, and he holds qualifications from Birkbeck, University of London, in management, as well as qualifications in Strategic Leadership and Management from the Tavistock and Portman NHS Trust. Richard Curen also works in private practice as a psychotherapist and as a consultant and clinical supervisor in statutory, private, and third sector organisations. He runs reflective practice groups and supervises teams of individual clinicians across the United Kingdom. Previously, he held a post as Honorary Psychotherapist in the Fitzjohn's Unit at the Tavistock and Portman NHS Trust, working with personality-disordered, severely ill, and complex patients. He is a Board Member of the International Association for Forensic Psychotherapy and a member of the Institute of Psychotherapy and Disability and of the National Organisation for the Treatment of Offenders. He is a Registered Member of the British Association for Counselling and Psychotherapy, and he has published widely and spoken at international conferences. He has also trained other professionals throughout Europe.

Ronald Doctor trained as a psychiatric register on the University College London Psychiatric Training Scheme and then became Senior Registrar at the Tavistock and Portman NHS Trust, where he had the good fortune to be tutored by Dr Estela Welldon. At the same time, he trained at the Institute of Psycho-Analysis in London. He now works as Consultant Psychiatrist in Medical Psychotherapy at the West London Mental Health NHS Trust and as a psychoanalyst in private practice. He has held a number of roles in both undergraduate and postgraduate medical education, which have included that of College Tutor for the Charing Cross Core Psychiatric Training, as well as that of Training Programme Director of the West London Higher Training in Medical and Forensic Psychotherapy, and as Site Coordinator of undergraduate medical education at Imperial College in the University of London, where he has also held the post of Honorary Clinical Lecturer. He has also held positions in the Psychotherapy Faculty of the Royal College of Psychiatrists, including that of Academic Secretary, during which time he and Estela Welldon organised a successful joint conference on "Terror in the Mind" in Venice, Italy, sponsored by the Royal College of Psychiatrists and the International Association for Forensic Psychotherapy. He has also served as Chair of the Association for Psychoanalytic Psychotherapy in the NHS, which spearheaded the inauguration of the Savoy Conference; and he has served as Treasurer of the International Association for Forensic Psychotherapy. Additionally, he has been the Chair of the NHS Liaison Committee of the British Psychoanalytical Society. He has edited two books: *Dangerous Patients: A Psychodynamic Approach to Risk Assessment and Management*, and *Murder: A Psychotherapeutic Investigation*, both published in the Karnac Books "Forensic Psychotherapy Monograph Series".

Brett Kahr has worked in the mental health field for over thirty-years, during which time he had the privilege of being one of Dr Estela Welldon's students in the late 1980s and early 1990s. He is Senior Fellow at Tavistock Relationships at the Tavistock Institute of Medical Psychology in London and also Senior Clinical Research Fellow at the Centre for Child Mental Health, in London. He is Consultant Psychotherapist to The Balint Consultancy and, additionally, Consultant in Psychology to The Bowlby Centre. Trained in psychology, psychotherapy, and also in medical history, he is Trustee of the Freud Museum London and also of Freud Museum Publications. In 2009, he received an appointment as Honorary Visiting Professor in the Department of Media, Culture and Language in the School of Arts at the University of Roehampton, attached to the Arts and Humanities Research Council network "Media and the Inner World", in recognition of his contributions to psychoanalysis and the media, having previously served as Consultant Psychotherapist to BBC Radio 2 and as Spokesperson for the BBC mental health campaign "Life 2 Live". In 2017, he became Visiting Professor in the Faculty of Media and Communication at Bournemouth University. Author or editor of nine books, his study *D. W. Winnicott: A Biographical Portrait* won the Gradiva Award for Biography, and his book *Sex and the Psyche* became a Waterstone's Non-Fiction Bestseller and a *Sunday Times* Book Club selection. His book *Tea with Winnicott* was chosen as one of the "Books of the Year" by *The Guardian* newspaper. He serves as Series Editor of the Karnac Books "Forensic Psychotherapy Monograph Series" and as Series Co-Editor of "The History of Psychoanalysis Series" and also of "The Library of Couple and Family Psychoanalysis". His most recent book, *Coffee with Freud*, appeared in early 2017 and will be followed by an historical study, *Winnicott's* Anni Horribiles: *The Creation of 'Hate in the Counter-Transference'*. A registrant of both the British Psychoanalytic Council and the United Kingdom Council for Psychotherapy, he maintains a private practice for individuals and couples in Hampstead, North London.

Paul Kassman is the Director of Changing the Game CiC [Community Interest Company], a community sector organisation that develops and delivers therapeutically orientated interventions for gang members within the criminal justice system. Since 1989 he has worked in the community in London as a youth worker as well as a worker with drug users and offenders in the youth offending and probation services. Before setting up Changing the Game, Paul Kassman held policy roles within local government authorities and, latterly, at the office of the Mayor of London. Here he led on work designed to tackle gangs and youth violence, coordinating funding across local authorities, as well as working with criminal justice sector partners in the Police, Probation and Youth Justice Board to develop strategic approaches to address the impact of gangs in London. The programme Changing the Game, developed alongside Dr Carine Minne of the Portman Clinic, represents a new approach to gang members and their specific narratives.

Gill McGauley trained as a physician at St Bartholomew's Hospital Medical School in London and as a psychiatrist at St Thomas's Hospital in London. She then trained in medical psychotherapy at St George's Hospital in London, where she also worked as a Senior Registrar in Forensic Psychiatry. In addition to her work in psychotherapy, with a special interest in forensics, she also developed research expertise in attachment theory as applied to offending behaviour, and she obtained a major grant to study attachment representations in personality-disordered offender patients, which became the basis of her MD degree, completed under the supervision of Professor Peter Fonagy at University College London. She spent much of her professional life working and teaching at St George's Hospital Medical School in London, and, owing to her interest in medical education, she rose to the post as Head of the Centre for Clinical Education; she also held the position of Chair of the National Reference Group for Training and Education in Forensic Psychotherapy. Gill McGauley also served as Consultant Forensic Psychotherapist at Broadmoor Hospital, developing and chairing its first Department of Forensic Psychotherapy. After she left Broadmoor Hospital, she worked in two women's prisons—HM Prison Holloway and HM Prison Bronzefield—where she set up psychotherapy groups as well as a special project for high-risk female offenders. In 2016, she became Professor of Forensic Psychotherapy and Medical Education in the Central and North West London Foundation NHS Trust. Additionally, she held the post as Chair of the National Reference Group for Training and Education in Forensic Psychotherapy. She is also a past President of the International Association for Forensic Psychotherapy and, additionally, a recipient of the National Teaching Fellowship award from the Higher Education Academy. Her many publications include *Forensic Mental Health: Concepts, Systems, and Practice*, co-edited by Dr Annie Bartlett. Shortly before her death, she co-edited a textbook on *Forensic Psychotherapy* with Dr Jessica Yakeley. Sadly, Professor McGauley died in 2016, after a short illness, only weeks after having delivered her inaugural professorial lecture. Professor McGauley will be much missed by her many friends and colleagues in the field of forensic psychotherapy, which she developed over so many years.

David Millar is a retired Child and Adolescent Psychotherapist. He worked in the National Health Service in Essex for over thirty-five years in both out-patient and in-patient services. He undertook his child psychotherapy training and, later, his adult psychotherapy training at the Tavistock Clinic, in London, and he also trained in forensic psychotherapy at the Portman Clinic. Previously, he had worked in Tottenham, North London, for many years, as a teacher and a social worker. He is a founding member of the Centre for Psychoanalytic Studies at the University of Essex and a founding member of the International Association for Forensic Psychotherapy. David Millar has lectured widely in the United Kingdom and overseas. He is currently preparing a volume of his collected papers on the theme of hate.

Carine Minne is Consultant Psychiatrist in Forensic Psychotherapy at the Portman Clinic, Tavistock and Portman NHS Trust, in London and also at Broadmoor Hospital, West London Mental Health Trust. She trained as a psychoanalyst at the Institute of Psycho-Analysis, and she is a member of the British Psychoanalytical Society. In her work, she brings together the disciplines of forensic psychiatry and psychoanalysis to work both directly with offender patients in different settings and also, indirectly, through teaching, training, and lecturing to professionals from various disciplines, nationally and internationally. She is the Vice-President of the International Association for Forensic Psychotherapy. With Paul Kassman, she has developed "Changing the Game", a project designed to provide a therapeutic intervention specifically for gang members in prisons, in which group members have engaged one hundred per cent. Minne and Kassman will be adapting this project for delivery to gang members in the community.

Anna Motz is a psychoanalytic psychotherapist and Consultant Clinical and Forensic Psychologist with over twenty-five years of clinical experience with violent patients and the staff teams who work with them. She has a particular expertise in working with female offenders with histories of violence and trauma. She is Consultant for the Institute of Mental Health, for whom she has developed and delivered MSc, BSc, and in-house training programmes for staff working with women with personality disorders within the criminal justice and mental health services as part of the Knowing and Understanding Framework, and she delivers these trainings within clinics and prison settings. Anna Motz is the author of *The Psychology of Female Violence: Crimes Against the Body*, now in its second edition, as well as *Managing Self-Harm*, and also *Toxic Couples: The Psychology of Domestic Violence*. Her forthcoming book is entitled *Trauma: Women, Difference and the*

Criminal Justice System. She is Clinical Lead for the Family Assess-ment and Safeguarding Service, Oxford Health NHS Foundation Trust, where she evaluates and treats parents whose children are at risk of harm, and she acts as expert witness to the courts and presents evidence in both care proceedings and in criminal cases. A former President of the International Association for Forensic Psychotherapy, she is a supervisor for the Anna Freud Centre's mentalization-based treatment groups for men with antisocial personality disorder, as part of a randomised control trial. She is also a Visiting Lecturer at the Tavistock Centre as well as for the Clinical Psychology Doctoral Programme at the University of Oxford.

NEW HORIZONS
IN FORENSIC PSYCHOTHERAPY

Introduction

Estela at La Scala

Brett Kahr

A healthy star

Estela Valentina Welldon certainly knows how to make an impression.

I cannot be certain as to the reason quite why, back in 1936, her parents christened her "Estela Valentina", but she has undoubtedly come to live up to both of her forenames.

"Estela", derives from the Latin "stella", and subsequently from the Spanish "estrella", which translate as "star" or "heavenly body". We do not know the particular resonances associated with the moniker "Estela" in her birthplace, Mendoza, in Argentina, but nowadays, at least according to the "Urban Dictionary", the name "Estela" "only belongs to an attractive, outgoing, girl with a great smile who just wants to have a good time".[1] In modern Spanish-speaking countries, "*estrella*" also refers to celebrities and film stars.

Her second title, "Valentina", comes to us from the Latin "valens", which translates as "healthy" and "strong".

Anyone who has ever spent more than thirty seconds with Dr Estela Valentina Welldon will appreciate how our much-loved and much-cherished teacher, mentor, friend, and *inspiratrice* has come to embody these names, for we know of no stronger or more glittering star.

To those of us who have known Estela for nearly the whole of our professional lifetimes, as I have had the good fortune to do, it seems both extraordinary and shocking that on 3 November 2016, this remarkable woman celebrated her eightieth birthday. Apart from a few intimates, none of her colleagues had quite realised that she would soon be entering her *ninth* decade, because she still possesses all the vigour that we associate—perhaps unfairly—with youths in their twenties and thirties. In spite of her age, Estela still attends far more lectures, conferences, committee meetings, book launches, parties, and family gatherings than anyone else . . . and does so with unparalleled style, panache, humour, and joy.

Estela among the opera divas

How does one best describe Estela Welldon to those who have never had the privilege of meeting her? Although I have many wonderful tales to tell, none better captures the essence of Estela than our evening in Milan.

Roughly ten years ago, my wife—a professional singer—performed at La Scala, one of the world's most spectacular opera houses. To our delight, the management offered her some box seats for the opening gala. Having had the privilege of attending many of my wife's débuts, I invariably receive one or two complimentary tickets, but rarely a box, and rarely one at La Scala! As my wife and I discussed whom we might invite to share these special seats, she and I immediately blurted out "Estela!" simultaneously, because we knew of no one who would relish the experience more.

Over the decades, Estela and I have attended many operas and classical concerts in London, whether at the Royal Opera House, the London Coliseum, or the Barbican Centre; but I had never had the pleasure of inviting her to one of my wife's performances outside Great Britain before, and certainly not to Italy—Estela's spiritual home. Estela accepted the invitation with her typical enthusiasm, far more excited by the prospect that my wife had received an invitation to perform at La Scala than for her own pleasure at being our honoured guest in the grand, curtained box.

On the appointed evening, Estela arrived at La Scala looking absolutely stunning. Had I a better knowledge of female fashions, I could, perhaps, offer a fuller description of her clothes. Alas, I cannot tell you exactly what she wore, but she looked truly beautiful: elegant, stylish, and tasteful, and in no way grand or upstaging the women singing that night. Estela had, as always, judged her wardrobe perfectly.

During the performance, Estela sipped champagne and enjoyed the evening thoroughly, as did I; and afterwards, we went backstage, past the fearsome security guards, and collected my wife from her dressing room, before proceeding to a post-opening-night party organised by the management.

Although Estela now speaks fluent Italian, at that point she had not yet mastered the language and still took lessons, so I did worry as to how she would fare at the party: a boisterous, boozy affair packed with opera singers, musicians, managers, Italian financiers, and assorted spouses from all over the world.

But I had worried in vain. Within a matter of minutes, Estela sat down at one of the large tables, with a delicate, fluted champagne glass in hand, and before long a throng of some of the most glamorous, well-attired opera divas encircled her, asking her questions about *her* dress! One of my wife's co-stars, a gorgeous young Japanese singer, whispered in my ear, "Who *is* that woman? She's *so* amazing!"

Over the course of the evening, everyone came to pay homage to Dr Welldon, the Argentinean-born, London-based, Italian-speaking forensic psychiatrist whose thick accent proved no barrier towards either comprehension or enchantment.

My wife and I smiled. I certainly did not need to look after Estela at this post-show party. She managed superbly well on her own.

These talented singers had, only hours before, kept the large, packed audience of some three thousand people at the Teatro alla Scala completely enraptured. And now Estela, who has never sung a note in her life, kept the entertainers entertained—indeed, enthralled. I know of no other mental health professional who possesses such an extraordinary capacity to engage and to enliven. I watched in awe. And Estela did very little, other than tell a story or two in a calm, quiet voice . . . but with a musicianship of delivery that would rival the best conductors and composers.

The next morning we rang Estela at her hotel and asked whether she would like to join us for lunch. To our regret, she had to refuse, as she had only just received a similar invitation from the director of the opera—one of the busiest men in the world, and one who does not socialise lightly. A sceptic might wonder why on earth he would wish to have lunch with a foreign psychiatrist, whom he had only just met the night before, when he could have spent time planning his next ten productions with the management of La Scala? And yet, he chose

Estela as his dining companion, and the two remained in contact for years to come. I must confess that the news of Estela's midday plans hardly came as a surprise: we knew only too well that she emits such an aura that even those with no free time in their diaries always create a space for her!

At St. Bartholomew's Hospital

Estela Welldon's remarkable capacity to relate to people, to debate with people, and to inspire people reached its professional apotheosis when, in 1992, she hosted the first conference of the International Association for Forensic Psychotherapy (IAFP). With great organisational genius, Estela founded the IAFP by gathering together all of her friends, colleagues, and students with whom she had worked over the decades; and she managed, without much difficulty, to entice us all together, to explore whether psychoanalytic thinking could inform mental health work with dangerous offender patients, in the hope of providing a more humane, less punitive approach to care and rehabilitation. Naturally, we responded with alacrity and filled the large lecture theatre at St. Bartholomew's Hospital in London to capacity.

As this inaugural conference unfolded, those of us in the audience sat enraptured as we listened to a stellar cast of psychotherapists, psychiatrists, psychoanalysts, and police officers speak about their work in high-security hospitals, prisons, and courtrooms. With a characteristic eye on the future, Estela had extended invitations not only to forensic celebrities of the day, such as the pre-eminent Dr Murray Cox, but also to students in training, several of whom served as speakers on the platform.

In many respects this landmark conference mirrored the now legendary parties that Estela hosts regularly at her home.

Often, when attending dinners at the houses of fellow mental health professionals, one arrives with a certain amount of trepidation, often wishing that one had refused the invitation in advance. One then spends two hours engaged in somewhat pretentious conversation about the failings of the Labour Party while eating perfectly decent, but not very inspiring, food, and while drinking perfectly adequate, but not very special, wines. The other guests will invariably be members from one's own training organisation, with very few "outsiders" in attendance.

Estela's parties could not be more different. The best wines flow freely, and the tables heave with the most scrumptious delicacies that one can find nowhere else. And the guests, ranging in age from twenty to ninety-five years, include not only mental health professionals from every institution and every school of thought imaginable (including Lacanians) but also musicians, politicians, writers, singers, photographers, sculptors, film stars, academics, judges, peers of the realm, as well as impecunious students and trainees. The musicians in attendance will often perform "live", and later in the evening Estela displays her remarkable skill as a tango dancer!

The launch conference of the IAFP at St. Bartholomew's Hospital benefited hugely from Estela's extraordinary personality and from her years of training, knowing how, precisely, to throw the best of parties. Consequently, with a carefully chosen "cast list" and with riveting "performances" from the speakers, the IAFP début proved to be a "smash hit" and since that time, like all good shows, has enjoyed a long "run".

Estela looked after the delegates well, not only with excellent papers (i.e., "food for thought") but also with excellent comestibles. I shall never forget that just before lunchtime Dr Timothy Scannell, then Consultant Psychiatrist at St. Bartholomew's Hospital and one of the conference hosts (and, of course, one of Estela's greatest friends), stood up and spent at least ten minutes, perhaps longer, advising the audience in great detail about the best restaurants in the local area. Estela knew only too well that Tim, her fellow connoisseur of fine foods and wines, would steer us in the right direction; and she came to appreciate that in order for us to tolerate a long conference full of weighty papers about murderers, arsonists, rapists, and paedophiles, the delegates would have to be well cared for during mealtimes.

I hope that one can begin to appreciate the parallels between Estela in her hostess role as Honorary President for Life of the International Association for Forensic Psychotherapy, Estela as party-giver, and Estela, also, as guest at the Teatro alla Scala in Milan. On each of these occasions, I have had the privilege of marvelling at a woman who knows how to make an impression, who knows how to bring people together, and who knows how to forge and sustain intimate relationships over very long periods of time.

Indeed, as I write this little tribute, the members of the IAFP have just begun to depart for Gent, in Belgium, in time for the twenty-fifth anniversary conference! The IAFP has now flourished for two-and-a-half decades and will, in all likelihood, continue its work for many, many decades, if not centuries, to come . . . and all because of Estela.

How to plan a Festschrift in secrecy

Shortly after Estela's seventy-eighth birthday, I conceived the wish to prepare a Festschrift in honour of her upcoming eightieth anniversary, as a tiny expression of my love and gratitude for this woman who has taught me so much, over so long, with the most unstinting honesty and generosity. First of all, I approached Daniel Welldon, Estela's son, and received his warm blessing to pursue the project, insisting that he provide us with one of his wonderful photographs of his mother for the cover of the book.

I then spoke with Oliver Rathbone, the Publisher and Managing Director of Karnac Books, who shares my deep admiration for Estela Welldon and for her work, and who, in 2011, published Estela's landmark volume *Playing with Dynamite: A Personal Approach to the Psychoanalytic Understanding of Perversions, Violence, and Criminality* (Welldon, 2011), which appeared in the "Forensic Psychotherapy Monograph Series", for which Estela has served as Honorary Consultant since its inception. Oliver not only commissioned this Festschrift for Estela's eightieth birthday, but also, with great generosity, agreed to keep the book a secret so that we could present the finished product to Estela as a proper birthday surprise. I know of very few publishers who would willingly miss out on the opportunity for "advance publicity"; hence, Oliver deserves special credit for his thoughtfulness and kindness.

With the "green light" from the Welldon family and from Karnac Books, I then wrote to eight of the busiest forensic mental health professionals in town—Gwen Adshead, Alan Corbett, Richard Curen, Ronald Doctor, Gill McGauley, David Millar, Carine Minne, and Anna Motz—all of whom share my love for Estela and all of whom would claim Estela as their great, if not *greatest*, teacher. I invited each to contribute a chapter, explaining carefully and emphatically that in order to have the book printed in time for Estela's birthday, everyone would have to promise to meet the stringent deadline.

To my delight, each of the eight contributors responded to my request immediately. And as a bonus Carine Minne co-opted her colleague Paul Kassman as co-author of a wonderful chapter about psychotherapeutic work with gang members.

Happily, everyone submitted his or her chapter in good time! Having edited books previously, I can tell you that this constitutes a world record, as editors of multi-authored texts must invariably spend most of their time chasing chapter-writers. Fortunately, all of the authors had committed themselves to honouring Estela by contributing to this Festschrift, and consequently, in spite of their gargantuan workloads in hospitals, prisons, and clinics, each of them has produced a sterling chapter that pays tribute to Estela's work and to her legacy.

Professor Gwen Adshead, the distinguished forensic psychiatrist and fellow Welldon admirer, completed a draft of her chapter almost immediately, and, with great thoughtfulness, she sent me a copy for my preliminary reactions. Gwen wrote a characteristically excellent, scholarly chapter, which places Estela Welldon's work squarely within the tradition of attachment theory; and it reads beautifully. I wrote back to Gwen enthusing about her chapter, explaining that I had only one reservation: throughout the draft chapter, she continued to refer to Dr Welldon not by her professional title but, rather, quite informally, as "Estela". I expressed a concern that in an academic, professional publication of this sort, it might seem too chatty to call the great lady by her first name. Gwen graciously wrote back to tell me that she would be happy to make any adjustments that might be required.

Over the next few months, the remaining seven chapters arrived. And to my delight, each and every author described our dedicatee in similar fashion as "Estela", rather than as "Welldon" or "Dr Welldon". Fortified by this group consensus, I happily agreed that throughout the course of this Festschrift we will all come to know the subject of our discussion by her first name, "Estela", meaning, quite simply, "star". And it seems most fitting that we should all be on a first-name basis with Estela, for she possesses that wonderful ability to make each of us feel as though we have a special relationship with her. One can only imagine how much her patients must have benefited, and still benefit, from this quality over more than fifty years of sustained clinical work.

In the pages that follow, readers will have the opportunity to learn about Estela's work, her contributions to forensic psychotherapy, and the ways in which her ideas, her teachings, and her writings have inspired the next generation of forensic practitioners to develop, expand, and apply Welldonian work in creative new directions. All of the authors of the chapters—once young Welldon students—have now become significant movers and shakers in the forensic mental health world, and I believe that none of us would have become as dynamic and as impactful without the guiding hand and loving encouragement afforded by Estela Valentina Welldon.

The chapters—all written with clarity and fortitude (including, I hope, my own)—speak for themselves. Our authors address a range of topics, providing descriptions of moving clinical encounters, contributions to theory and practice, applications of Welldonian work, and so much more. Throughout the course of these essays readers will come to learn about the new horizons in forensic psychotherapy (and its love-child, "forensic disability psychotherapy") as practised in hospitals, in prisons, in child guidance clinics, and even in private psychotherapy practices. We will engage with new developments in attachment theory, in traumatology, in gender studies, in research methodologies, and so much more. The very wide range of styles and accents contained herein represents not only the creativities of my colleagues, but also the ways in which Estela both engages with and celebrates diversity and richness in size and scope and accent.

Estela Welldon can easily trace her professional descent from Sigmund Freud. Her own training analyst, the brilliant Professor Horacio Etchegoyen, had undertaken his own training analysis with Dr Heinrich Racker, who had previously undergone analyses with, *inter alia*, Dr Jeanne Lampl-de Groot and Dr Theodor Reik—both patients of Sigmund Freud. Etchegoyen pursued a further analysis with Dr Donald Meltzer, who had the distinction of being Melanie Klein's last patient. Mrs Klein undertook *her* analysis with Dr Sándor Ferenczi and with Dr Karl Abraham: two of Sigmund Freud's closest colleagues. Hence, in terms of her analytic lineage, Estela can claim descent as a direct great-granddaughter of Freud several times over. Estela also studied at the world-famous Menninger Clinic in Topeka, Kansas, and enjoyed the protection of Dr Karl Menninger himself, analysed by Dr Franz Alexander and by Dr Ruth Mack Brunswick: the former, an analysand of Dr Hanns Sachs, one of the members of Freud's inner circle, and the latter, one of Freud's special patients and colleagues. "Dr Karl" had also met Freud in person, back in 1934 (e.g., Friedman, 1990). Thus, Estela Welldon sits staunchly within the very history of psychoanalysis itself.

In view of Estela's location amid these great pioneers, I can attest that she maintains a strong interest in the origins of the psycho-analytic profession, and, over the years, she has deeply encouraged me—indeed, gently nagged me on occasion—in my own endeavours as a psychoanalytic historian. Thus, in the first section of this Festschrift, I offer a painfully brief history of forensic psychoanalysis in what I have come to conceptualise as the "Pre-Welldonian Era". This chapter merely hints at some of the great contributions upon which Estela and her contemporaries have built, and this will, I hope, form the basis of a more detailed work in due course.

In the second section of this volume, which introduces readers to the landscape of modern forensic psychotherapy, David Millar treats us to one of the most heart-breaking but also most heart-warming and moving clinical accounts that I have ever read, about a young person called "Sanjay" who endured an immense amount of painful abuse and traumatisation in early childhood from multiple perpetrators. In later life, Sanjay internalised this violence by cutting his own skin with a knife and by sticking a burning cigarette into his eye, in a desperate attempt to gain some small degree of control over the management of his own body. Millar has provided us with the perfect clinical introduction to this Festschrift, because his case encapsulates the very essence of the day-to-day practice of forensic psychotherapy, treating the abused child within the abusive adult. In his chapter, Millar introduces us to the concept of "pasteurisation", noting sagaciously that our forensic patients have endured trauma of an infectious nature, and that the forensic psychotherapist must struggle to find a way of introducing the patient to something cleaner and fresher.

Afterwards, Gwen Adshead, a consummate forensic practitioner, pays tribute to Estela Welldon as the mother of our profession by reviewing Welldon's radical challenge to the orthodox psychoanalytic theory of perversion as a male preserve. Adshead explores Welldon's clinical researches—quite shocking when first presented to groups of male psychiatrists and psychoanalysts—which foreground the role of women in the genesis of forensic psychopathology. Helpfully, Adshead then demonstrates that much of Welldon's (1988) work, first advanced in her book *Mother, Madonna, Whore: The Idealization and Denigration of Motherhood*, has since received a great deal of empirical support from child development researchers and from those steeped in attachment theory. Adshead also argues for the expansion of psychological services for women offenders in distress.

In the third section, three distinguished colleagues explore the role of forensic psychotherapeutic work in the hospital setting. Ronald Doctor provides us with a truly jaw-dropping account of horrific acts of violence and about the complex way in which criminality becomes revealed in the course of psychodynamic investigation. Doctor also highlights the ways in which mental health professionals often succumb either to condemnation or to disbelief when working with extremely troubled and traumatised forensic patients. With great courage and honesty, he provides an extremely useful account of the painful countertransferential burdens that we, as clinicians, must struggle to endure in working with such tremendous psychological horror.

Thereafter, Gill McGauley, drawing upon her lengthy professional experience in hospital settings, reminds us that, for many perpetrators of violence, their days begin quite normally . . . and then, at quite unexpected moments, these men and women will commit unspeakably ghastly crimes. McGauley introduces us to the notion of the "prodrome", exploring the period leading up to the outbreak of the forensic moment in the mind of the patient, providing us with an astute and detailed diagnostic understanding of how broken attachment patterns and violent fantasies suddenly erupt into dangerous actions, which she has conceptualised as rather doomed attempts at self-cure.

Next, Anna Motz, who has embraced and developed Welldon's work on female offenders most creatively, provides a rich description of the chilling way in which early trauma and deprivation render human beings not only more vulnerable to the perpetration of forensic acts, but also far more likely to choose violent sexual partners. Her deft discussion of the toxic couple offers a chilling reminder of the ways in which psychopathology can be transmitted both spousally and then, after the birth of children, transgenerationally.

In the fourth section, Carine Minne and Paul Kassman report on their innovative intervention in a prison setting, examining the ways in which they have worked with highly violent gang members. The prisoners who participated in their novel psychotherapeutic group— mostly black men from impoverished, deprived immigrant families, besieged by broken attachments—had experienced, throughout their developmental years, racist attacks as well as copious "micro-aggressions", being regarded as inferior because of the colour of their skin. With tremendous compassion and sensitivity, the authors then investigate how these young boys would join gangs in a desperate effort to provide themselves with a false layer of security. Through their bold and sustained participation in this psychotherapeutic and psychoeducational project, many of these men became increasingly aware of the impact of their crimes and turned, in later years, to university study and to other healthier activities.

In the fifth section, the authors tackle the previously neglected subject of forensic disability psychotherapy—a growing area of concentration and interest within the wider forensic mental health community—studying the nature of men and women with intellectual disabilities who have committed offences, often of a sexual nature. Alan Corbett draws heavily upon the work both of Estela Welldon—the mother of forensic psychotherapy—and of Valerie Sinason—the mother of disability psychotherapy—to provide a helpful integration of these two specialities. Corbett offers particular appreciation not only of Welldon's efforts to work with offenders and with victims, but also celebrates her reluctance to split these categories in two, recognising that every offender will have suffered victimisation and that, likewise, every victim will have the capacity to retaliate by perpetrating an offence. Corbett praises Welldon as the inspirational, colourful psychotherapist whose vitality provides a brilliant contrast to the rather monochrome internal world of so many abused and disabled individuals.

In similar vein, Richard Curen, a fellow progenitor of the forensic disability psychotherapy movement, offers a thoroughly detailed and revealing analysis of the nature of risk assessment with a disabled offender, which often serves as the necessary prelude to more sustained, ongoing psychoanalytic work. Curen provides us with a vast amount of clinical evidence—at times grimly chilling—reminding us that our patients do not become perpetrators accidentally. In careful clinical tones, he traces the all too numerous traumata that had propelled his patient to commit ghastly sexual crimes.

In the sixth and final section of this Festschrift, I offer a clinical chapter of my own, providing an account of the way in which training in forensic psychotherapy becomes absolutely indispensable for working in a community-based independent practice. We tend to think of forensic psychotherapy as the sole preserve of the institutionally based clinician, but I hope to underscore that a forensic sensibility and a forensic lens can greatly enhance one's capacities to work with the criminal aspects of patients whose crimes will never be reported to the police.

The horror of loss

Tragically, during the editorial process two of our cherished contributors, Professor Gill McGauley and Dr Alan Corbett, died. With cruel irony, both succumbed to the very same fatal illness. Heartbreakingly, neither Alan nor Gill had reached the age of sixty years.

In view of the verve and zest with which both Gill and Alan had replied to my initial invitation to write chapters, and in view of the fact that both enjoyed truly rich professional and personal lives, no one could have foreseen the double tragedy that two middle-aged people, each in the prime of life and at the peak of creative potency, would be snatched away.

Certainly, none of us could have foreseen that Estela would lose two of her most prized students and that the Corbett and McGauley families and, indeed, the mental health profession at large, would have to endure the passing of two such remarkably loving and brilliant people. The unfair deaths of Gill and Alan cast a horrible shadow over our hope of providing a Festschrift of pure joy for Estela.

But those of us who have had the privilege of studying with Estela, of training with her, and of learning from her know only too well that Estela never idealises the world and never assumes that pleasure will shield us from pain or that life will be untouched by death. As a full-time forensic mental health specialist, Estela knows, only too chillingly, that horror—often *violent* horror—may befall anyone at any time. And because of this clear recognition of the reality principle, she has taught us to immerse ourselves in the world with full gusto, knowing that trauma and tragedy cannot be avoided on the human journey.

Estela at eighty

The queen of indefatigability, Estela Welldon remains a far more energetic, creative, and productive member of the mental health community than anyone else in our midst. In spite of her devotion to her family and to her friends, and her love of opera and travel, she still finds time to work with patients, to facilitate clinical supervision, to lecture all over the world, and to minister to her professional "baby": the much-cherished International Association for Forensic Psychotherapy, the organisation that she founded more than twenty-five years ago.

On Saturday, 5 November 2016—two days after her actual birthday—a large number of family, friends, and colleagues gathered in the Great Hall at BMA House, the headquarters of the British Medical Association, in Central London, to celebrate the great lady's eightieth year. As ever, Estela dressed magnificently, and she kept her audience enchanted, as a multitude of pictures of her life, taken by her extremely talented son, the photographer Dan Welldon, flashed on the screen behind her. At this wonderful party, Estela launched not one, but *two* new books, namely, *Sadomasochism in Art and Politics* (Welldon, 2016), an expansion of her earlier book on *Sadomasochism* (Welldon, 2002), and her beautifully, if provocatively, illustrated tome *Sex Now Talk Later* (Welldon, 2017), which encapsulates the very essence of Welldonianism. These new books now sit joyfully on the increasingly large shelf of Estela's writings, taking pride of place beside her classics, such as *Mother, Madonna, Whore: The Idealization and Denigration of Motherhood* (Welldon, 1988) and her much beloved *Playing with Dynamite: A Personal Approach to the Psychoanalytic Understanding of Perversions, Violence, and Criminality* (Welldon, 2011), not to mention the rich and useful edited volume, *A Practical Guide to Forensic Psychotherapy* (Welldon and Van Velsen, 1997).

At this memorable party, guests also learned that the Wellcome Library in London—the leading medical library in the United Kingdom—has agreed to house Estela's professional papers as part of their unparalleled archive of seminal figures in the history of health care. Currently in the process of being catalogued, these papers will become available to researchers in due time and will sit alongside the collections of such world-renowned figures in mental health as Dr John Bowlby, Mrs Melanie Klein, and Dr Donald Winnicott, as well as stellar figures in the history of medicine, including Sir Christopher Andrewes, Sir Ernst Chain, Sir Henry Dale, Sir George Godber, Sir Henry Head, Professor Archibald Hill, Sir William Arbuthnot Lane, Sir Thomas Lewis, Lord Moran of Manton [Charles McMoran Wilson], Sir George Pickering, Dr Marie Stopes, Dame Janet Vaughan, and others of this calibre.

To dearest Estela, we hope that you will enjoy these essays of tribute and love, and we all wish you a very happy eightieth birthday! On behalf of the fellow contributors and all of your many friends and colleagues around the world, we thank you for your generous lifetime of work, and we hope that the essays contained herein will serve as but a tiny expression of our deep appreciation for all that you have offered to us, and continue to do so.

NOTE

[1] www.urbandictionary.com/define.php?term=Estela [accessed on 2 April 2016].

REFERENCES

Friedman, Lawrence J. (1990). *Menninger: The Family and the Clinic*. New York: Alfred A. Knopf.

Welldon, Estela V. (1988). *Mother, Madonna, Whore: The Idealization and Denigration of Motherhood*. London: Free Association Books.

Welldon, Estela V. (2002). *Sadomasochism*. Duxford, Cambridge: Icon Books.

Welldon, Estela V. (2011). *Playing with Dynamite: A Personal Approach to the Psychoanalytic Understanding of Perversions, Violence, and Criminality*. London: Karnac Books.

Welldon, Estela V. (2016). *Sadomasochism in Art and Politics*. London: Author.

Welldon, Estela V. (2017). *Sex Now Talk Later*. London: Karnac Books.

Welldon, Estela V., and Van Velsen, Cleo (Eds.) (1997). *A Practical Guide to Forensic Psychotherapy*. London: Jessica Kingsley Publishers.

PART I

FORENSIC PSYCHOTHERAPY
IN THE PRE-WELLDONIAN ERA

"No intolerable persons" or "lewd pregnant women": towards a history of forensic psychoanalysis

Brett Kahr

> Do you not think that rage is a sickness of the soul?
>
> Claudius Galenus of Pergamon, "The Diagnosis and Treatment of the
> Affections and Errors Peculiar to Each Person's Soul", n.d.
> (Galen, n.d., p. 258).

> Shame and Diſgrace cauſe moſt violent paſſions, and bitter pangs.
>
> Democritus Junior [Robert Burton], *The Anatomy of Melancholy: What it
> is, with All the Kinds Causes, Symptomes, Prognostickes, & Seuerall Cures of
> it. In Three Partitions, with their Seuerall Sections, Members & Subſections,
> Philosophically, Medicinally, Historically, Opened & Cut Up*, 1660, Partition 1,
> Section 2, Member 3, Subſection 6. (Democritus Junior, 1660, p. 99).

The cruel treatment of the offender patient

Throughout much of history, human beings have treated offenders—vagrants, villains, outlaws, gangsters, hooligans, thugs, crooks, racketeers, or killers—with the utmost sadism, often punishing such people with a viciousness that far exceeded the original crime (Phillips, 1857; Bauman, 1996; Evans, 1996; Lyons, 2003; Hillner, 2015; Swain, n.d.; cf. Shepherd, 2016).

Consider the case of the famous literary character "Jean Valjean", the protagonist of Victor Hugo's classic nineteenth-century multi-volume novel *Les Misérables*, first published in 1862. Desperate to feed his starving family, Valjean stole a loaf of bread; tragically, after his conviction, he had to endure nearly twenty years of incarceration as a result of this so-called crime.

During the medieval period, for instance, anyone who transgressed the codes of Christian convention would not only be humiliated and stigmatised, but also prevented from receiving any charitable assistance. In the thirteenth century, the hospital of St. John the Baptist in Oxford stipulated that it would not admit "mulieres lasciuas pregnantes" (Innocent IV, 1246, p. 3) [lewd pregnant women], or "leprosos" (Innocent IV, 1246, p. 3) [lepers] or "paraliticos" (Innocent IV, 1246, p. 3) [cripples], let alone "furiosos" (Innocent IV, 1246, p. 3) [madmen]. In the fifteenth century, in similar vein, the hospital of St. John in Bruggewater (later known as Bridgewater), in Somerset, insisted that,

> No lepers, lunatics, or persons having the falling sickness or other contagious disease, and no pregnant women, or sucking infants, and no intolerable persons, even though they be poor and infirm, are to be admitted in the house; and if any such be admitted by mistake, they are to be expelled as soon as possible. [Bekynton, 1457, p. 289]

While our ancestors during the Middle Ages often treated the marginalised with shameful neglect, throughout the early modern period those who perpetrated offences would be subjected to the most inhumane forms of cruelty and torture. For instance, during Elizabethan times, miscreants would be subjected to a range of horrifying punishments, which included being flung into a windowless pit, or manacled to a rack, or placed in hand-crushing iron gauntlets, before being hanged, disembowelled, quartered, and beheaded, or even burned at the stake. Some offenders would be squashed to death by a process known as the *peine forte et dure*, a form of execution sanctioned in England since at least the year 1275 (Parry, 1933). Those convicted of the crime of poisoning, in particular, would often be boiled to death (Hutchinson, 2005). Such cruelties persisted in diabolical fashion for centuries to come (e.g., Gatrell, 1994; McKenzie, 2007).

Even physicians behaved cruelly, assaulting the bodies of criminals both before and after death. During the sixteenth century, Antonio Musa Brassavola, an Italian *medicus*, recommended that doctors

should test out new drugs on those condemned as criminals (Copeman, 1960). And it would be by no means unusual for the bodies of
those executed to be subjected to anatomical dissections after their
decease (e.g., Rütten, 2011).

As ever, William Shakespeare encapsulated the Tudor attitude
towards criminality with superb literary concision. In his play *The
Tragedy of Hamlet, Prince of Denmark*, written, in all likelihood, sometime between 1599 and 1602, the king, "Claudius", exclaims, "And
where th'offense is, let the great axe fall" (Act IV, Scene v, 219). Such
a remark typifies quite chillingly the attitude towards perpetrators
throughout much of the last millennium.

The neglect and abuse of offenders continued unrelentingly in the
centuries that followed. And in spite of some valiant efforts by prison
reformers, such as the remarkable eighteenth-century Englishman
John Howard, who exposed the ghastly, unhygienic conditions that
convicts endured (e.g., Howard, 1958; Southwood, 1958; Freeman,
1978; Radzinowicz, 1978), one struggles, when combing the historical record, for much evidence of any compassion and understanding
towards those who, for whatever reason, perpetrated acts of criminality.

In the nineteenth century, the progenitors of forensic psychiatry endeavoured to provide a more sophisticated approach to the
problem of homicidal insanity and other manifestations of criminal
violence by proclaiming offenders as mentally deranged. But the
vast majority of medical specialists who worked at the interface
between alienism and the law regarded lunatic perpetrators as suffering from hereditarian or constitutional predispositions (Colaizzi,
1989; cf. Rafter, 1997, 2008; Wetzell, 2000; Horn, 2003; Davie, 2005;
Bondio, 2006; Jalava, Griffiths, and Maraun, 2015)—a philosophy that
would, potentially, discourage researchers from exploring intrafamil-
ial aetiological factors in the development of offending behaviours.
The German physician, Professor Dr Johannes Lange (1929), *Ober-
arzt* [senior physician] at the Krankenhaus in München-Schwabing,
epitomised this tradition of biologising criminals; in his study of
twins, he underscored the hereditary nature of offending behaviour,
conceptualising crime as a manifestation of one's inherited destiny.
Furthermore, many criminologists construed illegal behaviours not
only in genetic terms, but also in racial terms, claiming, for instance,
that Jewish people or black people would be more likely to commit
offences than Christians or Caucasians (e.g., Berkowitz, 2006; cf.
Gilman, 1993).

Virtually no nineteenth-century medical professionals examined the early childhood experiences of the dangerous patient. This lack of interest in psychogenesis prevails to this day, and for many workers in the criminological field, the proto-biological approach remains paramount (e.g., Haycock, 2014).

Sigmund Freud and the humanisation of crime

The history of forensic psychotherapy begins, of course, with the contributions of Sigmund Freud, whose stupendous insights into the human mind and its violent depths have provided every mental health worker with an indispensable platform, whether or not one identifies oneself as a card-carrying Freudian.

We do not know when the young Viennese physician first became familiar with the study of criminology, but, while studying in France, during the last months of 1885 and the first months of 1886, Freud certainly attended the autopsies at the Paris morgue, where he had the opportunity to learn from Professeur Paul Brouardel (Freud, 1886), a pioneer of forensic medicine. Although we know little of the details of the autopsies that Freud observed, we can deduce, on the basis of some of Brouardel's publications, that the future father of psychoanalysis might well have witnessed the impact of acts of violence, including infanticide (Brouardel, 1897). Freud would have had occasion to absorb the works of Brouardel not only from his visits to the morgue, but also from having had the privilege of meeting him at one of the famous *soirées* hosted by Freud's neurological mentor, Professeur Jean-Martin Charcot (Freud, 1914).

It would not be long before Freud discovered the cruel underbelly of most human beings, having taken the time and the effort to listen to the narratives of his patients without interrupting them, as so many physicians of that era would have done. Appalled by the neglect and cruelty of the vast majority of late-nineteenth-century psychiatrists and other physicians, many of whom practised brutal acts of genital surgery in their attempt to deal with the neuroses (e.g., Church, 1893; Sims, 1893), Freud sought a more sympathetic route (cf. Kahr, 2013, 2017). By developing and perfecting the technique of the "talking cure" (quoted in Breuer, 1895, p. 23), Sigmund Freud learned how to elicit detailed, free-associative confessions from his analysands, and he soon came to appreciate that even the most seemingly kindly person harbours cruel thoughts and fantasies (e.g., Freud, 1900).

One might argue that Freud espoused a uniquely tolerant position towards the criminal. He eschewed the easy splitting of human beings into the violent and the non-violent, and consequently, he became far more compassionate and far less punitive in his approach to those whose psychopathology had prompted them to engage in criminal enactments.

The psychoanalytic investigation of the overtly forensic patient may well have begun in earnest on 6 February 1907, when members of Freud's Wednesday evening study group—the forerunner of the Wiener Psychoanalytische Vereinigung [Vienna Psycho-Analytical Society]—held a discussion on the psychology of vagrancy. During the course of the meeting, Professor Freud bemoaned that mentally ill offenders, many of whom become vagrant, would often be treated cruelly; and, according to Herr Otto Rank, Freud's secretary and keeper of the minutes, the founder of the psychoanalytic movement expressed his sorrow at the "unsinnige Behandlung dieser Leute (soweit sie Demenz zeigen) in Gefängnissen" (quoted in Rank, 1907b, p. 101), which translates as the "nonsensical treatment of these people in prisons (in so far as they are demented)" (quoted in Rank, 1907c, p. 108).

From this point onwards, Freud's interest in adopting a stance of concern and care for the criminal progressed. And while one cannot possibly do justice to the range and scope of his contributions in the context of a chapter-length study, we can, nevertheless, highlight a few seminal moments in Freud's career as a practitioner, as a writer, and as a polemicist.

Freud (1916a) considered the problem of criminality most notably, perhaps, in his famous essay "Einige Charaktertypen aus der psychoanalytischen Arbeit", published in *Imago* (the journal devoted to the study of applied psychoanalysis): a text better known by its English title, "Some Character-Types Met with in Psycho-Analytic Work" (Freud, 1916b). Although Freud devoted the bulk of this article to a study of characterology—investigating the whole personality of the individual, rather than solely specific symptoms—he also wrote sagaciously about criminal aspects of the human being in considerable detail and from a number of surprising angles.

In the first section of his three-part essay, Freud explored the question of people who regard themselves as exceptions to the rule, and he concentrated in some depth on the character of the late-medieval English villain Richard, Duke of Gloucester, as depicted in William Shakespeare's immortal play, *The Tragedy of King Richard the Third*:

Containing His treacherous Plots again∫t his brother Clarence: the pittiefull murther of his innocent nephewes: his tyrannicall v∫urpation: with the whole cour∫e of his dete∫ted life, and mo∫t de∫erued death. As it hath beene lately Acted by the Right honourable the Lord Chamberlaine his ∫eruants, written circa 1592. Freud noted that Richard suffered from bodily handicaps and infirmities, which left him "rudely stamp'd" (Act I, Scene i, 16)—so much so that "dogs bark at me as I halt by them" (Act I, Scene i, 23)—causing him to develop considerable shame and aggression, which prompted him to become murderous. As Shakespeare's protagonist laments, "And therefore, since I cannot prove a lover / To entertain these fair well-spoken days, / I am determined to prove a villain" (Act I, Scene i, 28–30). Thus, Freud made an important contribution to the study of forensic psychology *avant la lettre* through his recognition that murderers begin their careers as damaged youngsters.

In the second section of this 1916 classic, devoted to the study of those wrecked by success, Freud observed quite cunningly that many individuals will suffer a sense of breakdown *not* after they have *failed* in their efforts, as one might imagine, but, rather, after they have *succeeded*. For instance, Freud explored the mental disorder of "Lady Macbeth"—another famous Shakespearean character—and concluded that her illness developed after she had committed her crimes, rather than beforehand. In this respect, Freud has helped us to understand that violence and psychopathology often accompany one another, and that many criminals will become even more unwell after the commission of the offence.

In the third and final section of this psychological masterpiece, entitled famously, "Die Verbrecher aus Schuldbewußtsein" ["Criminals from a Sense of Guilt"], Sigmund Freud reflected upon a subset of his psychoanalytic patients, who, in spite of leading ostensibly respectable lives of probity, would confess in the course of treatment that they had, in earlier years, committed crimes such as theft, fraud, as well as arson. Thus, Freud reminded us that one could readily be an upstanding member of society and also, at the very same time, a forensic perpetrator. Additionally, he observed that many analysands reported that they had experienced a great sense of relief after having committed an offence, as many had carried the burden of guilt at feeling quite criminal without knowing the reason why. The commission of the crime thus reduced the painful tension between the internal guiltiness and the external guiltlessness (cf. Nunberg, 1926).

Freud concluded this hugely engaging essay by reflecting that most human beings must battle with internal criminal urges, not least, those of parricide and incest. In other words, Freud argued that if his notion of the Oedipus complex should have any merit, then we would come to find that everyone wishes to sleep with someone forbidden—perhaps the mother—and that everyone also wishes to kill someone—perhaps the parent of the opposite sex!

This meaty contribution, "Einige Charaktertypen aus der psycho-analytischen Arbeit", which has only just celebrated its centenary, deserves the very closest attention of anyone interested in expanding his or her understanding of the criminal mind. In many respects, this relatively short essay, drawn from literary studies and from Freud's own clinical work with essentially neurotic analysands, still provides perhaps the single most inspiring set of wide-ranging ideas about how and why human beings become perpetrators.

Freud's desire to understand the criminal within the ordinary man—the little Oedipus who wishes to kill a parental rival (e.g., Freud, 1912a, 1912b, 1912c, 1913a, 1913b, 1913c)—in no way precluded his interest in those who committed dangerous offences in *reality*, not simply in *fantasy*. Indeed, Freud harboured no illusions about the potential for violence not only among perpetrators, but also among those who imprisoned such offenders and who did so, often, in a truly sadistic manner.

Certainly, the brutal treatment of the criminal hardly surprised Freud; late in life, he wrote to the German literary critic and political dissident Professor Georg Fuchs (1931), congratulating him on the publication of his book *Wir Zuchthäusler: Errinerungen des Zellenge-fangenen Nr. 2911* [*We Convicts: Memories of the Prisoner in Cell Number 2911*]—a searing critique of penal institutions, based on Fuchs's own incarceration. As Freud (1931b, p. x) explained,

> Ich könnte zum Beispiel den Satz nicht unterschreiben, daß die Behandlung der Strafgefangenen eine Schande für unsere Kultur ist. Im Gegenteil, würde mir eine Stimme sagen: sie ist ganz in Einklang mit unserer Kultur, notwendige Äußerung der Brutalität und des Unverstandes, die die gegenwärtige Kulturmenschheit beherrschen.

> [I could not, for example, subscribe to the sentence that the way prisoners are treated is a disgrace to our civilization. On the contrary, a voice would tell me: it is quite in accord with our civiliza-tion, a necessary manifestation of the brutality and the folly that dominate present civilized mankind. (Freud, 1931c, p. 199)]

Freud's correspondence also contains numerous clues to his long-standing interest in forensic psychotherapeutic matters. Thanks to the researches of the literary scholar Professor Rubén Gallo (2012), we have come to learn that Freud maintained his interest in criminal psychology, during the 1930s, through his exchange of letters with the Mexican judge Señor Raúl Carrancá y Trujillo, who attempted to psychoanalyse offenders in his own office, learning about their dreams, their slips of the tongue, and their sexual fantasies. Carrancá y Trujillo maintained that judges must understand the criminal mind and its unconscious; and he even rallied for the creation of a "Laboratory of Criminal Psychology". Interestingly, after Freud's death, Carrancá y Trujillo actually presided at the trial of none other than Jacques Mornard (alias Ramón Mercader), apprehended for the murder of Leon Trotsky in 1940. In fact, psychoanalytic thinking infiltrated this trial, and the criminologist Dr Alfonso Quiroz Cuarón and the forensic psychiatrist Dr José Gómez Robleda actually conducted hundreds of hours of interviews with Mornard and administered various tests, including the Rorschach inkblot as well as word reaction tests; they also undertook both dream analysis, as well as handwriting analysis, eventually producing a 1,332-page report. The work of Carrancá y Trujillo and those he inspired—encouraged by Freud himself—remains a vital, though little-known, chapter in the history of forensic psychoanalysis.

Freud also corresponded with other international colleagues who maintained an interest in the relationship between psychoanalysis and criminality. In 1933, he wrote to an Englishwoman, Dr Grace Pailthorpe, a sometime analysand of Dr Ernest Jones (Roazen, 2000), who, it seems, required further psychoanalytic treatment. Freud (1933) could not oblige Dr Pailthorpe himself; instead, he recommended that she might communicate with his colleague, Dr Ruth Mack Brunswick, who also shared an interest in criminological topics. During the previous year, Dr Pailthorpe (1932) had produced a special report under the auspices of the Medical Research Council on *Studies in the Psychology of Delinquency*, published by His Majesty's Stationery Office: one of the first full-length psychoanalytically inspired forensic texts written by a Briton. Pailthorpe recommended psychotherapy as a treatment possibility for those who had committed crimes, suggesting, somewhat conservatively perhaps, that Freudian psychoanalysis might be of use in approximately 19% of cases!

Sigmund Freud's interest in helping victims of crime could in no way be described as armchair or academic in nature. Indeed, in

1922, a former Freud family servant molested his own daughter; subsequently, the servant's son, Ernst Haberl, attempted to rescue his half-sister by shooting the father—albeit non-fatally—in the process. Freud not only engaged the services of the lawyer Dr Valentin Teirich to defend the youth, but he even paid the legal expenses. Dr Teirich arranged for a plea of temporary insanity, and as a result the defendant, Ernst Haberl, did not go to prison (Jones, 1957; Aichhorn, 2014).

Certainly, Freud enjoyed studying the subject of crime, not only in his practice, but also during his moments of leisure. And it cannot be accidental that in later years he deeply relished reading the mystery novels that featured the aristocratic detective "Lord Peter Wimsey", portrayed so elegantly by Dorothy L. Sayers in her many popular novels (Jones, 1957).

Additionally, Freud would, from time to time, welcome visiting forensic specialists from overseas for a visit to the Berggasse in Vienna, often twice in the same month. We know from Freud's (1992) diary entries that on 3 February 1930, Professor Nerio Rojas, an expert in forensic medicine from Buenos Aires, in Argentina, called upon the founder of psychoanalysis. And not long thereafter, on 26 February 1930, Professor Gregorio Berman from Córdoba—a fellow Argentinean—also a forensic physician, sought Freud out as well.

Although the father of psychoanalysis never worked in a prison or in any other overtly forensic setting, he did have direct clinical knowledge of at least two paedophile patients. Though it is not widely known and very little cited in the literature, Freud conducted the supervision of the treatment of a child sexual offender undertaken by his Viennese disciple Dr Theodor Reik (Natterson, 1966; cf. Kahr, 1991). He also worked with a paedophile directly: a British man sent by the courts to Vienna in lieu of a prison sentence (Kahr, 2010). Regrettably, to the best of our knowledge Freud never wrote papers on either of these cases. Nevertheless, he certainly knew a great deal about paedophilia and about the sexual molestation of children from the direct reports of his adult patients who, while undergoing psychoanalysis, spoke of their early years (e.g., Freud, 1895, 1896, 1905). He even commented on the subject of paedophilic tendencies at a meeting of the Wiener Psychoanalytische Vereinigung in 1907, discussing, *inter alia*, the harming of little girls, as well as the capacity of some people to become aroused by pregnant women (Rank, 1907a).

Strikingly, in spite of Freud's long-standing interest in what we would now refer to as forensic psychotherapy or forensic psychoanalysis, his physical health prevented him from accepting an invitation that might well have changed the course of this field of endeavour. On 21 May 1924, two American teenagers, Nathan Leopold, Jr., and Richard Loeb, both sons of well-to-do businessmen, endeavoured to commit the "perfect crime" (Darrow, 1932, p. 228) by abducting a fourteen-year-old boy, Robert Franks, and then murdering him, having bludgeoned his skull with a chisel. The wealthy parents of the assailants engaged the services of the celebrated lawyer Clarence Darrow (1922), author of a tract on the humane treatment of criminals, desperate that he might orchestrate the acquittal of their felonious sons. In the hope of demonstrating that Leopold and Loeb had executed their crime while temporarily insane, Darrow sought the testimony of pioneering psychiatrists in the United States of America, including Dr Bernard Glueck, Sr., Dr William Healy, and Dr William Alanson White, the latter one of the co-founders of *The Psychoanalytic Review: A Journal Devoted to an Understanding of Human Conduct*—the first psychoanalytic periodical published in the English language.

Everyone hoped that Sigmund Freud, too, would come to Chicago, Illinois, and deliver evidence on behalf of the accused murderers. But in spite of exceptionally lucrative offers (e.g., Bonaparte, 1926; Seldes, 1953; Jones, 1957), the ageing Professor Freud (1924a, 1924b) refused to travel overseas, having only recently received his diagnosis of carcinoma (Schur, 1972; Romm, 1983; cf. Kahr, 2005, 2007). Had Freud joined the media circus of the trial (Baatz, 2008), one can only imagine the potential for the dissemination of psychoanalytic ideas among legal professionals.

Not long before his death, Freud provided an expert commentary, albeit from the comfort of his desk, about the case of a young Austrian student, Philipp Halsmann, accused of having murdered his father. In 1929, the court in Innsbruck had charged the young Herr Halsmann with murder; but Professor Josef Kupka, a specialist in jurisprudence at the Universität zu Wien [University of Vienna] harboured doubts about the young man's guilt; consequently, he marshalled Freud to provide a testimonial, even though Freud had never met the accused. Freud realised that, in view of the growing popularity of his theories about the Oedipus complex, certain persons might draw upon his work in an uncritical manner. And so, in 1931, he published a short essay on the Halsmann case in the journal *Psychoanalytische Bewegung* [*Psycho-Analytical Movement*] (Freud, 1931a). In this he wrote, in no uncertain terms—and quite hopefully so—that although a man may harbour murderous wishes towards his own father—a universal phenomenon—this in no way suggests that he will actually engage in murder. Freud fully recognised the strong difference between an unconscious fantasy and a forensic reality.

Freud could be very compassionate towards those who committed crimes and those accused of having done so. But he could also find such people irritating.

According to Dr Edoardo Weiss, a long-standing disciple and the progenitor of the psychoanalytic movement in Italy, Sigmund Freud struggled to further his interest in forensic matters owing to his countertransferential disdain towards those who had committed violent acts. As Weiss (n.d., p. 2) explained, "Although he had great consideration for human weaknesses he was not free of his reaction toward patients who had anti-social or criminal tendencies." Further, Weiss (n.d., p. 2) noted that, "He also disliked sexual perversions, alcoholism and other addictions" and maintained an "intolerance of what one would call "immoral psychopathy", which is considered to be a constitutional ego defect not very accessible to psychoanalysis" (Weiss, n.d., p. 2). Certainly, one must appreciate that, in addition to Freud's enthusiasm for the study of forensic issues, he also maintained a certain ambivalence as well.

Although criminality remained only one of Freud's numerous interests and preoccupations, he certainly provided us with the very foundations of the discipline that would come to be known, subsequently, as forensic psychotherapy. Not only did he make numerous observations about the nature of the criminal mind, he also bequeathed to us many vital working concepts that still assist us in the diagnosis and treatment of the forensic mind—not least the notion of the well-developed superego or moral function (Freud, 1923), which most criminals lack. Furthermore, Freud argued for tremendous compassion in our approach to those who have committed offences.

Perhaps Freud's attitude—on the whole an unusually compassionate and non-condemnatory one—can best be summarised in a most pointed comment to one of his patients. During the 1930s, Dr Joseph Wortis, an American psychiatrist, underwent psychoanalysis in Vienna with Sigmund Freud as part of his professional development. On 1 November 1934, Wortis—a highly accomplished physician in his own right—confessed to certain character faults, whereupon Freud replied, "We are not here to judge, not even if you were a criminal" (quoted in Wortis, 1954, p. 55).

The contributions of the early psychoanalysts

Inspired by Sigmund Freud's interest in, and preoccupation with, matters of violent offending, many of his pioneering disciples followed suit. Indeed, on 10 April 1907, Dr Fritz Wittels delivered a paper at one of Freud's Wednesday night seminars about the psychology of a murderer, analysing—albeit at a distance—the case of Tatjana Leontieva, a woman who attempted to assassinate the Tsarist official Peter Durnovo but ended up killing another man instead. Wittels attempted to unearth the repressed sexual underpinnings of this murder, but, never having met Leontieva in person, he struggled to do so. Consequently, the minutes of the meeting sound more classically psychiatric than psychodynamic, with the author having diagnosed the Russian murderess as both hysterical and paranoiac (Rank, 1907d). Nonetheless, Wittels would maintain his early interest in criminal psychology over the course of his career (e.g., Wittels, 1928, 1929a, 1929b, 1937a, 1937b, 1938).

Other early psychoanalytic adherents elaborated upon these initial forays. For instance, in 1911, Herr Adolf Josef Storfer (1911) published a monograph on the psychodynamics of parricide. And on 6 March 1912, Alfred Freiherr von Winterstein (1912), an early member of the Wiener Psychoanalytische Vereinigung, spoke to his colleagues about the potential scope of psychoanalytic investigations, arguing that the Freudian lens should be applied not only to the field of art, linguistics, morality, mythology, pedagogy, religion, and sociology, but also to the study of criminology.

Other Viennese colleagues who contributed to the discussion around forensic matters included Dr Paul Federn—one of Freud's first adherents—who had maintained a long-standing interest in the psychology of sadism and masochism (e.g., Federn, 1913) and who, some years later, published a tract on the psychology of revolution, daring to question whether people who engage in strikes should be regarded as criminals or, instead, as visionaries (Federn, 1919).

Dr Hanns Sachs, originally trained as a lawyer, became a fervent opponent of the death penalty, which he regarded as an expression of group sadism (Moellenhoff, 1966). Likewise, Dr Hermine von Hug-Hellmuth (1915) published an essay on fetishistic psychopathology (long before Professor Sigmund Freud's (1927a) contribution to this topic). Dr Wilhelm Reich (1927) questioned the widely held views about sexual perversions as mere indications of moral degeneration. And Dr Theodor Reik wrote about a variety of criminological topics such as the nature of confession (e.g., Reik, 1925) and the psychology of murder (e.g., Reik, 1932). Freud certainly knew of much, if not all, of this work, as many of his colleagues presented him with copies of their books. Reik, for instance (1925), inscribed his monograph on the obsession to confess crimes: "Meinem verehrten und geliebten Lehrer" [My adored and beloved teacher]. Reik's text still exists today in the library of the Freud Museum London.

Two of the earliest adherents of the psychoanalytic movement, Dr Wilhelm Stekel and Dr Alfred Adler, both fell famously foul of Freud. Nevertheless, each deserves to be remembered for having bequeathed important contributions to the psychoanalytically orientated study of forensic mental health. Stekel (1911), for instance, had long maintained a preoccupation with the sexual perversions; and even after his lamentable break-up with Freud, he continued to research the topic thoroughly. He founded a periodical that appeared irregularly during the 1920s and 1930s, *Fortschritte der Sexualwissenschaft und Psychanalyse* [*Progress in Sexual Science and Psycho-Analysis*], which featured numerous contributions to the study of forensic matters, surveying such topics as criminal psychology (Lippmann, 1926), sadomasochism (Schindler, 1926), kleptomania (Friedmann, 1928), and even the psychoanalytic treatment of offender patients more broadly (Sonnenschein, 1928).

Adler, a onetime president of the Wiener Psychoanalytische Vereinigung, eventually came to found his own movement, known as "*Individualpsychologie*" [individual psychology]. With his new colleagues, Adler undertook a number of clinical investigations into the study of criminality, and in 1931 he devoted a whole issue of his publication, the *Internationale Zeitschrift für Individualpsychologie* [*International Journal of Individual Psychology*], which he edited, to the study of forensic matters. Adler (1931) himself contributed the lead article on the treatment of the criminal personality, and many other colleagues offered their own particular perspectives (e.g., Beck, 1931; Bohne, 1931; Jacoby, 1931; Löwy, 1931; Nägele, 1931; Schlesinger, 1931; Schmidt, 1931; Sorge-Boehmke, 1931; Vértes, 1931; Vislick-Young, 1931). This special issue of Adler's journal also included an essay written by Herr Fritz Kleist (1931) who, quite creatively, offered both individual treatment and group therapy in a prison in the German town of Celle, near Hannover.

Perhaps most famously of all, Herr August Aichhorn (1925), a sometime schoolteacher who specialised in working with troubled adolescents and who eventually became a practising psychoanalyst, published a study of delinquent youths, for which Freud (1925a) wrote a foreword. Aichhorn's interest in delinquency had developed quite early in his own life when he encountered youths from deprived backgrounds who worked in his father's bakery. Apparently, these young rascals often stole Aichhorn's pocket money and also taught him their patois (Mohr, 1966). Thus, Aichhorn acquired a very intimate familiarity with this particular sub-culture of disadvantaged people.

Quite pioneeringly, Aichhorn established an institution for delinquent boys in the Austrian town of Ober-Hollabrunn (Aichhorn, 1925; Eissler, 1949). He also came to practise more traditional psychoanalysis and, over the years, his patients included not only those who exhibited rebellious, often violent, behaviours, but also those who engaged in sexually perverse activities. Indeed, at least one of his patients worked as a pimp (Mohr, 1966).

Aichhorn certainly went to great efforts to come to know his juvenile patients and, often, their families, as thoroughly as possible. His disciple, Dr Kurt Eissler (1949, p. xi), referred to Aichhorn as an "impassioned psychologist" who conducted memorable interviews with youngsters and who, over the course of his working life, could achieve great psychotherapeutic success. Eissler explained that

> As a great artist has supreme command over his instrument, be it a flute or a harp, so can Aichhorn play his instrument, the human personality. In the shortest time he can turn a squanderer into a miser, a thief into a scrupulously honest fellow, a blackmailer into a defender of law and order. [1949, p. xii]

Aichhorn listened to the stories of his patients with tremendous attentivity, and he recorded the precise detail of their narratives. With the exception of Sigmund Freud's case histories, most psychiatric literature in the nineteenth century, and even into the early twentieth century, adopted a patrician attitude, dismissing the patient's thoughts in short sentences. Rarely would one encounter such direct quotations from the patient's narrative. But Aichhorn, following the example set by Freud (1909) in his case of "kleiner Hans" ["Little Hans"], provided extensive quotations from the juvenile delinquents themselves: a true indication of the seriousness with which he treated those in his care.

By conducting lengthy clinical interviews with young offenders and their relatives, Aichhorn (1925, p. 91) managed to elicit full histories of the often violent roots of the children's psychopathology, underscoring the aetiological role of *"psychischen Traumen"* [psychic traumas]. For instance, he described in considerable detail the case of a delinquent boy whose father had died after the child's twelfth birthday. In the wake of this bereavement, the boy began to sleep in the father's place in the parental bed, becoming a surrogate husband to his mother. Two year's later, this mother—a factory worker—died in a tragic accident, mangled to death in a piece of machinery. Upon hearing that he had become an orphan, the poor teenager fainted. Forbidden to attend his mother's funeral, he struggled with his unarticulated grief and eventually became a vagrant and a delinquent. Whereas other clinicians at the time would have regarded the boy's forensic psychopathology as a sign of illness, August Aichhorn (1925)—anticipating later conceptualisations by Dr Donald Winnicott (1968)—came to regard the boy's delinquency as rather hopeful, in that his acting-out behaviours might well have saved him from having plunged into a severe melancholia.

Whereas other workers advocated staunch punishment and enforced labour, Aichhorn explained that such methods would serve only to reinforce the early punition experienced by these young people in their families of origin. Consequently, he provided an alternative by working psychoanalytically.

Aichhorn distinguished himself among his colleagues by intervening early with young delinquents, hoping that in doing so he might prevent them from becoming dangerous criminals in later life.

August Aichhorn expanded his work in the field of delinquency across the course of his career. In a subsequent contribution, he addressed the crucial question of treatment versus punishment, advocating, naturally, for the former, as did all psychoanalytically inspired workers (Aichhorn, 1932).

It would, of course, be far too restrictive to describe such developments in psychoanalytic criminology in Vienna as simply an elaboration of the ideas of Sigmund Freud. As one historian has argued, the movement grew, at least in part, out of a more widely shared effort to understand the nature of human cruelty, especially in light of the Great War of 1914–1918 (Finder, 2006).

Viennese psychoanalysts also became increasingly interested in, and concerned about, criminal offences, owing to the unexpected murder of one of their own stalwart colleagues.

On 9 September 1924, a young man called Rudolf Otto Hug broke into the Vienna home of his aunt, Dr Hermine Hug-Hellmuth, one of the pioneers of child psychoanalysis, and strangled her to death (cf. Anonymous, 1924). Although details about the precise nature of the relationship between the nephew and his aunt remain obscure, we do know that Hug-Hellmuth psychoanalysed her nephew at some point (MacLean, 1986; MacLean and Rappen, 1991), and one can only wonder whether this experience will have contributed to her ultimate strangulation—the apotheosis of a perverse negative transference. Extraordinarily, after Rudolf Hug's eventual release from prison, he applied to the Wiener Psychoanalytische Vereinigung for financial compensation, having claimed to be a victim of the psychoanalytic process. Dr Paul Federn referred Herr Hug to fellow psychoanalyst Dr Eduard Hitschmann for a consultation, and he, in turn, recommended that Hug undergo further psychoanalysis from Dr Helene Deutsch. Although this young murderer never embarked on treatment with Deutsch, he did stalk her; as a result, Helene Deutsch's husband, Dr Felix Deutsch, had to hire a private detective to provide protection for his wife (Deutsch, 1973).

The psychoanalytic approach to the study of what we would now refer to as forensic psychology also spread beyond Vienna, far and wide across Continental Europe and elsewhere. Dr Sándor Ferenczi (1909a, 1909b, 1910) from Budapest, an experienced forensic psychiatrist, worked vigorously to introduce psychodynamic concepts to colleagues in the legal profession. For instance, in October 1913 he addressed the "Reichsverein der Richter und Staatsanwälte" [State Society of Judges and Barristers] in Budapest, about the nature of psychoanalysis, reviewing the highlights of Freud's work over the previous two decades. Speaking with the passion of a Ciceronian orator, Ferenczi (1922, p. 110) argued that, "eine Zeit kommen muß" [a time must come] when psychoanalytic understanding of criminality will have to replace what he described as "der heute üblichen automatischen Strafmaßnahmen" (Ferenczi, 1922, p. 110) [the present-day usual automatic punitive sentences].

Some years later, Ferenczi (1919) published a short essay in Hungarian on psychoanalysis and criminology, which subsequently appeared alongside his speech to the judges and barristers in his German-language book *Populäre Vorträge über Psychoanalyse* [*Popular Lectures on Psycho-Analysis*] (Ferenczi, 1922). This brief contribution, less than four pages in length, deserves to be remembered as the clarion call for the development of what Ferenczi (1922, p. 114) called "einer psychoanalytischen Kriminologie" [a psycho-analytic criminology]. He claimed that, by investigating crime through a Freudian lens, one would be able to improve upon those worthy but, nonetheless, superficial approaches to the prevention and treatment of crime then in vogue. With tremendous prescience, Ferenczi noted that the conscious confessions of the offender will never fully explain the motivations of a crime, and that one must, in contrast, seek its unconscious origins.

In this essay on psychoanalytic criminology, Ferenczi recommended that Freudian practitioners should visit convicted felons in prisons and should analyse them *in situ* in order to conduct research on the nature of the criminal mind. He underscored that, in view of the cruelty with which many prison guards treated the intimates, "eine analytische Kriminaltherapie" (Ferenczi, 1922, p. 116) [an analytic criminal therapy] would be preferred. In many respects, Ferenczi's elegant statement anticipates virtually all of the fundamental tenets of contemporary forensic psychotherapeutic theory and practice.

In Berlin, home of the first psychoanalytic training institute, Dr Franz Alexander pioneered the study of psychoanalytic criminology with tremendous fervour. Alexander transmitted his work not only through publications, but also via lectures delivered both in Germany and abroad. In 1922, quite early in his career, Alexander (1925) treated a kleptomaniacal patient—Fräulein "E.R."—under the auspices of the low-cost clinic, the Poliklinik für psychoanalytische Behandlung nervöser Krankheiten [Polyclinic for Psycho-Analytical Treatment of Nervous Illnesses] of the Berliner Psychoanalytische Vereinigung [Berlin Psycho-Analytical Society]. He even served as an expert witness in a court case, offering testimony about a suspected offender; and when he did so, the judges "gave full attention" (Eitingon, 1925b, p. 141). Interest in this particular case flourished; and in the wake of Franz Alexander's pioneering courtroom experience, the Berliner Psychoanalytisches Institut [Berlin Psycho-Analytical Institute] received further requests for psychoanalytic consultation on legal cases, and Dr Max Eitingon (1925b), one of Freud's loyal devotees, provided expert testimony in a subsequent case.

Most notably, Dr Franz Alexander forged a collaboration with Dr Hugo Staub, a criminologist who later trained as a psychoanalyst in his own right. Together, the two men taught a course entitled "Kriminalistische Arbeitsgemeinschaft" [Criminal Working Group], which contributed to the publication of their groundbreaking book on forensic matters (Alexander and Staub, 1929a, p. [5]) and would, they hoped, serve as the basis for the development of the field of "einer psychoanalytischen Kriminologie" [a psycho-analytic criminology] (cf. Alexander and Staub, 1929b). No doubt Alexander, Hungarian-born and trained in Germany, drew inspiration from the works of his fellow countryman Sándor Ferenczi, in whose forensic analytic footsteps he followed.

Franz Alexander and Hugo Staub (1929a, p. [7]) recognised that many sceptics might regard a psychological approach to the study of criminology as little more than "eine luxuriöse Verschwendung" [a luxurious waste]—as if by offering compassion they might thereby come to minimise the crime. But these authors demonstrated quite powerfully that a psychological lens provides the most sophisticated route for understanding. These two pioneers of psychoanalytically orientated criminology explained that acts of violence do not stem from rational thought; often the offender patient will have absolutely no idea as to why he or she might have committed an illegal act. Therefore, Alexander and Staub argued for a detailed study of the hidden, unconscious motivations underlying crime.

Boldly, Alexander and Staub (1929a, p. 76) spoke out against retaliatory approaches; they argued that "Bestrafung ist psychologisch unsinnig und ist soziologisch schädlich" [punishment is psychologically futile and is sociologically harmful]. In fact, they recognised that, unconsciously, punishment might even serve as an incentive to some of the more masochistically orientated offenders. Instead, they championed psychoanalytic treatment as a means of intervening successfully with criminals (cf. Staub, 1931c).

These authors also argued for the introduction of psychology into the courtroom, noting that judges must concern themselves not only with the criminal act, but also with the criminal himself or herself, and that psychodynamic psychology would help the courts to appreciate factors that contribute to perpetration. Alexander and Staub (1929a, p. 17) underscored that, "Richten ohne Psychologie ist nicht denkbar" [Passing sentence without psychology is unthinkable].

Perhaps above all, Franz Alexander and Hugo Staub championed the humanity of the criminal. They fiercely rejected the notion that perpetrators of illegal activity should be dismissed as being organically different from ordinary men and women. In fact, they mounted a critique of the nineteenth-century biologisation of violent behaviour, explaining this trend in criminological discourse as little more than a narcissistic wish to regard the offender as totally other, and as a member of a different race, thereby allowing ordinary non-criminals to consider themselves superior. As loyal Freudians, aware of the ugly depths of the human unconscious, Alexander and Staub underscored that each human being has the potential to become a criminal. Of course, not everyone will break the law, but, they noted, many people will still engage in aggressivity through such activities as football, boxing, bullfights, duelling, and, of course, by going to war!

In spite of the lack of psychological training among legal professionals, the work of Alexander and Staub proved to be increasingly impactful, and it soon attracted the attention of judges and criminal lawyers throughout Germany (Zilboorg, 1931).

In 1930, both men visited the Wiener Psychoanalytische Vereinigung and presented their work to their Austrian colleagues, with Freud himself in attendance. As Freud (1930a) wrote to Princesse Marie Bonaparte:

> Letzten Donnerstag waren Alexander und Dr Staub, sein Mitarbeiter, Gäste unseres Vereinsabends. Es war sehr animirt. Alex. erzählte von analytsichen Eingriffe bei kriminellen Fällen, Staub machte mehrere sehr kluge Bemerkungen dazu.

> Last Thursday, Alexander and Dr Staub, his collaborator, were guests at our Society-meeting. It was very lively. Alex. told about analytic interventions in criminal cases, Staub added some very sagacious remarks. [Freud, 1930b]

After emigrating to the United States, Alexander developed his psychocriminological work, delivering, *inter alia*, a public lecture on "Psychic Factors in Crime" on behalf of the Institute for Psychoanalysis in Chicago, Illinois (Brown, 1987). He also collaborated with the American pioneer Dr William Healy on a book entitled *Roots of Crime: Psychoanalytic Studies* (Alexander and Healy, 1935a). Additionally, he wrote a paper about a teenage murderer (Alexander, 1937), among other contributions (cf. Alexander, 1925, 1929, 1930; Alexander and Healy, 1935b, 1935c). Furthermore, he would eventually become one of the international advisers to *The British Journal of Delinquency*.

Other German workers who facilitated the growth of this field included Dr Clara Happel (1925, 1926), who published a case report about a male paederast and genital exhibitionist, and Dr Ernst Simmel, one of the most distinguished pioneers of hospital-based psychoanalytic treatment, who worked with sadistic sexual offenders in the Sanatorium Schloß Tegel on the outskirts of Berlin (Lewy, 1947). And, quite impressively, the Berlin physician and novelist, Dr Alfred Döblin (1924) used both graphological analysis and dream analysis in his investigation of murderers in prison (cf. Fuechtner, 2011).

The discipline of psychoanalytic criminology proved increasingly potent in the German-speaking world—so much so that, in 1931, the journal *Imago*, devoted to the applications of psychoanalysis, sponsored an entire "Sonderheft" [special issue] on the subject of "Kriminologie" [criminology], with contributions from stalwarts Dr Franz Alexander (1931a, 1931b), Dr Hugo Staub (1931a, 1931b), as well as from Dr Siegfried Bernfeld (1931), who explored the problem of the superego in offenders. A young newcomer, Dr Erich Fromm, who would ultimately become one of the most profound psycho-analytic writers about social issues and the author of a huge text on destructiveness (Fromm, 1973), contributed an essay on the psychol-ogy of the criminal (Fromm, 1931), lambasting punishment. So also did one Herr Friedrich Haun (1931), who, likewise, questioned the value of retributive sentencing in the treatment of psychopaths. Of the many papers published herein, Franz Alexander's (1931b) case history of a young waiter, remains, perhaps, of greatest interest for its deft and cunning clinical analysis. Alexander explored the psycho-dynamics of a man who committed regular criminal acts by engaging chauffeurs to take him on long automobile journeys, and who would then abscond from these vehicles without paying his bill! Alexander traced this criminality to the fact, in part, that the waiter's stepfather had tried to chase him out of the family home when he was youngster; and in an effort to master this trauma, the patient in question would, quite unconsciously, take charge of any potential abandonment by fleeing from the parental figures of the chauffeurs before they could send him away for not having settled his account.

Perhaps German-language psychoanalytic criminology reached its apotheosis in 1926, with the appearance of the feature-length popular film *Geheimnisse einer Seele* [*Secrets of a Soul*], directed by Georg Wilhelm Pabst. This film, to which Dr Karl Abraham and Dr Hanns Sachs served as consultants, helped to popularise psychoa-nalysis as a method of treatment (e.g., Abraham, 1925; Freud, 1925b, 1925c; cf. Chodorkoff and Baxter, 1974; Ries, 1995). In the film, a man develops a phobia of knives in the wake of the murder of a neighbour. Unable to find relief from this symptom, the protagonist undergoes psychoanalysis and discovers that the knife phobia—triggered by the murder—prevented him from enacting his pre-existing unconscious rage towards his wife for not having given him a baby. After several months of psychoanalysis, the man is cured of his knife phobia and manages to impregnate his spouse; and the film closes with a happy scene of the proud man, with his wife and child. In many respects, *Geheimnisse einer Seele* provided concrete evidence of the keen inter-est of psychoanalytic workers in both actual forensic murder and in fantasied murder, and in the complex interplay between them.

In France, Princesse Marie Bonaparte (1927) undertook detailed studies of several murderers, including Marie Lefebvre, whom she interviewed for more than four hours in prison in Lille on 14 January 1927 (cf. Bonaparte, 1929), as well as Peter Kürten, known as the "Vampire of Düsseldorf" (Bonaparte, 1952). Sigmund Freud (1927b) warmly encouraged his royal disciple; and after her visit to Madame Lefebvre in prison, he wrote, "Zu Wahrheit wissen wir sehr wenig von den Bedingungen eines Verbrechens" ["In truth, we know very little about the preconditions of a crime" (Freud, 1927c)].

Alas, not everyone supported the princess's endeavours to study dangerous criminals. In 1931, Marie Bonaparte had hoped to interview a man called Matoschka—a sadist who became aroused by railway accidents. In an effort to facilitate Bonaparte's work, Freud spoke to the French ambassador, Comte Bertrand Clauzel, at a performance given by Freud's friend, the French *diseuse* Yvette Gilbert; however, after this conversation, Freud (1931d) had to write to the French princess that, "Graf Claudel [sic] (der französische Gestande) hat mich angesprochen u mir erzählt, dass er Ihre Verbrecherinteressen leider nicht fördern kann" [Count Claudel [sic] (the French envoy) addressed me and told me, that, unfortunately, he is unable to promote your interest in criminals (Freud, 1931e)].

Undeterred, Bonaparte continued to campaign vigorously against capital punishment, and with the assistance of Professor Franz Alexander and Dr Isadore Ziferstein, she petitioned Edmund Brown, the Governor of California, to release the robber, kidnapper, and rapist Caryl Chessman, then on Death Row, from the California State Prison in San Quentin. Bonaparte even sent a pleading letter to the American President, John Fitzgerald Kennedy, but to no avail (Bertin, 1982).

And in Switzerland, the loyal clergyman, Pfarrer Oskar Pfister (1915) contributed an early psychoanalytic essay on the topic of arson. Cunningly, Pfister explored the relationship between fire-setting and sublimation.

During the 1920s, Freudian theory impacted upon criminological studies as far east as India and as far west as South America. On 30 July 1925, Dr Girindrashekhar Bose (sometimes spelled Girindrasekhar Bose), the founder and first President of the Indian Psycho-Analytical Society, addressed the Calcutta Parliament on the subject of psychoanalysis and criminality (Anonymous, 1926); he also spoke to the Bengal Legislative Assembly on the same topic (Hartnack, 2001), and he even taught a course on psychoanalysis and crime at India's Principal Detective School (Hartnack, 2001). Moreover, Bose provided expert witness testimony for the defence in what one colleague described as a "sensational political murder case" (Banerji, 1925, p. 242), as a result of which Indian jurists began to develop a greater interest in psychoanalytic concepts.

In 1945, Bose published a book entitled *Everyday Psycho-Analysis*; this contained a very illuminating chapter on "Crime and Psycho-Analysis", in which he defined criminality as a disease that deserves psychological treatment, rather than punishment. As Bose (1945, p. 61) pleaded, "You cannot punish a criminal any more than you can punish a diseased individual. But you can certainly correct him and prevent him from doing mischief to others." Bose (1945, p. 62) warned that those who strive to punish others might well be suffering from a "lust of revenge". Aware that many Indians conceptualised criminality as the consequence of "spirit-possession" (Bose, 1945, p. 65), this pioneering psychoanalyst regarded acts of delinquency, in contrast, as motivated by private psychological factors and argued that psychoanalysis could assist not only in the treatment of dangerous individuals, but also in the prevention of delinquency in the first place.

Contemporaneously, on 20 August 1925, Dr Sarasilal Sarkar, a civil surgeon in Noakhali, Bengal, and an early member of the Indian Psycho-Analytical Society, delivered a talk to his colleagues on "Psychology of a Murderer" (Anonymous, 1926).

And in South America, Dr Juan Ramón Beltrán—an Argentinean physician—practised Freudian psychology in a prison setting, providing treatment, rather than punishment, to one of the inmates. Beltrán's work had so impressed Dr Karl Abraham (1924a, p. 766), the founder of the psychoanalytic movement in Germany, that he wrote to Freud enthusiastically, "Der Autor hat in einer Strafanstalt einen wegen Mordes Verurteilen ziemlich weitgehend und sehr verständnisvoll analysiert! So etwas muß aus Südamerika zu uns kommen!" ["In a prison the author has analysed quite deeply, and, with much understanding, a man sentenced for murder! This sort of thing has to come to us from South America!" (Abraham, 1924b, p. 505)]. Not long thereafter, during the second quarter of 1925, Abraham himself delivered three lectures on "Psychoanalytische Theorie des Verbrechens. (Für Juristen, Mediziner und Pädagogen)" ["Psycho-Analytical Theory of Crime. (For Jurists, Physicians, and Paedagogues) (Eitingon, 1925a, p. 503)] at the Berliner Psychoanalytisches Institut.

Due to the pioneering efforts of the émigré psychoanalyst Dr Clara Lazar-Geroe, dynamic forensic psychology began to penetrate the shores of Australia. In 1941, for instance, Lazar-Geroe (1942), one of the leaders of the Melbourne Institute for Psychoanalysis, offered three evenings of instruction on the "Psychoanalytic Approach to Juvenile Delinquency" to a study group sponsored by the Children's Court Probation Officers, in which participants discussed case material. Additionally, Lazar-Geroe's colleague, Dr Anita Muhl, presented a report about a delinquent boy to a group of psychiatrists.

Forensic psychoanalysis even reached the Middle East. For instance, in 1950, Dr Gerda Barag (1950), one of the founders of the psychoanalytic movement in Palestine and, later, Israel, published a case of kleptomania treated psychodynamically.

Freudian ideas certainly spread to North America as well, in large measure due to the efforts of the British-born émigré Dr William Healy, who worked as a child psychiatrist, first, at the Juvenile Psychopathic Institute in Chicago, Illinois (e.g., Sumner, Sims, Baum, Blaustein, Callaghan, et al., 1911), and later at the Judge Baker Foundation in Boston, Massachusetts (Healy and Bronner, 1922; cf. Horn, 1989). Healy had studied psychoanalysis in Vienna with Freud's trusted disciple Dr Helene Deutsch; he then undertook psychoanalysis with Dr Franz Alexander (Gardner, 1972, 1978; Snodgrass, 1984), incorporating the fruits of these experiences into his work with delinquent children in America (Gardner, 1972, 1978; Snodgrass, 1984).

In Healy's (1912) early work, such as his monograph on *Case Studies of Mentally and Morally Abnormal Types*, he eschewed lengthy psychoanalytic explanations about the delinquent children whom he encountered, but he did, nevertheless, provide rich case histories, which contain copious evidence of the deprived and often cruel backgrounds from which these young criminals hailed. In the tradition of Freud (and subsequently Aichhorn), Healy supplied detailed quotations from the narratives of the young offenders themselves. For instance, with reference to a fifteen-year-old delinquent girl, Healy (1912, p. 7) reported her "Own Story" and quoted this young person as having endured a painful relationship with her father. As the girl explained, "He never liked me. He wanted me put in a Home when I was little" (quoted in Healy, 1912, p. 7). Other cases in this text brim with tragic stories of early bereavement and of a lack of adequate emotional care.

In 1915, Healy, then Director of the Psychopathic Institute in Chicago and also Associate Professor of Mental and Nervous Diseases at the Chicago Policlinic, published a hefty landmark volume, entitled *The Individual Delinquent: A Text-Book of Diagnosis and Prognosis for All Concerned in Understanding Offenders* (Healy, 1915). As the supratitle of Healy's book indicates, he undertook a meticulous study of the delinquent as an "*Individual*", rather than as an object, having deeply appreciated that one must take time to study each unique person with great care. One of the very first American clinicians to champion Freud's method, Healy (1915, p. 120) stated boldly that, "The therapeutic effects of the application of the psychoanalytic method to the study of offenders prove in some instances nothing short of brilliant. Such results would warrant from every standpoint the expenditure of much effort" (cf. Healy, 1917).

Over the years, Healy immersed himself increasingly in the world of psychoanalysis, and he gradually became one of the leading disseminators of Freudian theory in the United States (Healy, Bronner, and Bowers, 1930). He also participated in the aforementioned trial of Leopold and Loeb as one of the expert witnesses. Following in the footsteps of August Aichhorn, William Healy helped to pioneer forensic child psychology, exploring the environmental causes, such as impoverished home environments, of delinquency in the young (e.g., Healy and Bronner, 1926; Healy and Alper, 1941).

Other early American pioneers of forensic psychodynamics included Dr Marion Kenworthy of the Bureau of Children's Guidance in New York City, who presented a talk on "Problems in Delinquency" before the New York Psychoanalytic Society on 31 January 1922 (Stern, 1922), as well as Dr Bernard Glueck, who spoke to that same organisation several months later, on 25 April 1922, on the subject of "Clinical Problems of the Psychopathic Personality" (Stern, 1922). Dr William Alanson White (1923) published an important book on *Insanity and the Criminal Law*; Dr Clarence Oberndorf (1939) studied the psychopathology of voyeurism; and the Hungarian-born Dr Sandor Lorand (1940), a stalwart member of the New York Psychoanalytic Society, investigated kleptomania; while Dr Gregory Zilboorg (1954), a Russian-born émigré to the United States, wrote at length on the psychology of crime more generally. In Topeka, Kansas, Dr Karl Menninger (1968) spoke bluntly against the cruelties of punishment. And, perhaps most famously of all, Dr Robert Lindner (1944), a psychoanalytically orientated psychologist who had undertaken his training analysis with Freud's disciple Dr Theodor Reik and who worked in the United States Penitentiary in Lewisburg, Pennsylvania, wrote a landmark book entitled *Rebel Without a Cause . . .: The Hypnoanalysis of a Criminal Psychopath*, which opened up new depths in the understanding of the offender patient and became the basis for a highly popular Hollywood film, *Rebel Without a Cause* (with no subtitle), released in 1955, starring James Dean in the title role (cf. Lindner, 1952, 1956).

The British School of Forensic Psychoanalysis

Building upon the foundations established by the Austrians, Germans, and others, the British, in particular, contributed substantially to the growth of psychoanalytic research in the fields of crime and perversion. Dr Montague David Eder, possibly the first person to practise psychoanalysis in Great Britain, worked at the Clinic for Juvenile Delinquents (Jones, 1936). And Dr Maurice Hamblin Smith, an early Associate Member of the British Psycho-Analytical Society, made huge strides as a pioneering prison psychiatrist. Smith held the post of Medical Officer at HM Prison Winson Green in Birmingham from 1920 until 1933 and also served as a sometime Lecturer at the Bethlem Royal Hospital. He advocated fervently that offenders should receive treatment in hospitals, rather than punishment in prisons (Smith, 1924). His achievements, most notably his landmark book on *The Psychology of the Criminal* (Smith, 1922; cf. Smith, 1933), enjoyed the appreciation of Dr Ernest Jones—the dean of British psychoanalysts—who wrote,

> Dr Hamblin Smith may justly be called the leading medical criminologist in England, and his pioneering work in the Birmingham courts and prisons is attracting wide attention among those concerned with prison reform. It is a matter for congratulation that a man of such distinction in his special field should be perspicacious and courageous enough to recognise the fundamental importance of psycho-analysis for his work. [Jones, 1923, p. 346]

Other early British psychoanalysts who immersed themselves in this arena included Dr James Glover—one of Karl Abraham's analysands—who lectured to the Penal Reform League on the psychology of punishment as early as 12 December 1919 (Jones, 1927), and Mr Cyril Burt, a psychologist who embraced psychoanalysis during the early part of his long career and encountered two cases of attempted fratricide while working at the London County Council (Flügel, 1921). Burt (1923, 1925) came to specialise in research on retardation; he became an unwitting pioneer in the field that would eventually come to be known as "forensic disability psychotherapy" (Kahr, 2014, p. xiii; cf. Corbett, 2014, 2016; Kahr, 2016b) by having delivered a talk on

"Delinquency and Mental Defect" to a joint meeting of the Medical Section and the Education Section of the British Psychological Society on 25 April 1923. And Dr William Stoddart (1923), one of the earliest psychoanalysts in Great Britain and a founder member of the British Psycho-Analytical Society in 1919, also presented a talk on this same subject alongside Cyril Burt.

The British mental health community welcomed contributors from abroad, such as the distinguished American psychodynamic forensic psychiatrist Dr Bernard Glueck, who delivered a talk on "Current Tendencies in American Criminology" to the psychoanalytically orientated Medical Section of the British Psychological Society on 23 November 1926 (British Psychological Society, 1928). The following year, Frau Melanie Klein, the Viennese-born and Berlin-trained child psychoanalyst, newly immigrated to London, addressed the Medical Section on 23 March 1927, on the subject of "Criminal Tendencies in Normal Children" (British Psychological Society, 1928), subsequently published under that very title (Klein, 1927). An experienced psychoanalyst, Melanie Klein (1932) recognised only too powerfully the sadistic fantasies so prevalent in the minds of youngsters, and she argued passionately that if children could receive psychoanalytic treatment, they might be less likely to become criminals in later life.

Not all of the contributors to the psychological study of criminality in the United Kingdom held membership in the British Psycho-Analytical Society. During the post–World War I era, a large medico-psychological movement emerged and spawned an army of creative psychodynamically orientated physicians. Indeed, during the 1920s and 1930s, staff at the Tavistock Clinic in London treated many delinquents. Shortly after the opening of the Tavistock Square Clinic for Functional Nervous Disorders—its earlier incarnation—the medical director, Dr Hugh Crichton Miller, spoke to the institution's Council of Administration about the importance of providing treatment for young thieves, urging that colleagues must endeavour to explore the hidden reasons why a person would engage in such stealing. A pioneer of preventative forensic psychotherapy, Crichton Miller urged that, "If we can find out the answer to that question we may possibly save the community from having on its hands in years to come one more incorrigible criminal" (quoted in Dicks, 1970, pp. 18–19).

The Tavistock Clinic also treated adult patients, of course. One man—a homosexual—attended for three-times-weekly psychotherapy; however, owing to his potential dangerousness, he arrived cuffed to a warder, with another warder standing guard. Apparently, this gentleman frightened some of the other patients in the waiting room; but fortunately, as treatment progressed, the warders began to dispense with the handcuffs (Dicks, 1970)!

During the early years, staff at the Tavistock Clinic identified quite a number of forensic patients and, eventually, conducted a follow-up study of 168 of these cases of both actual delinquents and potential delinquents, 104 of whom had benefited from three years or more of treatment. According to the results of this unpublished study, those who struggled with sexual deviations such as genital exhibitionism and sexual assault did improve greatly; and many of those who had engaged in acts of stealing subsequently refrained from doing so. Dr Henry Dicks (1970, p. 79), a long-serving psychiatrist at the clinic, recalled, "The general opinion of the staff at the Tavistock at that time was that delinquent behaviour was not a disease, but a symptom."

Among this group of forward-thinking British medical psychologists, Dr Ronald Grey Gordon made a particularly sagacious contribution to the study of delinquency from a psychoanalytic perspective. In his tract on miscreant youth, Gordon critiqued the prevalent view that naughty behaviour stems from biological factors. For instance, he quoted the case of a woman who brought her daughter to hospital, explaining that, "Our Emily can't tell the truth because she has got adenoids" (quoted in Gordon, 1928, p. 13). Dr Gordon expressed great dismay not only at the medicalisation of crime, but also towards its cruel treatment, castigating the widespread use of birching and other forms of futile retaliation then in vogue. In clear tones, Gordon (1928, p. 22) opined that, "really retributive punishment must be destructive and can have no place in the treatment of children".

Instead, Dr Gordon argued that crime results from deeper causes and carries more symbolic meanings. In his analysis of the case of a schoolboy who stole spectacles—indeed, *only* spectacles, nothing else—Gordon ascertained that this boy felt very guilty about masturbation and believed that others could tell from the expression on his face that he had indulged in onanism. Hence, in order to protect himself, he purloined glasses so that other people would have difficulty seeing his shameful expression up close!

Anticipating the work of both Dr John Bowlby and Dr Donald Winnicott, this lone medical psychologist—very much an independent voice—argued that home life occupies a far greater role in the genesis of juvenile delinquency than factors such as housing, opportunity, or provocation. Indeed, based on his clinical experience, Ronald Gordon (1928, p. 44) came to discover that the family life of many young criminals could only be described as sheer "hell". And to counteract such backgrounds, Gordon (1928, p. 79) insisted that, "If the home is utterly impossible, machinery must be easily put in motion to provide the child with a better one."

Gordon (1928, p. 61) adopted a sympathetic position towards classical psychoanalysis tinged with a slight suspicion, concluding that, "Psychotherapy may do much for such children and Psychoanalysis claims a great deal, but it is much too early to be sure of the good or ill effects of this complex procedure." Perhaps in view of Gordon's position as a sceptical sympathist, his work failed to gain wider acceptance within the psychoanalytic community and remains virtually forgotten to this day.

But amid this profusion of creative voices within the growing psychodynamic movement, three individuals, in particular—Dr Edward Glover, Dr John Bowlby, and Dr Donald Winnicott—completely transformed the landscape of forensic mental health in Great Britain during the 1930s and beyond. Each of these men deserves a book-length tribute, at least, and one deeply regrets that we can provide only a mere hint of the enormity of their contributions in the context of this broad overview of the history of forensic psychoanalysis.

Edward Glover, a Scot, trained in Berlin, where he undertook treatment from Dr Karl Abraham, as had his brother, fellow psychoanalyst Dr James Glover. Upon his return to Great Britain, Edward Glover gradually became the indispensable amanuensis to Dr Ernest Jones; throughout the 1920s and 1930s, these two men ruled the British Psycho-Analytical Society double-handedly (e.g., Kahr, 1995, 2016a). Edward Glover developed an interest in criminology quite early in his psychoanalytic career; and on 5 December 1924, he lectured to the Howard League for Penal Reform. Alas, he had to endure a great deal of ignorance and suspicion from the naïve audience. James Strachey, the pioneering British psychoanalyst, attended Glover's lecture and reported afterwards that,

> in the middle of it the clear ringing tones of an upper class lady's voice were heard—old Lady Dyke-Acland: "Might we have those two words again please, so as to get them clear?" . . . "Sadism and Masochism" . . . "Will you spell them please?" . . . "S–A–D–I . . ." I thought the poor man's nerve was going after that.—The discussion was awful,—sheer emotionalism. [Strachey, 1924, p. 141]

In 1932, Glover helped to establish The Association for the Scientific Treatment of Delinquency and Crime, which developed out of The

Association for the Scientific Treatment of Criminals, founded one year earlier, in 1931, by a small group of pioneers, including the aforementioned Dr Grace Pailthorpe, who had played a seminal role, as well as Dr Ernest Thomas Jensen (1915), a sometime specialist in tropical diseases and, formerly, a Physician to the Special Hospital for Officers at Kensington Palace Green, who wrote about the role of fear in the genesis of diseases such as alimentary toxaemia. The organisation eventually restyled itself as The Institute for the Scientific Treatment of Delinquency, known by its initials, the ISTD (Rumney, 1992a), and, ultimately, as the Institute for the Study and Treatment of Delinquency.

This institution explored the possibility of offering psychoanalytically informed psychotherapy to those individuals whose psychopathology had propelled them to commit crimes. In 1933, the ISTD sponsored the creation of a Psychopathic Clinic, which operated from a rented room in the West End Hospital for Nervous Diseases on Welbeck Street, in Central London. The very first patient—a violent forty-seven-year-old woman who had assaulted her employer—attended for her inaugural session on 18 September 1933 (Rumney, 1992b). In 1937, the fledgling clinic moved nearby, into new premises on Portman Street, and eventually adopted the name Portman Clinic (Rumney, 1992c), still in existence today, which gradually became the leading psychoanalytically orientated outpatient service for the treatment of those struggling with perversion or delinquency.

The ISTD endeavoured to promote research into the causes of crime and its prevention, as well as to encourage psychological treatment, rather than punition; and in its early days, both Professor Sigmund Freud and Dr Carl Gustav Jung served as sponsors. Eventually, the ISTD launched a periodical, *The British Journal of Delinquency*, edited by Dr Edward Glover, in collaboration with the criminologist Professor Hermann Mannheim and the child psychiatrist Dr Emanuel Miller. A number of psychoanalytically orientated colleagues served on its Advisory Board, including Miss Anna Freud, as well as the noted geneticist and early supporter of psychoanalysis in Great Britain, Professor Lionel Penrose. The first volume included several overtly psychoanalytic articles on criminality, including Miss Hedwig Schwarz's (1950) study of a case of stealing, and Mr Hans Zulliger's (1951) examination of the unconscious causes of theft. Eventually, the journal became transformed, in 1960, into *The British Journal of Criminology: Delinquency and Deviant Social Behaviour* (Rumney, 1992b). The work of the I.S.T.D. has persevered to the present day under the auspices of the Centre for Crime and Justice Studies in London, established in 1999.

As early as 19 October 1932, Glover approached his colleagues on the Board of the Institute of Psycho-Analysis—the training arm of the British Psycho-Analytical Society—to enquire which members might be in a position to offer their services to the newly established ISTD. The Board recommended that Dr Marjorie Franklin, Mrs Melanie Klein, and her daughter Dr Melitta Schmideberg, as well as Miss Helen Sheehan-Dare, Dr Karin Stephen, Dr Cyril Wilson, and Dr Sybille Yates might be suitable possibilities (British Psychoanalytical Society, 1925–1945), many of whom would, in the end, make notable contributions to forensic psychoanalysis. Both Marjorie Franklin and Melitta Schmideberg became key figures at the ISTD, and Cyril Wilson would work as a Consultant in Psychotherapy at the Broadmoor Criminal Lunatic Asylum (Winnicott, 1958b), the forerunner of the noted forensic institution Broadmoor Hospital, in Crowthorne, Berkshire. In addition, Glover collaborated with physicians from the Tavistock Clinic, such as Dr Basil Crowhurst Archer, Dr James Hadfield, and Dr Emanuel Miller, who also made contributions to the ISTD (Dicks, 1970).

Glover wrote extensively, both about perversion and crime (e.g., Glover, 1932, 1933, 1936, 1956, 1964) and about the abolition of the death penalty (e.g., Glover, 1960, 1961); and together with Hermann Mannheim and Emanuel Miller, he edited a collection of *Papers on Psychopathy* on behalf of the ISTD (Glover, Mannheim, and Miller, 1951). Most notably, he produced a volume entitled *Selected Papers on Psycho-Analysis: Volume II: The Roots of Crime* (Glover, 1960), a rich collection of papers that explored such diverse topics as the history of forensic psychology; the aetiology, diagnosis, and treatment of the criminal psychopath; the psychology and psychopathology of prostitution; and much more besides.

Across a long professional career as clinician, author, administrator, and ambassador for forensic matters, Edward Glover undertook an immense amount of work on behalf of the criminal patient. Unsurprisingly, the Portman Clinic inaugurated an annual memorial lecture in Glover's honour.

John Bowlby's investigation of the links between early loss and deprivation and the subsequent delinquency that results from such traumata requires little introduction. Based on his child psychiatric experience, Bowlby observed that youngsters who commit crimes will invariably have endured parental loss during the first years of life. This prescient idea has now achieved widespread recognition.

Bowlby began to publish in this arena as early as 1940 (e.g., Bowlby, 1940a, 1940b), and he produced his landmark papers on the forty-four juvenile thieves some four years thereafter (Bowlby, 1944a, 1944b); two years later, he transformed this work into monograph form (Bowlby, 1946). His research on the pathogenic effects of loss derived not only from his direct clinical work in child guidance, but also from his collaboration with fellow pioneering child psychiatrists Emanuel Miller and Donald Winnicott, who shared his concerns about the potentially deleterious effects of evacuating London's children at the outset of the Second World War (Bowlby, Miller, and Winnicott, 1939; cf. Bathurst, Brown, Bowlby, Bullen, Fairbairn, et al., 1941; Kahr, 2015). Indeed, the pathogenic nature of separation and loss would form the very backdrop of Bowlby's entire *oeuvre* across his long and productive professional lifetime (e.g., Bowlby, 1951a, 1951b, 1969, 1973, 1979, 1980; Bowlby and Robertson, 1953).

Donald Winnicott's contribution to the study of forensic matters can only be described as enormous. With characteristic modesty, he claimed Sigmund Freud as the font of all wisdom; and in a lecture on "Psycho-Analysis and the Sense of Guilt", delivered in honour of Freud's centenary in 1956, Winnicott (1958a, pp. 31–32) explained that, "More than anyone else it was Freud who paved the way for the understanding of antisocial behaviour and of crime as a *sequel* to an unconscious criminal intention, and a symptom of a failure in child-care." Like Freud and Klein—his predecessors—and like Bowlby—his contemporary—Winnicott underscored that criminality begins in the nursery and in the mind (Kahr, 2001).

The great child psychoanalyst encountered violent youngsters at the very outset of his career. In rich detail, Winnicott recalled his earliest child training patient:

> For my first child analysis I chose a delinquent. This boy attended regularly for a year and the treatment stopped because of the disturbance that the boy caused in the clinic. I could say that the analysis was going well, and its cessation caused distress both to the boy and to myself in spite of the fact that on several occasions I got badly bitten on the buttocks. The boy got out on the roof and also he spilt so much water that the basement became flooded. He broke into my locked car and drove it away in bottom gear on the self-starter. The clinic ordered termination of the treatment for the sake of the other patients. He went to an approved school. [Winnicott, 1956, p. 306]

The ravages of the war helped Winnicott, like Bowlby, to appreciate more and more the ways in which separation and loss form the backbone of delinquency in the young. Indeed, throughout much of World War II, Winnicott served as a psychiatric consultant to the Government Evacuation Scheme, in which post he visited a number of children's hostels that housed those evacuees who suffered from such a multitude of psychological difficulties—including juvenile delinquency—that they could not be maintained in ordinary billets. These children would, *inter alia*, terrorise local townsfolk and even set fire to hay ricks (Winnicott and Britton, 1947; cf. Winnicott, 1943, 1945; Winnicott and Britton, 1944).

After the war, Winnicott (1948, p. 180) became a pioneer of preventative forensic mental health by lobbying for provision for what he described as "the early anti-social case": in other words, those children who posed a risk of becoming full-fledged offenders and who might, therefore, benefit from psychological treatment sooner rather than later.

Winnicott not only documented the clinical consequences of early separation and traumatisation, but he also attempted to disseminate this knowledge far and wide. On 1 September 1949, he wrote two separate letters to government officials about this matter. He complained to Mr R. S. Hazlehurst that, "Stealing has practically no more relation to poverty and want than civil murder has to persecution" (Winnicott, 1949a, p. 17); and likewise, he wrote to Mr S. H. Hodge that criminals actually suffer from psychological illness (Winnicott, 1949b)—still a relatively new notion at that time.

In 1956, Winnicott presented yet another landmark paper, "Study of the Antisocial Tendency", published more simply as "The Antisocial Tendency", in which he endeavoured to provide clinical strategies for the treatment of delinquent acts, incorporating his prior knowledge about its causation. Winnicott discussed the case of a little boy called "John", who had begun to steal from shops in a compulsive manner. Unlike many clinicians of that era who regarded theft as an indication of degeneracy or disease, Winnicott considered stealing as hopeful: a communication from the child that he or she might be missing something! Keen to help parents develop a better understanding of their children, Winnicott (1956, p. 307) did not rush John into five-times weekly child analysis; rather, he orchestrated a simple conversation with the boy's mother, in which he interpreted, "'Why not tell him that you know that when he steals he is not wanting the things that he steals but he is looking for something that he has a right to: that he is making a claim on his mother and father because he feels deprived of their love.' I told her to use language which he could understand." The grateful mother followed Winnicott's advice and wrote to him some time thereafter that,

> I told him that what he really wanted when he stole money and food and things was his mum; and I must say I didn't really expect him to understand, but he did seem to. I asked him if he thought we didn't love him because he was so naughty some-times, and he said right out that he didn't think we did, much. Poor little scrap! I felt so awful, I can't tell you. [Quoted in Winnicott, 1956, p. 307]

Winnicott's interest in the antisocial tendency persisted throughout much of his long career (e.g., Winnicott, 1962–1963, 1966), and in a little-known typescript on "Meet to Be Stolen From", he even dared to suggest that "theft is a form of love" (Winnicott, n.d., p. 1).

Years later, Winnicott would develop his notion of the delinquent act as a cry for help when, on 19 April 1967, he addressed the Borstal Assistant Governors' Conference at King Alfred's College in Winchester, Hampshire, on the subject of "Delinquency as a Sign of Hope". This paper appeared in print in 1968, most helpfully, in the *Prison Service Journal* (Winnicott, 1968), rather than in a psychoanalytic periodical, thus disseminating Freudian thinking more extensively among probation officers and others working in the penal system.

It will not be at all widely known that, among his many contributions to the forensic mental health field, Winnicott campaigned strongly against capital punishment: for many centuries an unshifting feature of the British penal system. When Francis Graham-Haiman (1950), Secretary to the Royal Commission on Capital Punishment, wrote to the Institute of Psycho-Analysis, soliciting views on the death penalty, Winnicott, then Scientific Secretary, coordinated the reply. The Institute of Psycho-Analysis prepared a formal memorandum arguing that, "We are of the opinion that the deterrent effect of capital punishment has been much overrated" (Institute of Psycho-Analysis, 1950, p. 3), and that, irrespective of the death penalty, many people would continue to kill—including psychotics, epileptics, low-grade mental defectives, those with brain injury or organic brain disease, sexual perverts, suicidal people, disturbed adolescents, as well as those in states of passion, including someone catching a spouse *in flagrante delicto*. Spearheaded by Winnicott, the Institute of Psycho-Analysis also explained that, for many suicidal patients, the continued persistence of capital punishment might even serve as a "positive incentive to murder" (Institute of Psycho-Analysis, 1950, p. 5). Impressively, Winnicott and the committee recommended that psychoanalysis should be provided instead of the death penalty and, moreover, that prevention of mental illnesses in the first place would be even better!

Donald Winnicott not only stressed the early childhood origins of delinquency and criminality, he also regarded offenders with optimism rather than pessimism: still a desirable, though not always attainable, quality for contemporary forensic mental health professionals. Perhaps above all, in true Freudian fashion, Winnicott encouraged patients with violent impulses to transform their thoughts into words, rather than enact them in a physically harmful way. When Mr Richard Balbernie (1969), a psychologically orientated teacher at the Cotswold Community, near the village of Ashton Keynes, Wiltshire, wrote to Winnicott in 1969, enquiring whether one should tolerate foul language from children, the aged psychoanalyst replied, "How much nicer is hate than murder and how silly we are if we mind when children scream out 'fuck' and other obscenities" (Winnicott, 1969; cf. Kahr, 1998).

Over the years, many other notable British-based practitioners made useful contributions that underscored the importance of psychodynamics in the treatment of offenders. Dr John Rickman (1932), one of the pillars of British psychoanalysis and British medical psychology more generally, contributed a short essay on the dynamics of crime. Miss Mary Chadwick (1932), a nurse who had trained as a psychoanalyst, wrote about delinquent children, as did the Adlerian child psychiatrist Dr Ethel Dukes and the physician and child psychotherapist Dr Margaret Lowenfeld, both of the Institute of Child Psychology in London (Lowenfeld and Dukes, 1938). And Dr Michael Bálint (1951), the Hungarian-born psychoanalyst who had emigrated from his homeland to escape the Nazi menace, wrote an important essay about the cruelty of punishing offenders (cf. Bálint, 1937).

The post-war creation of forensic psychotherapy

From its very inception, psychoanalytically orientated forensic practitioners challenged the deeply entrenched notions of original sin and of the necessity for punishment (Finder, 2006). The early psychoanalytic theoreticians of criminology stressed, by contrast, a number of new and, ultimately, seminal ideas. First and foremost, these clinical researchers hypothesised that criminal acts stem from early traumatic experiences that become repressed in the unconscious mind and that, in consequence, a criminal who engages in illegal activity has no conscious understanding of why he or she has committed such a breach. Secondly, the pioneering generation of psychoanalysts argued that we administer punishment *not* for rational reasons but, rather, in order to exact unconscious retribution. And thirdly, these psychoanalytic investigators argued for treatment instead of punishment, and, increasingly, for prevention of lifetime criminality through early intervention.

In spite of the vast amount of clinical activity and the profusion of publications, not to mention the creation of mental health services such as the Portman Clinic, the forensic psychoanalytic movement lacked a formal structure as well as a comprehensive training, let alone any international coalition. Consequently, the work of the pioneers—though influential within the confines of classical psychoanalysis—made little direct impact upon the wider psychiatric community. For instance, in 1934, the mainstream criminologists Professor Sheldon Glueck, Professor of Criminology at the Harvard Law School, and his wife, Dr Eleanor Glueck, progenitors of the "Harvard Crime Survey", concluded that, in spite of the work by Sigmund Freud, August Aichhorn, Franz Alexander, and others, "A carefully planned and adequately controlled attack upon the problems of criminogenesis and therapy from the psychoanalytic point of view still remains to be made" (Glueck and Glueck, 1934, pp. 282–283). Two years later, Sheldon Glueck (1936, pp. 243–244), underscored that, "the possibilities of psychoanalysis in treating psychoneurotic offenders have been little explored" and that Freudianism had in no way become standard.

Indeed, the psychoanalytic approach to criminal behaviour remained confined, for the most part, to specialist Freudian publications. Consequently, the early psychoanalysts had to struggle against those who adopted more mainstream psychiatric models.

Additionally, the progenitors of the forensic psychodynamic movement had to endure tremendous suspicion not only from fellow mental health workers, but also from the wider population, not least from the growing Nazi menace. Indeed, on 13 February 1936, *Das Schwarze Korps* [*The Black Corps*]—the official newspaper of the *Schutzstaffel* [S.S.]—published a not uncharacteristically vicious attack on the Freudians who treated criminals far too leniently. According to the SS newspaper, the "collection of race traitors, sexual degenerates, and common criminals" (Anonymous, 1936, p. 223) so prevalent in Germany "were still being coddled by psychoanalysts" (Anonymous, 1936, p. 223). According to the Nazis, these deviants did not merit psychotherapy but, rather, incarceration in concentration camps.

At least one pioneer of forensic psychoanalysis could not continue his important work, owing to the fact that he became a victim of the Nazis.

Dr jur. Géza Dukes—a lawyer by background—developed a strong interest in psychoanalysis, having studied under Dr Sándor Ferenczi (1915). On 6 February 1926, Dr Dukes delivered a talk to the Hungarian Psycho-Analytical Society on "Eine neue Strafrechtstheorie" ["A New Theory of Penal Law" (Ferenczi, 1926)]. Dukes attended as a guest; and in his talk, he criticised the work of the Viennese psychoanalyst Dr Theodor Reik, who had already written extensively on criminological topics (Hermann, 1926). A loyal sympathist to the psychoanalytic movement, Dukes would eventually come to translate Freud's (1923) tract Das Ich und das Es [The Ego and the Id] into Hungarian, in collaboration with Dr István Hollós (Freud, n.d. [1937]). Over time, Dukes devoted himself extensively to the study of forensic matters, and his immersion in this work culminated in the publication of an extremely useful, but little read, essay on "The Development of Psycho-Analytic Criminology" (Dukes, 1946), which appeared in The International Journal of Psycho-Analysis. Tragically, in spite of efforts by fellow psychoanalysts to rescue Dukes (Mészáros, 2014), he died in a concentration camp.

Nevertheless, many psychoanalytic workers persevered. In 1939, a group of American clinicians launched the Journal of Criminal Psychopathology, under the editorship of Dr Vernon Branham, a disciple of the early American psychoanalyst Dr William Alanson White. A leading specialist in work with delinquents, Branham founded the Section on Forensic Psychiatry of the American Psychiatric Association in 1933 (Overholser, 1952). He published a number of worthwhile contributions written by Freudian practitioners (e.g., Oberndorf, 1939; Lorand, 1940) in the Journal of Criminal Psychopathology; but, alas, this periodical did not survive for very long.

During the early 1950s, Dr Benjamin Karpman, a distinguished psychodynamic psychiatrist based at St. Elizabeth's Hospital in Washington, DC, who had already written on numerous subjects, including delinquency (Karpman, 1939), insanity (Karpman, 1942), the psychodynamics of exhibitionism (Karpman, 1948), and paedophilia (Karpman, 1950), collaborated with Dr Melitta Schmideberg to create a new periodical, the *Archives of Criminal Psychodynamics*. Although Schmideberg strove passionately to attract some of the world's top psychoanalytic clinicians as potential contributors, she did not always succeed. For instance, in 1953, she wrote to Donald Winnicott, whom she had known for over twenty years, and proclaimed,

> It is with great pleasure that I can personally announce to you the inauguration of a new Journal, which will be devoted exclusively to the study of criminal behavior. This field has been dominated too long by the non-analytic professionals, despite the discoveries of Freud in regards to psychodynamics. [Schmideberg, 1953]

She urged Winnicott to contribute an article; alas, he never quite managed to do so, and within a short time this periodical also foundered.

In fact, some of the psychoanalytic colleagues who gravitated towards forensic work developed a reputation for being quasi-forensic themselves as personalities. For instance, after Melitta Schmideberg emigrated from London to the United States in 1946, Dr Ernest Jones (1946, p. 59) wrote to his long-standing colleague, Dr Abraham Brill, "I hope Dr Schmideberg will stay in America. She has an excellent flair, probably because of personal reasons, for delinquents and is very intelligent. But she was a great nuisance in the Society and perhaps may find more scope in New York for her quarrelsomeness."

Very few psychodynamic forensic specialists succeeding in publishing their work in mainstream psychiatric or psychological periodicals, and this insularity also forestalled the development of the forensic psychotherapeutic profession. A rare exception includes Dr John Charsley Mackwood (1949), a medical psychotherapist at HM Prison Commission, based in Wormwood Scrubs Prison in London, who recommended psychotherapeutic interventions for offenders. Born in Colombo, in Ceylon (Anonymous, 1958), Mackwood spent the early part of his career working in general medical practice before gravitating towards prison psychiatry, having served previously as a clinical assistant at the Tavistock Clinic in London during the 1930s, during which time he became exposed to an eclectic mixture of Freudian, Jungian, Adlerian, and Stekelian approaches (Dicks, 1970).

Mackwood (1947) certainly championed the use of psychoanalytically orientated psychotherapy in the prison setting; but although he deeply appreciated the main tenets of psychoanalysis, Mackwood (1949, 1954) also recognised that traditional psychotherapy requires a great deal of time, and consequently he supported not only individual psychotherapy for inmates, but also group psychotherapy, which permitted a larger number of inmate patients to receive treatment. Mackwood even established a special unit at Wormwood Scrubs to protect those prisoners undergoing psychotherapy; and in the course of his work with these men he discovered that "the chief distinction between the neuroses and delinquency is that we find symptoms in the former and actions in the latter" (Mackwood, 1949, p. 13), noting, also, that psychotherapeutic interventions contribute to the containment of criminal acting-out.

Never formally trained in classical psychoanalysis, John Mackwood certainly personified the growing impact of psychodynamic thought within the forensic mental health profession more generally. A modest man, he came to appreciate that psychoanalysis must not be regarded as a magical panacea, and he cautioned that,

> The psycho-analytic method has uncovered a vast field of hidden motives behind human conduct, but one becomes aware of a level where the probes seem to be too blunt to be entirely satisfactory. And if this is so, it is not possible to lay claim to the possession of positive knowledge of all the motives behind delinquent behaviour. [Mackwood, 1949, p. 15]

Fortunately, psychoanalytic efforts soon began to penetrate mainstream popular culture, if not mainstream academic publications. Just as, back in 1926, the Continental psychoanalysts had impacted upon the public at large with the production of the German-language film *Geheimnisse einer Seele*, so, too, did their English-language counterparts—most spectacularly, through the work of Alfred Hitchcock. Spurred by the psychoanalytically sympathetic producer David O. Selznick, Hitchcock employed the services of Dr May Romm, a noted Russian-born American psychoanalyst, as psychiatric adviser to his 1945 film, *Spellbound*. Under the influence of psychoanalytic theory, this compelling motion picture engaged in a very deft manner not only with actual murder, but also with "accidental" murder and fantasied murder (Leff, 1987).

In 1960, Hitchcock completed his even more famous film, *Psycho*, an impactful cinematic exploration of a psychotic killer, which climaxes with a significant scene in which a dynamically orientated psychiatrist provides a detailed and serious theory as to why "Norman Bates" committed multiple murders dressed in the clothes of his deceased mother. The psychiatrist, "Dr. Fred Richmond", portrayed by the actor Simon Oakland, hypothesises that the protagonist, Mr Bates, jealous of his mother's new lover, perpetrated matricide—"the most unbearable crime of all"—and that as a result he attempted to master this tragedy by *becoming* his mother in his mind! The psychiatrist further explained that, whenever Norman Bates became sexually aroused by a woman, that part of him that had already identified with the deceased mother would become pathologically jealous; and thus, the mother-identified aspect of Norman Bates would be forced to kill off any potential female rival. Without mentioning the term "Oedipus complex", the psychiatrist nonetheless gave voice to a very traditional psychoanalytic hypothesis about the child's conflictual feelings of eroticism and murderousness towards parental figures. Hitchcock may thus be credited with a critical role in the dissemination of psychoanalytic ideas about the genesis of criminality.

As word began to spread gradually about the possibility that psychoanalysts and psychotherapists might be able to work successfully with dangerous criminals, the more conservative, more punitively orientated members of the establishment protested. Indeed, Noël Coward, the most celebrated songwriter in Great Britain for much of the mid-twentieth-century, lampooned the possibility of psychoanalysis for offender patients in the first chorus of his very biting song "Three Juvenile Delinquents", penned for his musical comedy *Ace of Clubs*, first performed in 1950, on the stage of the Cambridge Theatre in London. In this sarcastic number, Coward's delinquents dismiss psychoanalysts as ineffectual people who attempt to civilise criminals rather fruitlessly.

But from time to time, in contrast to Noël Coward's suspiciousness, sympathists would appear, often from unexpected quarters outside the mental health field. In 1940, Atwell Westwick, a Judge of the Superior Court of Santa Barbara, California, actually contributed a highly inspiring essay on "Criminology and Psychoanalysis" to *The Psychoanalytic Quarterly*, thus becoming perhaps the first judge to have committed himself in print to the advancement of the psychoanalytic cause. With tremendous foresight, Westwick (1940) conceded that punishment of the forensic patient remains a sheer waste of time; he dared to wonder,

> Can we not, in our well nigh hopeless and overwhelming struggle with the problems of delinquency and crime, profit by medical experience with the problems of health and disease? Will we not, eventually, terminate the senseless policy of sitting idly by until misbehavior occurs, often with irreparable damage, then dumping the delinquent into the juvenile court or reformatory and dumping the criminal into prison? [Westwick, 1940, p. 281]

This prescient legal professional argued that judges, probation officers, and social workers, as well as teachers and even parents, should actually receive training in psychoanalysis!

In spite of the lack of institutional support in the post-World War II era, a number of forward-thinking, psychoanalytically orientated professionals persevered in their attempt to introduce psychodynamic ideas into penal institutions and mental health clinics. For instance, in England, Dr Arthur Hyatt Williams (1964), a Kleinian psychoanalyst, practised psychotherapy with inmates in HM Wormwood Scrubs from the 1950s onwards, while Dr Ismond Rosen, a psychoanalyst trained in the Anna Freud school, laboured for many years at the Portman Clinic, specialising in the treatment of severe sexual deviations (e.g., Rosen, 1964b, 1979). Dr Rosen (1964a) has earned an important place in the history of forensic psychoanalysis for having edited the first landmark textbook on the sexual deviations, which included contributions not only from mental health professionals (e.g., Gillespie, 1964; Khan, 1964; Scott, 1964), but also from a lawyer (James, 1964) and even from a parliamentarian (Robinson, 1964).

From the 1970s onwards, Dr Murray Cox (1979, 1992a, 1992b) pioneered prison psychotherapy at HM Pentonville in London and also in the maximum secure institution of Broadmoor Hospital. And Dr Eileen Vizard, a child psychiatrist and psychoanalyst who worked for many years at the Tavistock Clinic, created the Young Abusers Project, in association with the Department of Health, the National Children's Home Action for Children, and the National Society for the Prevention of Cruelty to Children, providing preventative psychotherapy for young sexual offenders at risk of becoming career paedophiles (e.g., Mezey, Vizard, Hawkes, and Austin, 1991; Vizard, Monck, and Misch, 1995; Vizard, Wynick, Hawkes, Woods, and Jenkins, 1996; Vizard, 1997; Kahr, 2004).

Even noted politicians, such as the Welshman Leo Abse, a long-standing post-war Member of Parliament in the House of Commons—and brother of a psychoanalyst, Professor Wilfred Abse—campaigned for the more humane treatment of prisoners, for the abolition of the death penalty, and also for the decriminalisation of post-partum depressed mothers who committed infanticide (Kahr, 1996, 2009).

Among these great achievements, the work of Dr Estela Valentina Welldon stands out, perhaps above all, as truly exceptional. Not only did she alter our views about the nature of sexual perversion by recognising that women could behave as cruelly as men (e.g., Welldon,

1988, 1991, 1996, 2001, 2011), in particular towards their own bodies and towards the offspring of those bodies, but she also made a huge contribution to the proliferation of psychoanalytic ideas by developing the world's first formalised training in forensic psychotherapy—at the Portman Clinic in London—and through the creation of the International Association for Forensic Psychotherapy. Additionally, she developed the use of group psychotherapy and group analysis techniques as interventions that would enrich the range of treatment possibilities (e.g., Welldon, 1993, 2011).

Welldon not only launched the Diploma in Forensic Psychotherapy (later restyled as the Diploma in Forensic Psychotherapeutic Studies, and then, more recently, as the Diploma in Forensic Psychodynamic Psychotherapy), but she also obtained joint validation from both the British Postgraduate Medical Federation of the University of London and from the Faculty of Clinical Science of University College London, also part of the University of London—the first official recognition of forensic psychotherapy from an accredited institution of higher education! (Indeed, many of the contributors to this Festschrift—who include some of Welldon's earliest trainees and supervisees—hold this qualification with great pride.)

Through the sustained labours of Welldon, not only as clinician and creator, but also as teacher, author, administrator, ambassador, and popular disseminator, Great Britain now boasts several National Health Service consultancies in forensic psychotherapy. Additionally, the Royal College of Psychiatrists has established a Forensic Psychotherapy Special Interest Group; and the British Psychoanalytic Council has now recognised forensic psychodynamic psychotherapy as a professional category, validated under the auspices of the Forensic Psychotherapy Society. And in 2016, the University of London appointed Dr Gill McGauley as the world's first Professor of Forensic Psychotherapy and Medical Education—a post that she held all too briefly, owing to her untimely death only several months later.

As this volume represents, Welldon's students have transformed the landscape of the field, creating new sub-disciplines within the profession (e.g., Corbett, 2014, 2016). "Forensic psychotherapy" even boasts its own page on Wikipedia—the on-line encyclopaedia—a true measure of the discipline's standing in our modern, technologised world!

By having created institutional structures in this way, Welldon, and those who preceded her, laid the important groundwork for the

rich array of work undertaken by so many mental health professionals and legal professionals today.

In this chapter, one cannot hope to do justice to all the immense
contributions of psychoanalytic workers, from Freud to Welldon and
beyond, who have provided the very foundations for the future of
more enlightened treatments and interventions in the fields of criminology and forensic mental health. With regret, we must pass over
many of the truly seminal figures who have made rich discoveries
about violence and sexual perversion (such as Rosenthal, 1911; Stekel,
1912; Sadger, 1926; Forsyth, 1939; Penrose, 1939; Friedlander, 1947;
Federn and Meng, 1949; Jacobson, 1949; Johnson, 1949; Schmideberg, 1949; Simmel, 1949; Zulliger, 1949; Bromberg, 1951; Johnson
and Szurek, 1952; Freeman, 1955; Schmideberg, 1956; Zilboorg, 1956;
Freeman and Hoffman, 1970; deMause, 1974; Stoller, 1975, 1979; Binion, 1976), not to mention some of the more recent work by a vast
range of personalities who have done so (e.g., Bromberg and Small,
1983; Schreiber, 1983; Freeman, 1984; Strean and Freeman, 1991; Bar-
On, 1996; Pfäfflin, 1996; Williams, 1998; Skoler, 1998; Sinason, 2001,
2008a, 2008b, 2011, 2012; Kernberg, 2004; Cooney and Greenwood,
2005; Irvine, 2005; de Zulueta, 2006; Acquarone, 2008; Brafman, 2008;
Campher, 2008; Macleod, 2008; Sim, 2008; Aylward and Wooster,
2012; Stewart, 2016). We can only hope that a study such as this will
stimulate future historians and clinicians to embark upon additional
investigations.

Of course, it would be folly to imply in any way that each and
every attempt to humanise the legal system, or to abolish sadistic
forms of punishment, or to keep our world safe from those mentally
unwell people who commit crimes has been undertaken *exclusively*
by psychoanalytically informed members of the mental health professions. Humanitarians have for centuries endeavoured to transform
the landscape of crime. One need only cite, once again, Victor Hugo's
novel *Les Misérables*, published in 1862, or Oscar Wilde's incredibly
moving poem, "The Ballad of Reading Gaol", written in 1897, upon
his release from prison, to learn something about the ways in which
great writers have attempted to alter antiquated views of what constitutes a crime.

Perhaps few *littérateurs* ever captured the very essence of the
psychodynamics of criminality as well as did Mary Shelley, who,
in her remarkable tale of *Frankenstein; or, the Modern Prometheus: In
Three Volumes. Vol. II*, first published in 1818, spoke of the traumatic

origins of violence and of the role of humanity in its cure. In the ninth chapter of the second volume of the novel, the "creature" explains to "Victor Frankenstein" that, "I am malicious because I am miserable" and underscores further that, "If any being felt emotions of benevolence towards me, I should return them an hundred and an hundred fold; for that one creature's sake, I would make peace with the whole kind!"

Mary Shelley had long anticipated a similar observation about the roots of aggression provided more than a century later by Professor Sigmund Freud, who, while visiting the Sanatorium Schloß Tegel in the suburbs of Berlin, encountered a large, barking police dog in chains. When Freud's colleague, Dr Ernest Simmel, cautioned Freud—a dog-lover of long standing—against approaching too closely, Freud refused to heed such advice, and he released the animal instead. As Freud explained to Simmel, "If you had been chained up all your life you'd be vicious too" (quoted in Simmel, 1940, p. 174).

As early as 1945, Dr Girindrasekhar Bose (1945, p. 63), the leader of the psychoanalytic movement in India, lamented, "I am sorry the study of the individual criminal has not yet been deemed so fruitful a one as it assuredly promises to be." Prior to the formal development of forensic psychotherapy as an official discipline, very few workers regarded the childhood experiences of perpetrators as a proper arena of study. But in the wake of the remarkable efforts of psychoanalytic practitioners in both the pre-World-War-II and post-World-War-II eras, it has now become increasingly standard to appreciate that early life experiences impact profoundly upon the development of subsequent criminal behaviours.

Psychoanalytic practitioners have made immense contributions to the study of offending. Psychodynamic theoreticians and clinicians have appreciated, since the time of Freud and beyond, that violence represents a universal theme in the mind of every human being, and that the simple punishment of the designated offender will in no way abolish crime. Additionally, unlike the pre-Freudian criminologists, the psychoanalytically orientated forensic mental health professionals gave credence to motivation—especially unconscious motivation (Finder, 2006)—and have provided an increasingly rich theory of the aetiology of crime, often rooted in early violence, trauma, and separation. In doing so, psychoanalysts have removed criminal acts entirely from the discourses of heredity and race, so long prevalent in European criminology (Finder, 2006). Furthermore, forensic workers have developed fertile ways of intervening psychotherapeutically, both after the commission of a crime and also beforehand, in a preventative manner.

Although it has taken psychodynamic workers quite some time to establish themselves in the forensic field and also to transmit this hard-won knowledge about the deprivational origins of delinquency, we now have a platform upon which to stand—one that Estela Welldon and other pioneers from Sigmund Freud onwards have created and buttressed—offering us, at last, a more secure base for future endeavours and for creative breakthroughs.

REFERENCES

Abraham, Karl (1924a). Letter to Sigmund Freud. 25 May. In Sigmund Freud and Karl Abraham, *Briefwechsel 1907–1925: Vollständige Ausgabe. Band 2: 1915–1925*. Ernst Falzeder and Ludger M. Hermanns (Eds.), pp. 765–766. Vienna: Verlag Turia und Kant, 2009.

Abraham, Karl (1924b). Letter to Sigmund Freud. 25 May. In Sigmund Freud and Karl Abraham, *The Complete Correspondence of Sigmund Freud and Karl Abraham: 1907–1925. Completed Edition*. Ernst Falzeder (Ed.), Caroline Schwarzacher, Christine Trollope, and Klara Majthényi King (Transls.), pp. 505–506. London: H. Karnac (Books) / Other Press, 2002.

Abraham, Karl (1925). Letter to Sigmund Freud. 7 June. In Sigmund Freud and Karl Abraham, *Briefwechsel 1907–1925: Vollständige Ausgabe. Band 2: 1915–1925*. Ernst Falzeder and Ludger M. Hermanns (Eds.), pp. 818–819. Vienna: Verlag Turia und Kant, 2009.

Acquarone, Stella M. (2008). Violence and Babies. In Rosemary Campher (Ed.), *Violence in Children: Understanding and Helping Those Who Harm*, pp. 95–127. London: Karnac Books.

Adler, Alfred (1931). Die kriminelle Persönlichkeit und ihre Heilung: Ansprache, gehalten auf der Jahresversammlung der "Nationalen Komitees für Gefängnisse und Gefängnisarbeit", New York, 1930. *Internationale Zeitschrift für Individualpsychologie, 9*, 321–329.

Aichhorn, August (1925). *Verwahrloste Jugend: Die Psychoanalyse in der Fürsorgeerziehung. Zehn Vortäge zur ersten Einführung*. Vienna: Internationaler Psychoanalytischer Verlag.

Aichhorn, August (1932). Treatment Versus Punishment in the Management of Juvenile Delinquents. Frederick M. Sallagar (Transl.). In

Proceedings of the First International Congress on Mental Hygiene: Volume One, pp. 582–598. New York: International Committee for Mental Hygiene.

Aichhorn, Thomas (2014). "Ein Schuß gegen den Vater. Attentat eines Studenten": Sigmund Freud und der "Fall Ernst Haberl". *Luzifer-Amor*, *27*, Number *53*, 108–121.

Alexander, Franz (1925). Psychoanalytischen Gutachten vor Gericht. *Internationale Zeitschrift für Psychoanalyse, 11*, 128–129.

Alexander, Franz (1929). Strafbedürfnis und Todestrieb. *Internationale Zeitschrift für Psychoanalyse, 15*, 231–245.

Alexander, Franz (1930). Der Doppelmord eines 19jährigen. *Die psychoanalytische Bewegung, 2*, 80–93.

Alexander, Franz (1931a). Psychische Hygiene und Kriminalität. *Imago, 17*, 145–173.

Alexander, Franz (1931b). Ein besessener Autofahrer: Ein psychoanalytischen Gutachten. *Imago, 17*, 174–193.

Alexander, Franz (1937). A Double Murder Committed by a Nineteen Year Old Boy. *Psychoanalytic Review, 24*, 113–124.

Alexander, Franz, and Healy, William (1935a). *Roots of Crime: Psychoanalytic Studies*. New York: Alfred A. Knopf.

Alexander, Franz, and Healy, William D. (1935b). Ein Opfer der Verbrechermoral und eine nichtentdeckte Diebin: Zwei Analysen Krimineller. I. Der Fall Sigrid Amenson. *Imago, 21*, 5–43.

Alexander, Franz, and Healy, William (1935c). Ein Opfer der Verbrechermoral und eine nicht entdeckte Diebin: Zwei Analysen Krimineller. II. Der Fall Richard Vorland. *Imago, 21*, 158–206.

Alexander, Franz, and Staub, Hugo (1929a). *Der Verbrecher und seine Richter: Ein psychoanalytischer Einblick in die Welt der Paragraphen*. Vienna: Internationaler Psychoanalytischer Verlag.

Alexander, Franz, and Staub, Hugo (1929b). Der Kampf ums Recht. *Die psychoanalytische Bewegung, 1*, 117–122.

Anonymous (1924). Dr Hermine Hug-Hellmuth. *Internationale Zeitschrift für Psychoanalyse, 10*, 337–338.

Anonymous (1926). Indian Psycho-Analytical Society: Annual Report, 1925, pp. 291–293. In Max Eitingon (Ed.), *Bulletin of the International Psycho-Analytical Association. International Journal of Psycho-Analysis, 7*, 285–295.

Anonymous (1936). Concentration Camps and Their Inmates. In Anson Rabinbach and Sander L. Gilman (Eds.), *The Third Reich Sourcebook*, pp. 222–223. Berkeley, California: University of California Press, 2013.

Anonymous (1958). J. C. Mackwood, *M.C.*, M.R.C.S., L.R.C.P. *British Medical Journal*, 10 May, p. 1125.

Aylward, Peter, and Wooster, Gerald (2012). *Understanding Dunblane and Other Massacres: Forensic Studies of Homicide, Paedophilia, and Anorexia*. London: Karnac Books.

Baatz, Simon (2008). *For the Thrill of It: Leopold, Loeb, and the Murder That Shocked Chicago*. New York: Harper / HarperCollins Publishers.

Balbernie, Richard (1969). Letter to Donald W. Winnicott. 17 March. Box 7. File 10. Donald W. Winnicott Papers. Archives of Psychiatry, The Oskar Diethelm Library, The DeWitt Wallace Institute for the History of Psychiatry, Department of Psychiatry, Joan and Sanford I. Weill Medical College, Cornell University, The New York Presbyterian Hospital, New York, New York.

Bálint, Michael (1937). Ein Beitrag zum Fetischismus. *Internationale Zeitschrift für Psychoanalyse*, 23, 413–414.

Balint, Michael (1951). On Punishing Offenders. In George B. Wilbur, Warner Muensterberger, and Lottie M. Maury (Eds.), *Psychoanalysis and Culture: Essays in Honor of Géza Róheim*, pp. 254–279. New York: International Universities Press.

Banerji, Manmath N. (1925). The Indian Psycho-Analytical Society: Annual Report, 1924, pp. 240–242. In Max Eitingon (Ed.), *Bulletin of the International Psycho-Analytical Association. International Journal of Psycho-Analysis*, 6, 235–245.

Barag, Gerda (1950). From the Analysis of a Case of Cleptomania. In Moshe Wulff (Ed.), *Max Eitingon: In Memoriam*, pp. 222–235. Jerusalem: Israel Psycho-Analytical Society.

Bar-On, Dan (1996). Attempting to Overcome the Intergenerational Transmission of Trauma: Dialogue Between Descendants of Victims and of Perpetrators. In Roberta J. Apfel and Bennett Simon (Eds.), *Minefields in Their Hearts: The Mental Health of Children in War and Communal Violence*, pp. 165–188. New Haven, Connecticut: Yale University Press.

Bathurst, Georgina; Brown, Sibyl Clement; Bowlby, John; Bullen, G.A.; Fairbairn, Nancy; Isaacs, Susan; Mercer, N.S., Rooff, Madeline, and Thouless, Robert H. (1941). *The Cambridge Evacuation Survey: A Wartime Study in Social Welfare and Education*. Susan Isaacs, Sibyl Clement Brown, and Robert H. Thouless (Eds.). London: Methuen and Company.

Bauman, Richard A. (1996). *Crime and Punishment in Ancient Rome*. London: Routledge.

Beck, Oskar (1931). Ursache und Therapie bei verwahrlosten Jugendlichen. *Internationale Zeitschrift für Individualpsychologie*, 9, 396–402.

Bekynton, Thomas (1457). Register Entry 1062, pp. 287–290. In Thomas Bekynton (1443–1465), Bishop Bekynton's Register. In Thomas Bekynton, *The Register of Thomas Bekynton: Bishop of Bath and Wells. 1443–1465. Part I*. Henry C. Maxwell-Lyte and Michael C. B. Dawes (Eds.), pp. 1–427. n.p., 1934.

Berkowitz, Michael (2006). Unmasking Counterhistory: An Introductory Explanation of Criminality and the Jewish Question. In Peter Becker and Richard F. Wetzell (Eds.), *Criminals and Their Scientists: The History of Criminology in International Perspective*, pp. 61–84. Washington, DC: German Historical Institute, and Cambridge: Cambridge University Press.

Bernfeld, Siegfried (1931). Die Tantalussituation: Bemerkungen zum "kriminellen Über-Ich". *Imago, 17*, 252–267.

Bertin, Célia (1982). *La Dernière Bonaparte*. Paris: Librairie Académique Perrin.

Binion, Rudolph (1976). *Hitler Among the Germans*. New York: Elsevier Scientific Publishing Company.

Bohne, Gotthold (1931). Individualpsychologische Beurteilung krimineller Persönlichkeiten. *Internationale Zeitschrift für Individualpsychologie, 9*, 330–345.

Bonaparte, Marie (1926). Diary Entry, 8 January. *Journal d'analyse*. Cited in Célia Bertin, *La Dernière Bonaparte*, p. 259. Paris: Librairie Académique Perrin, 1982.

Bonaparte, Marie (1927). Le Cas de Madame Lefebvre. *Revue Française de Psychanalyse, 1*, 149–198.

Bonaparte, Marie (1929). Der Fall Lefebvre: Zur Psychoanalyse einer Mörderin. Rudolph Loewenstein (Transl.). *Imago, 15*, 15–62.

Bonaparte, Marie (1952). Some Biopsychical Aspects of Sado-Masochism. John Rodker (Transl.). *International Journal of Psycho-Analysis, 33*, 373–384.

Bondio, Mariacarla Gadebusch (2006). From the "Atavistic" to the "Inferior" Criminal Type: The Impact of the Lombrosian Theory of the Born Criminal on German Psychiatry. In Peter Becker and Richard F. Wetzell (Eds.), *Criminals and Their Scientists: The History of Criminology in International Perspective*, pp. 183–205. Washington, DC: German Historical Institute; Cambridge: Cambridge University Press.

Bose, Girindrashekhar (1945). *Everyday Psycho-Analysis*. Calcutta: Susil Gupta.

Bowlby, John (1940a). The Problem of the Young Child. In John Rickman (Ed.), *Children in War-Time: The Uprooted Child, the Problem of the Young Child, the Deprived Mother, Foster-Parents, Visiting, the Teacher's Prob-*

lems, *Homes for Difficult Children*, pp. 19–30. London: New Education Fellowship.

Bowlby, John (1940b). The Influence of Early Environment in the Development of Neurosis and Neurotic Character. *International Journal of Psycho-Analysis*, 21, 154–178.

Bowlby, John (1944a). Forty-Four Juvenile Thieves: Their Characters and Home-Life. *International Journal of Psycho-Analysis*, 25, 19–53.

Bowlby, John (1944b). Forty-Four Juvenile Thieves: Their Characters and Home-Life (II). *International Journal of Psycho-Analysis*, 25, 107–128.

Bowlby, John (1946). *Forty-Four Juvenile Thieves: Their Characters and Home-Life*. Covent Garden, London: Baillière, Tindall and Cox.

Bowlby, John (1951a). *Maternal Care and Mental Health: A Report Prepared on Behalf of the World Health Organization as a Contribution to the United Nations Programme for the Welfare of Homeless Children*. Geneva: World Health Organization.

Bowlby, John (1951b). Maternal Care and Mental Health. *Bulletin de l'Organisation Mondiale de la Santé / Bulletin of the World Health Organization*, 3, 355–533.

Bowlby, John (1969). *Attachment and Loss: Volume I. Attachment*. London: Hogarth Press and the Institute of Psycho-Analysis.

Bowlby, John (1973). *Attachment and Loss: Volume II. Separation. Anxiety and Anger*. London: Hogarth Press and the Institute of Psycho-Analysis.

Bowlby, John (1979). *The Making and Breaking of Affectional Bonds*. London: Tavistock Publications.

Bowlby, John (1980). *Attachment and Loss: Volume III. Loss. Sadness and Depression*. London: Hogarth Press and the Institute of Psycho-Analysis.

Bowlby, John; Miller, Emanuel, and Winnicott, Donald W. (1939). Evacuation of Small Children. *British Medical Journal*, 16 December, pp. 1202–1203.

Bowlby, John, and Robertson, James (1953). A Two-Year-Old Goes to Hospital. *Proceedings of the Royal Society of Medicine*, 46, 425–426.

Brafman, Abrahão H. (2008). Violence in Children. In Rosemary Campher (Ed.), *Violence in Children: Understanding and Helping Those Who Harm*, pp. 55–70. London: Karnac Books.

Breuer, Josef (1895). Beobachtung I. Frl. Anna O . . . In Josef Breuer and Sigmund Freud, *Studien über Hysterie*, pp. 15–37. Vienna: Franz Deuticke.

British Psychoanalytical Society (1925–1945). *Institute Board Meetings: 16.1.1925 to 30.4.1945*. Archives of the British Psychoanalytical Society, British Psychoanalytical Society, Byron House, Maida Vale, London.

British Psychological Society (1928). Proceedings of the British Psychological Society, Medical Section. *British Journal of Medical Psychology*,
8, 85–86.

Bromberg, Norbert, and Small, Verna Volz (1983). *Hitler's Psychopathology*.
New York: International Universities Press.

Bromberg, Walter (1951). A Psychological Study of Murder. *International
Journal of Psycho-Analysis, 32*, 117–127.

Brouardel, Paul (1897). *L'Infanticide*. Paris: Librairie J.-B. Baillière et Fils.

Brown, Theodore M. (1987). Alan Gregg and the Rockefeller Foundation's
Support of Franz Alexander's Psychosomatic Research. *Bulletin of the
History of Medicine, 61*, 155–182.

Burt, Cyril (1923). Delinquency and Mental Defect (II). *British Journal of
Medical Psychology, 3*, 168–178.

Burt, Cyril (1925). *The Young Delinquent*. London: University of London
Press.

Campher, Rosemary (2008). Neutralizing Terror. In Rosemary Campher
(Ed.), *Violence in Children: Understanding and Helping Those Who Harm*,
pp. 185–209. London: Karnac Books.

Chadwick, Mary (1932). The Neurotic Child. In *Proceedings of the First
International Congress on Mental Hygiene: Volume Two*, pp. 447–465.
New York: International Committee for Mental Hygiene.

Chodorkoff, Bernard, and Baxter, Seymour (1974). "Secrets of a Soul": An
Early Psychoanalytic Film Venture. *American Imago, 31*, 319–334.

Church, Archibald (1893). Removal of Ovaries and Tubes in the Insane
and Neurotic. *American Journal of Obstetrics and Diseases of Women and
Children, 28*, 491–498.

Colaizzi, Janet (1989). *Homicidal Insanity, 1800–1985*. Tuscaloosa, Alabama: University of Alabama Press.

Cooney, Emily, and Greenwood, Lynn (2005). Working with Adolescents
Who Want to Kill Themselves. In Lynn Greenwood (Ed.), *Violent Ado-
lescents: Understanding the Destructive Impulse*, pp. 73–85. London: H.
Karnac (Books).

Copeman, William S. C. (1960). *Doctors and Disease in Tudor Times*. London: Dawson's of Pall Mall / William Dawson and Sons.

Corbett, Alan (2014). *Disabling Perversions: Forensic Psychotherapy with People with Intellectual Disabilities*. London: Karnac Books.

Corbett, Alan (2016). *Psychotherapy with Male Survivors of Sexual Abuse: The
Invisible Men*. London: Karnac Books.

Coward, Noël (1950). Three Juvenile Delinquents. In Noël Coward, *Noël
Coward: The Complete Lyrics*. Barry Day (Ed.), pp. 262–263. London:
Methuen / Methuen Publishing, 1998.

Cox, Murray (1979). Dynamic Psychotherapy with Sex-Offenders. In Ismond Rosen (Ed.), *Sexual Deviation: Second Edition*, pp. 306–350. Oxford: Oxford University Press.

Cox, Murray (Ed.) (1992a). *Shakespeare Comes to Broadmoor: "The Actors are Come Hither". The Performance of Tragedy in a Secure Psychiatric Hospital*. London: Jessica Kingsley Publishers.

Cox, Murray (1992b). Forensic Psychiatry and Forensic Psychotherapy. In Murray Cox (Ed.), *Shakespeare Comes to Broadmoor: "The Actors Are Come Hither". The Performance of Tragedy in a Secure Psychiatric Hospital*, pp. 253–258. London: Jessica Kingsley Publishers.

Darrow, Clarence (1922). *Crime: Its Cause and Treatment*. New York: Thomas Y. Crowell Company Publishers.

Darrow, Clarence (1932). *The Story of My Life*. New York: Charles Scribner's Sons.

Davie, Neil (2005). *Tracing the Criminal: The Rise of Scientific Criminology in Britain. 1860–1918*. Oxford: Bardwell Press.

deMause, Lloyd (1974). The Evolution of Childhood. In Lloyd deMause (Ed.), *The History of Childhood*, pp. 1–73. New York: Psychohistory Press.

Democritus Junior [Robert Burton] (1660). *The Anatomy of Melancholy: What it is, with All the Kinds Causes, Symptomes, Prognostickes, & Seuerall Cures of it. In Three Partitions, with their Severall Sections, Members & Subjections, Philosophically, Medicinally, Historically, Opened & Cut Up*. London: H. Cripps.

Deutsch, Helene (1973). *Confrontations with Myself: An Epilogue*. New York: W.W. Norton and Company.

de Zulueta, Felicity (2006). Inducing Traumatic Attachment in Adults with a History of Child Abuse: Forensic Applications. *British Journal of Forensic Practice*, 8, 4–15.

Dicks, Henry V. (1970). *Fifty Years of the Tavistock Clinic*. London: Routledge and Kegan Paul.

Döblin, Alfred (1924). *Die beiden Freundinnen und ihr Giftmord*. Berlin: Verlag die Schmiede.

Dukes, Geza (1946). The Development of Psycho-Analytic Criminology. *International Journal of Psycho-Analysis*, 27, 145–151.

Eissler, Kurt R. (1949). A Biographical Outline. In Kurt R. Eissler, Susan H. Kubie, and Gertrud M. Kurth (Eds.), *Searchlights on Delinquency: New Psychoanalytic Studies. Dedicated to Professor August Aichhorn, on the Occasion of His Seventieth Birthday. July 27, 1948*, pp. ix–xiii. New York: International Universities Press.

Eitingon, Max (1925a). Berliner Psychoanalytische Vereinigung: II. Quartal 1925, pp. 502–503. In Max Eitingon (Ed.), *Korrespondenzblatt der Internationalen Psychoanalytischen Vereinigung. Internationale Zeitschrift für Psychoanalyse*, *11*, 501–528.

Eitingon, Max (1925b). Untitled Report. 4 September, pp. 139–141. In Anonymous, Report of the Ninth Psycho-Analytical Congress, pp. 119–143. *Bulletin of the International Psycho-Analytical Association. International Journal of Psycho-Analysis*, *7*, 119–143, 1926.

Evans, Richard J. (1996). *Rituals of Retribution: Capital Punishment in Germany. 1600–1987*. Oxford: Oxford University Press.

Federn, Paul (1913). Beiträge zur Analyse des Sadismus und Masochismus: I. Die Quellen des männlichen Sadismus. *Internationale Zeitschrift für ärztliche Psychoanalyse*, *1*, 29–49.

Federn, Paul (1919). *Zur Psychologie der Revolution: Die vaterlose Gesellschaft. Nach Vorträgen in der Wiener psychoanalytischen Vereinigung und im Monistenbund*. Vienna: Anzengruber-Verlag Brüder Suschitzky.

Federn, Paul, and Meng, Heinrich (1949). Psychoanalytic Prevention Versus Therapeutic Psychoanalysis. In Kurt R. Eissler, Susan H. Kubie, and Gertrud M. Kurth (Eds.), *Searchlights on Delinquency: New Psychoanalytic Studies. Dedicated to Professor August Aichhorn, on the Occasion of His Seventieth Birthday. July 27, 1948*, pp. 26–34. New York: International Universities Press.

Ferenczi, Sándor (1909a). Letter to Sigmund Freud. 30 June. In Sigmund Freud and Sándor Ferenczi, *Briefwechsel: Band I / 1. 1908–1911*. Eva Brabant, Ernst Falzeder, Patrizia Giampieri-Deutsch, and André Haynal (Eds.), pp. 129–130. Vienna: Böhlau Verlag / Böhlau Verlag Gesellschaft, 1993.

Ferenczi, Sándor (1909b). Letter to Sigmund Freud. 20 November. In Sigmund Freud and Sándor Ferenczi, *Briefwechsel: Band I / 1. 1908–1911*. Eva Brabant, Ernst Falzeder, Patrizia Giampieri-Deutsch, and André Haynal (Eds.), pp. 167–171. Vienna: Böhlau Verlag / Böhlau Verlag Gesellschaft, 1993.

Ferenczi, Sándor (1910). Letter to Sigmund Freud. 4 March. In Sigmund Freud and Sándor Ferenczi, *Briefwechsel: Band I / 1. 1908–1911*. Eva Brabant, Ernst Falzeder, Patrizia Giampieri-Deutsch, and André Haynal (Eds.), pp. 226–227. Vienna: Böhlau Verlag / Böhlau Verlag Gesellschaft, 1993.

Ferenczi, Sándor (1915). Letter to Sigmund Freud. 4 January. In Sigmund Freud and Sándor Ferenczi, *Briefwechsel: Band II / 1. 1914–1916*. Ernst Falzeder, Eva Brabant, Patrizia Giampieri-Deutsch, and André Haynal (Eds.), p. 100. Vienna: Böhlau Verlag / Böhlau Verlag Gesellschaft, 1996.

Ferenczi, Sándor (1919). Pszichoanalízis és kriminológia. In *A pszicho-analízis haladása: Értekezések*, pp. 126–128. Budapest: Dick Manó Kiadása.

Ferenczi, Sándor (1922). *Populäre Vorträge über Psychoanalyse*. Vienna: Internationaler Psychoanalytischer Verlag.

Ferenczi, Sándor (1926). Letter to Sigmund Freud. 21 February. In Sigmund Freud and Sándor Ferenczi. *Briefwechsel: Band III / 2. 1925 bis 1933*. Ernst Falzeder, Eva Brabant, Patrizia Giampieri-Deutsch, and André Haynal (Eds.), p. 79. Vienna: Böhlau Verlag / Böhlau Verlag Gesellschaft, 2003.

Finder, Gabriel N. (2006). Criminals and Their Analysts: Psychoanalytic Criminology in Weimar Germany and the First Austrian Republic. In Peter Becker and Richard F. Wetzell (Eds.), *Criminals and Their Scientists: The History of Criminology in International Perspective*, pp. 447–469. Washington, DC: German Historical Institute, and Cambridge: Cambridge University Press.

Flügel, John C. (1921). *The Psycho-Analytic Study of the Family*. London: International Psycho-Analytical Press.

Forsyth, David (1939). The Case of a Middle-aged Embezzler. *British Journal of Medical Psychology*, *18*, 141–153.

Freeman, John C. (Ed.) (1978). *Prisons Past and Future*. London: Heinemann / Heinemann Educational Books.

Freeman, Lucy (1955). *"Before I Kill More . . ."*. New York: Crown Publishers.

Freeman, Lucy (1984). The "Seeds" of Murder as Sown "in the Nursery". *Current Issues in Psychoanalytic Practice*, *1*, Number 2, 19–28.

Freeman, Lucy, and Hoffman, Lisa (1970). *The Ordeal of Stephen Dennison*. Englewood Cliffs, New Jersey: Prentice-Hall.

Freud, Sigmund (1886). "Bericht": Ueber meine mit Universitäts-Jubiläums-Reisestipendium unternommene Reise nach Paris und Berlin. Oktober 1885—Ende März 1886. In Josef Gicklhorn and Renée Gicklhorn, *Sigmund Freuds akademische Laufbahn im Lichte der Dokumente*, pp. 82–89. Vienna: Verlag Urban und Schwarzenberg, 1960.

Freud, Sigmund (1895). Katharina . . . . In Josef Breuer and Sigmund Freud, *Studien über Hysterie*, pp. 106–116. Vienna: Franz Deuticke.

Freud, Sigmund (1896). L'Hérédité et l'étiologie des névroses. *Revue Neurologique*, *4*, 161–169.

Freud, Sigmund (1900). *Die Traumdeutung*. Vienna: Franz Deuticke.

Freud, Sigmund (1905). *Drei Abhandlungen zur Sexualtheorie*. Vienna: Franz Deuticke.

Freud, Sigmund (1909). Analyse der Phobie eines 5jährigen Knaben. *Jahrbuch für psychoanalytische und psychopathologische Forschungen, 1,* 1–109.

Freud, Sigmund (1912a). Über einige Übereinstimmungen im Seelenleben der Wilden und der Neurotiker: I. Die Inzestscheu. *Imago, 1,* 17–33.

Freud, Sigmund (1912b). Über einige Übereinstimmungen im Seelenleben der Wilden und der Neurotiker: II. Das Tabu und die Ambivalenz der Gefühlsregungen. *Imago, 1,* 213–227.

Freud, Sigmund (1912c). Über einige Übereinstimmungen im Seelenleben der Wilden und der Neurotiker: II. Das Tabu und die Ambivalenz der Gefühlsregungen. *Imago, 1,* 301–333.

Freud, Sigmund (1913a). *Totem und Tabu: Einige Übereinstimmungen im Seelenleben der Wilden und der Neurotiker.* Vienna: Hugo Heller und Compagnie.

Freud, Sigmund (1913b). Über einige Übereinstimmungen im Seelenleben der Wilden und der Neurotiker: III. Animismus, Magie und Allmacht der Gedanken. *Imago, 2,* 1–21.

Freud, Sigmund (1913c). Über einige Übereinstimmungen im Seelenleben der Wilden und der Neurotiker: IV. Die infantile Wiederkehr des Totemismus. *Imago, 2,* 357–408.

Freud, Sigmund (1914). Zur Geschichte der psychoanalytischen Bewegung. *Jahrbuch der Psychoanalyse, 6,* 207–260.

Freud, Sigmund (1916a). Einige Charaktertypen aus der psychoanalytischen Arbeit. *Imago, 4,* 317–336.

Freud, Sigmund (1916b). Some Character-Types Met with in Psycho-Analytic Work. E. C. Mayne and James Strachey (Transls.). In Sigmund Freud, *The Standard Edition of the Complete Psychological Works of Sigmund Freud: Volume XIV. (1914–1916). On the History of the Psycho-Analytic Movement. Papers on Metapsychology and Other Works.* James Strachey, Anna Freud, Alix Strachey, and Alan Tyson (Eds. and Transls.), pp. 311–333. London: Hogarth Press and the Institute of Psycho-Analysis, 1957.

Freud, Sigmund (1923). *Das Ich und das Es.* Vienna: Internationaler Psychoanalytischer Verlag.

Freud, Sigmund (1924a). Letter to George Seldes. 29 June. In George Seldes, *Tell the Truth and Run,* p. 107. New York: Greenberg, 1953.

Freud, Sigmund (1924b). Letter to George Seldes. 29 June. In Ernest Jones, *The Life and Work of Sigmund Freud: Volume 3. The Last Phase. 1919–1939,* p. 103. New York: Basic Books, 1957.

Freud, Sigmund (1925a). Geleitwort. In August Aichhorn, *Verwahrloste*

Jugend: Die Psychoanalyse in der Fürsorgeerziehung. Zehn Vortäge zur ersten Einführung, pp. 3–6. Vienna: Internationaler Psychoanalytischer Verlag.

Freud, Sigmund (1925b). Letter to Karl Abraham. 9 June. In Sigmund Freud and Karl Abraham, *Briefwechsel 1907–1925: Vollständige Ausgabe. Band 2: 1915–1925*. Ernst Falzeder and Ludger M. Hermanns (Eds.), pp. 823–824. Vienna: Verlag Turia und Kant, 2009.

Freud, Sigmund (1925c). Letter to Karl Abraham. 10 August. In Sigmund Freud and Karl Abraham, *Briefwechsel 1907–1925: Vollständige Ausgabe. Band 2: 1915–1925*. Ernst Falzeder and Ludger M. Hermanns (Eds.), pp. 833–834. Vienna: Verlag Turia und Kant, 2009.

Freud, Sigmund (1927a). Fetischismus. *Internationale Zeitschrift für Psychoanalyse, 13*, 373–378.

Freud, Sigmund (1927b). Letter to Marie Bonaparte. 19 January. Box 137. Folder 7. Sigmund Freud Papers. Sigmund Freud Collection. Manuscript Reading Room, Room 101, Manuscript Division, James Madison Memorial Building, Library of Congress, Washington, DC.

Freud, Sigmund (1927c). Letter to Marie Bonaparte. 19 January. Hermann Nunberg and Margarethe Nunberg (Transls.). Box 137. Folder 6. Sigmund Freud Papers. Sigmund Freud Collection. Manuscript Reading Room, Room 101, Manuscript Division, James Madison Memorial Building, Library of Congress, Washington, DC.

Freud, Sigmund (1930a). Letter to Marie Bonaparte. 20 February. Box 137. Folder 7. Sigmund Freud Papers. Sigmund Freud Collection. Manuscript Reading Room, Room 101, Manuscript Division, James Madison Memorial Building, Library of Congress, Washington, DC.

Freud, Sigmund (1930b). Letter to Marie Bonaparte. 20 February. Hermann Nunberg and Margarethe Nunberg (Transls.). Box 137. Folder 6. Sigmund Freud Papers. Sigmund Freud Collection. Manuscript Reading Room, Room 101, Manuscript Division, James Madison Memorial Building, Library of Congress, Washington, DC.

Freud, Sigmund (1931a). Die Fakultätsgutachten im Prozeß Halsmann. *Psychoanalytische Bewegung, 3*, 32–34.

Freud, Sigmund (1931b). Geleitworte: Prof. Dr. S. Freud, Wien. In Georg Fuchs, *Wir Zuchthäusler: Erinnerungen des Zellengefangenen Nr. 2911*, pp. x–xi. Munich: Albert Langen.

Freud, Sigmund (1931c). Letter to Georg Fuchs. n.d., pp. 199–200. In Kurt R. Eissler, A Hitherto Unnoticed Letter by Sigmund Freud. *International Journal of Psycho-Analysis, 42*, 197–204, 1961.

Freud, Sigmund (1931d). Letter to Marie Bonaparte. 15 December. Box 137. Folder 7. Sigmund Freud Papers. Sigmund Freud Collection.

Manuscript Reading Room, Room 101, Manuscript Division, James Madison Memorial Building, Library of Congress, Washington, DC.

Freud, Sigmund (1931e). Letter to Marie Bonaparte. 15 December. Hermann Nunberg and Margarethe Nunberg (Transls.). Box 137. Folder 6. Sigmund Freud Papers. Sigmund Freud Collection. Manuscript Reading Room, Room 101, Manuscript Division, James Madison Memorial Building, Library of Congress, Washington, DC.

Freud, Sigmund (1933). Letter to Grace Pailthorpe. 8 November. Box 38. Folder 10. Sigmund Freud Papers. Sigmund Freud Collection. Manuscript Reading Room, Room 101, Manuscript Division, James Madison Memorial Building, Library of Congress, Washington, DC.

Freud, Sigmund (1992). *The Diary of Sigmund Freud: 1929–1939. A Record of the Final Decade.* Michael Molnar (Ed. and Transl.). London: Hogarth Press.

Freud, Sigmund (n.d. [1937]). *Az ősvalami és az én.* István Hollós and Géza Dukes (Transls.). Budapest: Pantheon Kiadás.

Friedlander, Kate (1947). *The Psycho-Analytical Approach to Juvenile Delinquency: Theory. Case-Studies. Treatment.* London: Kegan Paul, Trench, Trubner and Company.

Friedmann, Max (1928). Zur Psychanalyse und gerichtlichen Begutachtung der Kleptomanie. *Fortschritte der Sexualwissenschaft und Psychanalyse, 3,* 96–115.

Fromm, Erich (1931). Zur Psychologie des Verbrechers und der strafenden Gesellschaft. *Imago, 17,* 226–251.

Fromm, Erich (1973). *The Anatomy of Human Destructiveness.* New York: Holt, Rinehart and Winston.

Fuchs, Georg (1931). *Wir Zuchthäusler: Erinnerungen des Zellengefangenen Nr. 2911.* Munich: Albert Langen.

Fuechtner, Veronika (2011). *Berlin Psychoanalytic: Psychoanalysis and Culture in Weimar Republic Germany and Beyond.* Berkeley, California: University of California Press.

Galen (n.d.). The Diagnosis and Treatment of the Affections and Errors Peculiar to Each Person's Soul. Peter N. Singer (Transl.). In Galen, *Galen: Psychological Writings. Avoiding Distress. Character Traits. The Diagnosis and Treatment of the Affections and Errors Peculiar to Each Person's Soul. The Capacities of the Soul Depend on the Mixtures of the Body.* Peter N. Singer (Ed.), Vivian Nutton, Daniel Davies, Peter N. Singer, and Piero Tassinari (Transls.), pp. 237–314. Cambridge: Cambridge University Press, 2013.

Gallo, Rubén (2012). A Wild Freudian in Mexico: Raúl Carrancá y Trujillo. *Psychoanalysis and History, 14,* 253–268.

Gardner, George E. (1972). William Healy: 1869–1963. *Journal of the American Academy of Child Psychiatry*, *11*, 1–29.

Gardner, George E. (1978). William Healy: 1869–1963. In George E. Gifford, Jr. (Ed.), *Psychoanalysis, Psychotherapy, and the New England Medical Scene, 1894–1944*, pp. 251–272. New York: Science History Publications / USA: Neale Watson Academic Publications.

Gatrell, Vic A. C. (1994). *The Hanging Tree: Execution and the English People. 1770–1868*. Oxford: Oxford University Press.

Gillespie, William H. (1964). The Psycho-Analytic Theory of Sexual Deviation with Special Reference to Fetishism. In Ismond Rosen (Ed.), *The Pathology and Treatment of Sexual Deviation: A Methodological Approach*, pp. 123–145. London: Oxford University Press.

Gilman, Sander L. (1993). *Freud, Race, and Gender*. Princeton, New Jersey: Princeton University Press.

Glover, Edward (1932). The Psychology of Crime: V. *British Journal of Medical Psychology*, *12*, 270–272.

Glover, Edward (1933). The Relation of Perversion-Formation to the Development of Reality-Sense. *International Journal of Psycho-Analysis*, *14*, 486–504.

Glover, Edward (1936). *The Dangers of Being Human*. London: George Allen and Unwin.

Glover, Edward (1956). Psycho-Analysis and Criminology: A Political Survey. *International Journal of Psycho-Analysis*, *37*, 311–317.

Glover, Edward (1960). *Selected Papers on Psycho-Analysis: Volume II. The Roots of Crime*. London: Imago Publishing Company.

Glover, Edward (1961). Foreword. In Elizabeth Orman Tuttle, *The Crusade Against Capital Punishment in Great Britain*, pp. ix–x. London: Stevens and Sons, and Chicago, Illinois: Quadrangle Books.

Glover, Edward (1964). Aggression and Sado-Masochism. In Ismond Rosen (Ed.), *The Pathology and Treatment of Sexual Deviation: A Methodological Approach*, pp. 146–163. London: Oxford University Press.

Glover, Edward; Mannheim, Hermann, and Miller, Emanuel (Eds.) (1951). *Papers on Psychopathy*. London: Institute for the Study and Treatment of Delinquency / Baillière Tindall and Cox.

Glueck, Sheldon (1936). *Crime and Justice*. Boston, Massachusetts: Little, Brown, and Company.

Glueck, Sheldon, and Glueck, Eleanor T. (1934). *One Thousand Juvenile Delinquents: Their Treatment by Court and Clinic*. Cambridge, Massachusetts: Harvard University Press.

Gordon, Ronald G. (1928). *Autolycus or the Future for Miscreant Youth*. London: Kegan Paul, Trench, Trubner and Company, and New York: E.P. Dutton and Company.

Graham-Haiman, Francis (1950). Letter to the Institute of Psycho-Analysis. 13 January. GO/BA/FO1/15. Archives of the British Psychoanalytical Society, British Psychoanalytical Society, Byron House, Maida Vale, London.

Happel, Clara (1925). Aus der Analyse eines Falles von Päderastie: Vortrag aus der I. Deutschen Psychoanalytischen Zusammenkunft in Würzburg, Oktober 1924. *Internationale Zeitschrift für Psychoanalyse, 11*, 206–211.

Happel, Clara (1926). Notes on an Analysis of a Case of Paederasty. *International Journal of Psycho-Analysis, 7*, 229–236.

Hartnack, Christiane (2001). *Psychoanalysis in Colonial India*. New Delhi: Oxford University Press.

Haun, Friedrich (1931). Sträfe für Psychopathen? *Imago, 17*, 268–302.

Haycock, Dean A. (2014). *Murderous Minds: Exploring the Criminal Psychopathic Brain: Neurological Imaging and the Manifestation of Evil*. New York: Pegasus Books.

Healy, William (1912). *Case Studies of Mentally and Morally Abnormal Types*. n.p.: Harvard Summer School.

Healy, William (1915). *The Individual Delinquent: A Text-Book of Diagnosis and Prognosis for All Concerned in Understanding Offenders*. Boston, Massachusetts: Little, Brown, and Company.

Healy, William (1917). *Mental Conflicts and Misconduct*. Boston, Massachusetts: Little, Brown, and Company.

Healy, William, and Alper, Benedict S. (1941). *Criminal Youth and the Borstal System*. New York: Commonwealth Fund, and London: Humphrey Milford / Oxford University Press.

Healy, William, and Bronner, Augusta F. (1922). *Judge Baker Foundation: Case Studies. Series I. Case 1*. Boston, Massachusetts: Judge Baker Foundation.

Healy, William, and Bronner, Augusta F. (1926). *Delinquents and Criminals: Their Making and Unmaking. Studies in Two American Cities*. New York: Macmillan Company.

Healy, William; Bronner, Augusta F., and Bowers, Anna Mae (1930). *The Structure and Meaning of Psychoanalysis: As Related to Personality and Behavior*. New York: Alfred A. Knopf.

Hermann, Imre (1926). Hungarian Psycho-Analytical Society: First Quarter, 1926, pp. 535–536. *Bulletin of the International Psycho-Analytical Association. International Journal of Psycho-Analysis, 7*, 531–537.

Hillner, Julia (2015). *Prison, Punishment and Penance in Late Antiquity*. Cambridge: Cambridge University Press.

Horn, David G. (2003). *The Criminal Body: Lombroso and the Anatomy of Deviance*. New York: Routledge / Taylor and Francis Books, Taylor and Francis Group.

Horn, Margo (1989). *Before It's Too Late: The Child Guidance Movement in the United States, 1922–1945*. Philadelphia, Pennsylvania: Temple University Press.

Howard, Derek L. (1958). *John Howard: Prison Reformer*. London: Christopher Johnson.

Hutchinson, Robert (2005). *The Last Days of Henry VIII: Conspiracy, Treason and Heresy at the Court of the Dying Tyrant*. London: Weidenfeld and Nicolson / Orion Publishing Group.

Innocent IV (1246). The Rule of the Hospital Drawn Up by Innocent IV. In Herbert E. Salter (Ed.), *A Cartulary of the Hospital of St. John the Baptist: Vol. III*, pp. 1–6. Oxford: Clarendon Press / Oxford University Press, 1917.

Institute of Psycho-Analysis (1950). *Memorandum Submitted by the Institute of Psycho-Analysis to the Royal Commission on Capital Punishment*. G10/ BA/F01/09. Archives of the British Psychoanalytical Society, British Psychoanalytical Society, Byron House, Maida Vale, London.

Irvine, Bruce (2005). Violence in Care. In Lynn Greenwood (Ed.), *Violent Adolescents: Understanding the Destructive Impulse*, pp. 57–72. London: H. Karnac (Books).

Jacobson, Edith (1949). Observations on the Psychological Effect of Imprisonment on Female Political Prisoners. In Kurt R. Eissler, Susan H. Kubie, and Gertrud M. Kurth (Eds.), *Searchlights on Delinquency: New Psychoanalytic Studies. Dedicated to Professor August Aichhorn, on the Occasion of His Seventieth Birthday. July 27, 1948*, pp. 341–368. New York: International Universities Press.

Jacoby, Heinz (1931). Wie ich zum Verbrecher wurde. *Internationale Zeitschrift für Individualpsychologie*, 9, 389–395.

Jalava, Jarkko; Griffiths, Stephanie, and Maraun, Michael (2015). *The Myth of the Born Criminal: Psychopathy, Neurobiology, and the Creation of the Modern Degenerate*. Toronto: University of Toronto Press.

James, Thomas E. (1964). Law and the Sexual Offender. In Ismond Rosen (Ed.), *The Pathology and Treatment of Sexual Deviation: A Methodological Approach*, pp. 461–492. London: Oxford University Press.

Jensen, Ernest T. (1915). Fear and Disease. *The Lancet*. 30 January, pp. 231–233.

Johnson, Adelaide M. (1949). Sanctions for Superego Lacunae of Adolescents. In Kurt R. Eissler, Susan H. Kubie, and Gertrud M. Kurth (Eds.), *Searchlights on Delinquency: New Psychoanalytic Studies. Dedicated to Professor August Aichhorn, on the Occasion of His Seventieth Birthday. July 27, 1948*, pp. 225–245. New York: International Universities Press.

Johnson, Adelaide M., and Szurek, Stanislaus A. (1952). The Genesis of Antisocial Acting Out in Children and Adults. *Psychoanalytic Quarterly, 21*, 323–343.

Jones, Ernest (1923). Book Review of Maurice Hamblin Smith. *The Psychology of the Criminal. International Journal of Psycho-Analysis, 4*, 346.

Jones, Ernest (1927). James Glover: 1882–1926. *International Journal of Psycho-Analysis, 8*, 1–7.

Jones, Ernest (1936). M. D. Eder: 1866–1936. *International Journal of Psycho-Analysis, 17*, 143–146.

Jones, Ernest (1946). Letter to Abraham A. Brill. 8 March. Cited in Paul Roazen (2000). *Oedipus in Britain: Edward Glover and the Struggle Over Klein*, p. 59. New York: Other / Other Press.

Jones, Ernest (1957). *The Life and Work of Sigmund Freud: Volume 3. The Last Phase. 1919–1939*. New York: Basic Books.

Kahr, Brett (1991). The Sexual Molestation of Children: Historical Perspectives. *Journal of Psychohistory, 19*, 191–214.

Kahr, Brett (1995). Interview with Ursula Bowlby. 29 January.

Kahr, Brett (1996). Interview with Leo Abse. 12 June.

Kahr, Brett (1998). An Unpublished Fragment by Donald Winnicott. *NewSquiggle, 2*, 7.

Kahr, Brett (2001). Winnicott's Contribution to the Study of Dangerousness. In Brett Kahr (Ed.), *Forensic Psychotherapy and Psychopathology: Winnicottian Perspectives*, pp. 1–10. London: H. Karnac (Books).

Kahr, Brett (2004). Juvenile Paedophilia: The Psychodynamics of an Adolescent. In Charles Socarides and Loretta R. Loeb (Eds.), *The Mind of the Paedophile: Psychoanalytic Perspectives*, pp. 95–119. London: H. Karnac (Books).

Kahr, Brett (2005). Why Freud Turned Down $25,000: Mental Health Professionals in the Witness Box. *American Imago, 62*, 365–371.

Kahr, Brett (2007). Why Freud Turned Down $25,000. In Jane Ryan (Ed.), *Tales of Psychotherapy*, pp. 5–9. London: Karnac Books.

Kahr, Brett (2009). Leo Abse: Pioneer of Political Psychoanalysis. In Ania Abse (Ed.), *Leo Abse: 22 April 1917—19 August 2008*, pp. 65–68. Pontypool, Torfaen: Pontypool Museum.

Kahr, Brett (2010). Four Unknown Freud Anecdotes. *American Imago, 67*, 301–312.

Kahr, Brett (2013). *Life Lessons from Freud*. London: Macmillan / Pan Macmillan, Macmillan Publishers.

Kahr, Brett (2014). Series Editor's Foreword: Towards Forensic Disability Psychotherapy. In Alan Corbett, *Disabling Perversions: Forensic Psychotherapy with People with Intellectual Disabilities*, pp. xiii–xxii. London: Karnac Books.

Kahr, Brett (2015). "Led Astray by Their Half-Baked Pseudo-Scientific Rubbish": John Bowlby and the Paradigm Shift in Child Psychiatry. *Attachment: New Directions in Psychotherapy and Relational Psychoanalysis, 9*, 297–317.

Kahr, Brett (2016a). Ursula Longstaff Bowlby (1916–2000): The Creative Inspiration Behind the Secure Base. *Attachment: New Directions in Psychotherapy and Relational Psychoanalysis, 10*, 223–242.

Kahr, Brett (2016b). Series Editor's Foreword. In Alan Corbett, *Psychotherapy with Male Survivors of Sexual Abuse: The Invisible Men*, pp. xiii–xviii. London: Karnac Books.

Kahr, Brett (2017). *Coffee with Freud*. London: Karnac Books.

Karpman, Ben (1939). The Delinquent as a Type and Personality. *Journal of Criminal Psychopathology, 1*, 24–33.

Karpman, Ben (1942). Widening the Concepts of Insanity and Criminality. *Journal of Criminal Psychopathology, 4*, 129–144.

Karpman, Ben (1948). The Psychopathology of Exhibitionism: Review of the Literature. *Journal of Clinical Psychopathology, 9*, 179–225.

Karpman, Benjamin (1950). A Case of Pedophilia (Legally Rape) Cured by Psychoanalysis. *Psychoanalytic Review, 37*, 235–276.

Kernberg, Otto F. (2004). *Aggressivity, Narcissism, and Self-Destructiveness in the Psychotherapeutic Relationship: New Developments in the Psychopathology and Psychotherapy of Severe Personality Disorders*. New Haven, Connecticut: Yale University Press.

Khan, M. Masud R. (1964). The Role of Infantile Sexuality and Early Object Relations in Female Homosexuality. In Ismond Rosen (Ed.), *The Pathology and Treatment of Sexual Deviation: A Methodological Approach*, pp. 221–292. London: Oxford University Press.

Klein, Melanie (1927). Criminal Tendencies in Normal Children. *British Journal of Medical Psychology, 7*, 177–192.

Klein, Melanie (1932). *Die Psychoanalyse des Kindes*. Vienna: Internationaler Psychoanalytischer Verlag.

Kleist, Fritz (1931). Erfahrungen eines Individualpsychologen im Strafvollzug. *Internationale Zeitschrift für Individualpsychologie, 9*, 381–388.

Lange, Johannes (1929). *Verbrechen als Schicksal: Studien an kriminellen Zwillingen*. Leipzig: Georg Thieme, Verlag.

Lazar-Geroe, Clara (1942). First Annual Report of the Melbourne Institute for Psychoanalysis for the Year 1941, pp. 613–615. In Notes. *Psychoanalytic Quarterly, 11*, 611–617.

Leff, Leonard J. (1987). *Hitchcock and Selznick: The Rich and Strange Collaboration of Alfred Hitchcock and David O. Selznick in Hollywood.* New York: Weidenfeld and Nicolson / Wheatland Corporation.

Lewy, Ernst (1947). Ernst Simmel: 1882–1947. *International Journal of Psycho-Analysis, 28*, 121–123.

Lindner, Robert M. (1944). *Rebel Without a Cause . . .: The Hypnoanalysis of a Criminal Psychopath.* New York: Grune and Stratton.

Lindner, Robert (1952). *Prescription for Rebellion.* New York: Rinehart and Company.

Lindner, Robert (1956). *Must You Conform?* New York: Rinehart and Company.

Lippmann, Werner (1926). Analyse eines Kriminellen: (Ein Beitrag zur Kriminalpsychologie). *Fortschritte der Sexualwissenschaft und Psychanalyse, 2*, 288–316.

Lorand, Sandor (1940). Compulsive Stealing: Contribution to the Psychopathology of Cleptomania. *Journal of Criminal Psychopathology, 1*, 247–253.

Lowenfeld, Margaret, and Dukes, Ethel (1938). Play Therapy and Child Guidance. *British Medical Journal.* 17 December, p. 1281.

Löwy, Ida (1931). Eindrücke beim Jugendgericht. *Internationale Zeitschrift für Individualpsychologie, 9*, 367–371.

Lyons, Lewis (2003). *The History of Punishment.* London: Amber Books.

Mackwood, John C. (1947). Discussion on the Social Aspects of Homosexuality. *Proceedings of the Royal Society of Medicine*, Section of Psychiatry, *40*, 591–592.

Mackwood, John C. (1949). The Psychological Treatment of Offenders in Prison. *British Journal of Psychology: General Section, 40*, 5–22.

Mackwood, John C. (1954). Psychotherapy in Prisons and Corrective Institutions: [*Abridged*]. *Proceedings of the Royal Society of Medicine*, Section of Psychiatry, *47*, 220–221.

MacLean, George (1986). A Brief Story About Dr Hermine Hug-Hellmuth. *Canadian Journal of Psychiatry / Revue Canadienne de Psychiatrie, 31*, 586–589.

MacLean, George, and Rappen, Ulrich (1991). *Hermine Hug-Hellmuth: Her Life and Work.* New York: Routledge / Routledge, Chapman and Hall.

Macleod, Roderick (2008). The Kick of Life. In Rosemary Campher (Ed.), *Violence in Children: Understanding and Helping Those Who Harm*, pp. 71–93. London: Karnac Books.

McKenzie, Andrea (2007). *Tyburn's Martyrs: Execution in England, 1675–1775*. London: Hambledon Continuum / Continuum Books.

Menninger, Karl (1968). *The Crime of Punishment*. New York: Viking Press.

Mészároz, Judit (2014). *Ferenczi and Beyond: Exile of the Budapest School and Solidarity in the Psychoanalytic Movement During the Nazi Years*. Thomas A. Williams (Transl.). London: Karnac Books.

Mezey, Gillian; Vizard, Eileen; Hawkes, Colin, and Austin, Richard (1991). A Community Treatment Programme for Convicted Child Sex Offenders: A Preliminary Report. *Journal of Forensic Psychiatry, 2*, 11–25.

Moellenhoff, Fritz (1966). Hanns Sachs: 1881–1947. The Creative Unconscious. In Franz Alexander, Samuel Eisenstein, and Martin Grotjahn (Eds.), *Psychoanalytic Pioneers*, pp. 180–199. New York: Basic Books.

Mohr, George J. (1966). August Aichhorn: 1878–1949. Friend of the Wayward Youth. In Franz Alexander, Samuel Eisenstein, and Martin Grotjahn (Eds.), *Psychoanalytic Pioneers*, pp. 348–359. New York: Basic Books.

Nägele, Otto (1931). Kriminalität und Justiz. *Internationale Zeitschrift für Individualpsychologie, 9*, 350–357.

Natterson, Joseph M. (1966). Theodor Reik: b. 1888. Masochism in Modern Man. In Franz Alexander, Samuel Eisenstein, and Martin Grotjahn (Eds.), *Psychoanalytic Pioneers*, pp. 249–264. New York: Basic Books.

Nunberg, Hermann (1926). The Sense of Guilt and the Need for Punishment. *International Journal of Psycho-Analysis, 7*, 420–433.

Oberndorf, Clarence P. (1939). Voyeurism as a Crime. *Journal of Criminal Psychopathology, 1*, 103–111.

Overholser, Winfred (1952). Vernon C. Branham, M.D.: 1889–1951. *American Journal of Psychiatry, 108*, 640.

Pailthorpe, Grace W. (1932). *Studies in the Psychology of Delinquency*. London: His Majesty's Stationery Office.

Parry, Leonard A. (1933). *The History of Torture in England*. London: Sampson Low, Marston and Company.

Penrose, Lionel S. (1939). Mental Disease and Crime: Outline of a Comparative Study of European Statistics. *British Journal of Medical Psychology, 1*, 1–15.

Pfäfflin, Friedemann (1996). The Out-Patient Treatment of the Sex Offender. In Christopher Cordess and Murray Cox (Eds.), *Forensic Psychotherapy: Crime, Psychodynamics and the Offender Patient. Volume II. Mainly Practice*, pp. 261–271. London: Jessica Kingsley Publishers.

Pfister, Oskar (1915). Ist die Brandstiftung ein archaischer Sublimierungsversuch? *Internationale Zeitschrift für ärztliche Psychoanalyse, 3*, 139–153.

Phillips, Charles (1857). *Vacation Thoughts on Capital Punishments*. London: William and Frederick G. Cash.

Radzinowicz, Leon (1978). John Howard. In John C. Freeman (Ed.), *Prisons Past and Future*, pp. 7–13. London: Heinemann / Heinemann Educational Books.

Rafter, Nicole Hahn (1997). *Creating Born Criminals*. Urbana, Illinois: University of Illinois Press.

Rafter, Nicole (2008). *The Criminal Brain: Understanding Biological Theories of Crime*. New York: New York University Press.

Rank, Otto (Ed.) (1907a). Vortragsabend: Am 23. Januar 1907. In Herman Nunberg and Ernst Federn (Eds.), *Protokolle der Wiener Psychoanalytischen Vereinigung: Band I. 1906–1908*, pp. 77–86. Frankfurt am Main: S. Fischer / S. Fischer Verlag, 1976.

Rank, Otto (Ed.) (1907b). Vortragsabend: Am 6. Februar 1907. In Herman Nunberg and Ernst Federn (Eds.), *Protokolle der Wiener Psychoanalytischen Vereinigung: Band I. 1906–1908*, pp. 97–104. Frankfurt am Main: S. Fischer / S. Fischer Verlag, 1976.

Rank, Otto (Ed.) (1907c). Scientific Meeting on February 6, 1907. In Herman Nunberg and Ernst Federn (Eds.), *Minutes of the Vienna Psychoanalytic Society: Volume I: 1906–1908*. Margarethe Nunberg (Transl.), pp. 103–110. New York: International Universities Press, 1962.

Rank, Otto (Ed.) (1907d). Vortragsabend: Am 10. April 1907. In Herman Nunberg and Ernst Federn (Eds.), *Protokolle der Wiener Psychoanalytischen Vereinigung: Band I. 1906–1908*, pp. 150–156. Frankfurt am Main: S. Fischer / S. Fischer Verlag, 1976.

Reich, Wilhelm (1927). *Die Funktion des Orgasmus: Zur Psychopathologie und zur Soziologie des Geschlechtslebens*. Vienna: Internationaler Psychoanalytischer Verlag.

Reik, Theodor (1925). *Geständniszwang und Strafbedürfnis: Probleme der Psychoanalyse und der Kriminologie*. Vienna: Internationaler Psychoanalytischer Verlag.

Reik, Theodor (1932). *Der unbekannte Mörder: Von der Tat zum Täter*. Vienna: Internationaler Psychoanalytischer Verlag.

Rickman, John (1932). The Psychology of Crime: IV. *British Journal of Medical Psychology, 12*, 264–269.

Ries, Paul (1995). Popularise and/or Be Damned: Psychoanalysis and Film at the Crossroads in 1925. *International Journal of Psycho-Analysis, 76*, 759–791.

Roazen, Paul (2000). *Oedipus in Britain: Edward Glover and the Struggle Over Klein*. New York: Other Press.

Robinson, Kenneth (1964). Parliamentary and Public Attitudes. In Ismond Rosen (Ed.), *The Pathology and Treatment of Sexual Deviation: A Methodological Approach*, pp. 451–460. London: Oxford University Press.

Romm, Sharon (1983). *The Unwelcome Intruder: Freud's Struggle with Cancer*. New York: Praeger Publishers / CBS Educational and Professional Publishing, Division of CBS / Praeger Special Studies / Praeger Scientific.

Rosen, Ismond (Ed.) (1964a). *The Pathology and Treatment of Sexual Deviation: A Methodological Approach*. London: Oxford University Press.

Rosen, Ismond (1964b). Exhibitionism, Scopophilia and Voyeurism. In Ismond Rosen (Ed.), *The Pathology and Treatment of Sexual Deviation: A Methodological Approach*, pp. 293–350. London: Oxford University Press.

Rosen, Ismond (1979). The General Psychoanalytical Theory of Perversion: A Critical and Clinical Review. In Ismond Rosen (Ed.), *Sexual Deviation: Second Edition*, pp. 29–64. Oxford: Oxford University Press.

Rosenthal, Tatjana (1911). Karin Michaelis: "Das gefährliche Alter" im Lichte der Psychoanalyse. *Zentralblatt für Psychoanalyse*, 1, 277–294.

Rumney, David (1992a). Origin and Early Struggles. In Eve Saville and David Rumney, *"Let Justice Be Done!": Your National and International Crime Forum After its Diamond Jubilee Year. A History of the ISTD. A Study of Crime and Delinquency from 1931 to 1992*, pp. 1–9. London: Institute for the Study and Treatment of Delinquency.

Rumney, David (1992b). Owning Their Own Clinic. In Eve Saville and David Rumney, *"Let Justice Be Done!": Your National and International Crime Forum After its Diamond Jubilee Year. A History of the ISTD. A Study of Crime and Delinquency from 1931 to 1992*, pp. 10–12. London: Institute for the Study and Treatment of Delinquency.

Rumney, David (1992c). Under One Roof. In Eve Saville and David Rumney, *"Let Justice Be Done!": Your National and International Crime Forum After its Diamond Jubilee Year. A History of the ISTD. A Study of Crime and Delinquency from 1931 to 1992*, pp. 14–15. London: Institute for the Study and Treatment of Delinquency.

Rütten, Thomas (2011). Early Modern Medicine. In Mark Jackson (Ed.), *The Oxford Handbook of the History of Medicine*, pp. 60–81. Oxford: Oxford University Press.

Sadger, J. [Isidor] (1926). A Contribution to the Understanding of Sado-Masochism. *International Journal of Psycho-Analysis*, 7, 484–491.

Schindler, Walter (1926). Zur Dynamik des Sadomasochismus. *Fortschritte der Sexualwissenschaft und Psychanalyse*, 2, 127–195.

Schlesinger, Edmund (1931). Hat der Verbrecher Gemeinschaftsgefühl? *Internationale Zeitschrift für Individualpsychologie, 9*, 345–350.

Schmideberg, Melitta (1949). The Analytic Treatment of Major Criminals: Therapeutic Results and Technical Problems. In Kurt R. Eissler, Susan H. Kubie, and Gertrud M. Kurth (Eds.), *Searchlights on Delinquency: New Psychoanalytic Studies. Dedicated to Professor August Aichhorn, on the Occasion of His Seventieth Birthday. July 27, 1948*, pp. 174–189. New York: International Universities Press.

Schmideberg, Melitta (1953). Letter to Donald W. Winnicott. 6 November. PP/DWW/B/A/27. Donald Woods Winnicott Collection. Archives and Manuscripts, Rare Materials Room, Wellcome Library, Wellcome Collection, The Wellcome Building, London.

Schmideberg, Melitta (1956). Delinquent Acts as Perversions and Fetishes. *International Journal of Psycho-Analysis, 37*, 422–424.

Schmidt, Eugen (1931). Vorgeschichte eines Attentates. *Internationale Zeitschrift für Individualpsychologie, 9*, 358–367.

Schreiber, Flora Rheta (1983). *The Shoemaker: The Anatomy of a Psychotic*. New York: Simon and Schuster.

Schur, Max (1972). *Freud: Living and Dying*. New York: International Universities Press.

Schwarz, Hedwig (1950). Dorothy: The Psycho-Analysis of a Case of Stealing. *British Journal of Delinquency, 1*, 29–44.

Scott, Peter D. (1964). Definition, Classification, Prognosis and Treatment. In Ismond Rosen (Ed.), *The Pathology and Treatment of Sexual Deviation: A Methodological Approach*, pp. 87–119. London: Oxford University Press.

Seldes, George (1953). *Tell the Truth and Run*. New York: Greenberg: Publisher.

Shepherd, Jade (2016). "I am very glad and cheered when I hear the flute": The Treatment of Criminal Lunatics in Late Victorian Broadmoor. *Medical History, 60*, 473–491.

Sim, Camilla (2008). Non-Retaliation: Surviving a Violent 5-Year-Old. In Rosemary Campher (Ed.), *Violence in Children: Understanding and Helping Those Who Harm*, pp. 129–156. London: Karnac Books.

Simmel, Ernst (1940). Sigmund Freud: The Man and His Work. *Psychoanalytic Quarterly, 9*, 163–176.

Simmel, Ernst (1949). Incendiarism. In Kurt R. Eissler, Susan H. Kubie, and Gertrud M. Kurth (Eds.), *Searchlights on Delinquency: New Psychoanalytic Studies. Dedicated to Professor August Aichhorn, on the Occasion of His Seventieth Birthday. July 27, 1948*, pp. 90–101. New York: International Universities Press.

Sims, Henry Marion (1893). Hystero-Epilepsy: A Report of Seven Cases Cured by Surgical Treatment. *American Journal of Obstetrics and Diseases of Women and Children*, 28, 80–88.

Sinason, Valerie (2001). Children Who Kill Their Teddy Bears. In Brett Kahr (Ed.), *Forensic Psychotherapy and Psychopathology: Winnicottian Perspectives*, pp. 43–49. London: H. Karnac (Books).

Sinason, Valerie (2008a). Finding Abused Children's Voices: Junior-School Living Nightmares. In Rosemary Campher (Ed.), *Violence in Children: Understanding and Helping Those Who Harm*, pp. 211–227. London: Karnac Books.

Sinason, Valerie (2008b). When Murder Moves Inside. In Adah Sachs and Graeme Galton (Eds.), *Forensic Aspects of Dissociative Identity Disorder*, pp. 100–107. London: Karnac Books.

Sinason, Valerie (2011). Interview with Detective Chief Inspector Clive Driscoll. In Valerie Sinason (Ed.), *Attachment, Trauma and Multiplicity: Second Edition. Working with Dissociative Identity Disorder*, pp. 195–203. London: Routledge / Taylor and Francis Group, and Hove, East Sussex: Routledge / Taylor and Francis Group.

Sinason, Valerie (2012). Infanticide and Paedophilia as a Defence Against Incest: Work with a Man with a Severe Intellectual Disability. In John Adlam, Anne Aiyegbusi, Pam Kleinot, Anna Motz, and Christopher Scanlon (Eds.), *The Therapeutic Milieu Under Fire: Security and Insecurity in Forensic Mental Health*, pp. 175–185.

Skoler, Glen (1998). The Archetypes and Psychodynamics of Stalking. In J. Reid Meloy (Ed.), *The Psychology of Stalking: Clinical and Forensic Perspectives*, pp. 85–112. San Diego, California: Academic Press / Harcourt Brace and Company, Publishers.

Smith, Maurice Hamblin (1922). *The Psychology of the Criminal*. London: Methuen and Company.

Smith, Maurice Hamblin (1924). The Mental Conditions Found in Certain Sexual Offenders. *The Lancet*. 29 March, pp. 643–646.

Smith, Maurice Hamblin (1933). *The Psychology of the Criminal: Second Edition Revised*. London: Methuen and Company.

Snodgrass, Jon (1984). William Healy (1896–1963): Pioneer Child Psychiatrist and Criminologist. *Journal of the History of the Behavioral Sciences*, 20, 332–339.

Sonnenschein, Max (1928). Analyse eines Kriminellen. *Fortschritte der Sexualwissenschaft und Psychanalyse*, 3, 116–130.

Sorge-Boehmke, Elisabeth (1931). Eine dreizehnjährige Brandstifterin. *Internationale Zeitschrift für Individualpsychologie*, 9, 371–375.

Southwood, Martin (1958). *John Howard: Prison Reformer. An Account of His Life and Travels*. London: Independent Press.
Staub, Hugo (1931a). Psychoanalyse und Strafrecht: Vortrag vor der Berliner und Dresdener Anwaltsvereinigung. *Imago, 17,* 194–216.
Staub, Hugo (1931b). Einige praktische Schwierigkeiten der psychoanalytischen Kriminalistik. *Imago, 17,* 217–225.
Staub, Hugo (1931c). Zum Kampf um die Todesstrafe. *Psychoanalytische Bewegung, 3,* 448–456.
Stekel, Wilhelm (1911). Zur Psychologie des Exhibitionismus. *Zentralblatt für Psychoanalyse, 1,* 494–495.
Stekel, Wilhelm (1912). Kriminalität und Epilepsie. *Zentralblatt für Psychoanalyse, 2,* 206.
Stern, Adolph (1922). New York Psycho-Analytical Society, pp. 509–512. Reports of the International Psycho-Analytical Association. *International Journal of Psycho-Analysis, 3,* 500–520.
Stewart, Pamela Windham (2016). Interventions with Mothers and Babies in Prisons: Collision of Internal and External Worlds. In Stella Acquarone (Ed.), *Surviving the Early Years: The Importance of Early Intervention with Babies at Risk*, pp. 101–111. London: Karnac Books.
Stoddart, William H. B. (1923). Delinquency and Mental Defect (IV). *British Journal of Medical Psychology, 3,* 188–193.
Stoller, Robert J. (1975). *Perversion: The Erotic Form of Hatred*. New York: Pantheon Books.
Stoller, Robert J. (1979). Centerfold: An Essay on Excitement. *Archives of General Psychiatry, 36,* 1019–1024.
Storfer, Adolf J. (1911). *Zur Sonderstellung des Vatermordes: Eine rechtsgeschichtliche und völkerpsychologische Studie*. Vienna: Franz Deuticke.
Strachey, James (1924). Letter to Alix Strachey. 8 December. In James Strachey and Alix Strachey, *Bloomsbury/Freud: The Letters of James and Alix Strachey. 1924–1925*. Perry Meisel and Walter Kendrick (Eds.), pp. 141–142. New York: Basic Books, 1985.
Strean, Herbert S., and Freeman, Lucy (1991). *Our Wish to Kill: The Murder in All Our Hearts*. New York: St. Martin's Press.
Sumner, Dean Walter T.; Sims, Edwin W.; Baum, W.L.; Blaustein, David; Callaghan, J.F.; Dwyer, Anna; Evans, W.A., et al. (1911). *The Social Evil in Chicago: A Study of Existing Conditions with Recommendations by The Vice Commission of Chicago. A Municipal Body Appointed by the Mayor and the City Council of the City of Chicago and Submitted as its Report to the Mayor and City Council of Chicago*. Chicago, Illinois: Gunthorp-Warren Printing Company.

Swain, John (n.d.). *The Pleasures of the Torture Chamber*. London: Noel Douglas.

Vértes, Theodor (1931). Der Weg zum Verbrechen. *Internationale Zeitschrift für Individualpsychologie, 9*, 403–406.

Vislick-Young, Pauline (1931). Urbanisation: Ein Faktor der jugendlichen Kriminalität. *Internationale Zeitschrift für Individualpsychologie, 9*, 376–381.

Vizard, Eileen (1997). Adolescents Who Sexually Abuse. In Estela V. Welldon and Cleo Van Velsen (Eds.), *A Practical Guide to Forensic Psychotherapy*, pp. 48–55. London: Jessica Kingsley Publishers.

Vizard, Eileen; Monck, Elizabeth, and Misch, Peter (1995). Child and Adolescent Sex Abuse Perpetrators: A Review of the Research Literature. *Journal of Child Psychology and Psychiatry and Allied Disciplines, 36*, 731–756.

Vizard, Eileen; Wynick, Sarah; Hawkes, Colin; Woods, John, and Jenkins, Jill (1996). Juvenile Sex Offenders: Assessment Issues. *British Journal of Psychiatry, 168*, 259–262.

von Hug-Hellmuth, Hermine (1915). Ein Fall von weiblichem Fuß-, richtiger Stiefelfetischismus. *Internationale Zeitschrift für ärztliche Psychoanalyse, 3*, 111–114.

von Winterstein, Alfred Freiherr (1912). Zur Psychoanalyse des Reisens. *Imago, 1*, 489–506.

Weiss, Edoardo (n.d.). My Impressions of Sigmund Freud. Unpublished Typescript. Box 114. Folder 59. Sigmund Freud Papers. Sigmund Freud Collection. Manuscript Reading Room, Room 101, Manuscript Division, James Madison Memorial Building, Library of Congress, Washington, DC.

Welldon, Estela V. (1988). *Mother, Madonna, Whore: The Idealization and Denigration of Motherhood*. London: Free Association Books.

Welldon, Estela V. (1991). Psychology and Psychopathology in Women: A Psychoanalytic Perspective. *British Journal of Psychiatry, 158*, Supplement *10*, 85–92.

Welldon, Estela V. (1993). Forensic Psychotherapy and Group Analysis. *Group Analysis, 26*, 487–502.

Welldon, Estela V. (1996). Contrasts in Male and Female Sexual Perversions. In Christopher Cordess and Murray Cox (Eds.), *Forensic Psychotherapy: Crime, Psychodynamics and the Offender Patient. Volume II. Mainly Practice*, pp. 273–289. London: Jessica Kingsley Publishers.

Welldon, Estela (2001). Babies as Transitional Objects. In Brett Kahr (Ed.), *Forensic Psychotherapy and Psychopathology: Winnicottian Perspectives*, pp. 19–25. London: H. Karnac (Books).

Welldon, Estela V. (2011). *Playing with Dynamite: A Personal Approach to the Psychoanalytic Understanding of Perversions, Violence, and Criminality*. London: Karnac Books.

Westwick, Atwell (1940). Criminology and Psychoanalysis. *Psychoanalytic Quarterly, 9*, 269–282.

Wetzell, Richard F. (2000). *Inventing the Criminal: A History of German Criminology, 1880–1945*. Chapel Hill, North Carolina: University of North Carolina Press.

White, William A. (1923). *Insanity and the Criminal Law*. New York: Macmillan Company.

Williams, Arthur H. (1964). The Psychopathology and Treatment of Sexual Murderers. In Ismond Rosen (Ed.), *The Pathology and Treatment of Sexual Deviation: A Methodological Approach*, pp. 351–377. London: Oxford University Press.

Williams, Arthur H. (1998). *Cruelty, Violence, and Murder: Understanding the Criminal Mind*. Paul Williams (Ed.). Northvale, New Jersey: Jason Aronson.

Winnicott, Donald W. (1943). Delinquency Research. *New Era in Home and School, 24*, 65–67.

Winnicott, Donald W. (1945). The Return of the Evacuated Child. In Donald W. Winnicott. *The Child and the Outside World: Studies in Developing Relationships*. Janet Hardenberg (Ed.), pp. 88–92. London: Tavistock Publications, 1957.

Winnicott, Donald W. (1948). Children's Hostels in War and Peace: A Contribution to the Symposium on "Lessons for Child Psychiatry". Given at a Meeting of the Medical Section of the British Psychological Society, 27 February 1946. *British Journal of Medical Psychology, 21*, 175–180.

Winnicott, Donald W. (1949a). Letter to R. S. Hazlehurst. 1 September. In Donald W. Winnicott, *The Spontaneous Gesture: Selected Letters of D. W. Winnicott*. F. Robert Rodman (Ed.), p. 17. Cambridge, Massachusetts: Harvard University Press, 1987.

Winnicott, Donald W. (1949b). Letter to S. H. Hodge. 1 September. In Donald W. Winnicott, *The Spontaneous Gesture: Selected Letters of D. W. Winnicott*. F. Robert Rodman (Ed.), pp. 17–19. Cambridge, Massachusetts: Harvard University Press, 1987.

Winnicott, Donald W. (1956). The Antisocial Tendency. In Donald W. Winnicott, *Collected Papers: Through Paediatrics to Psycho-Analysis*, pp. 306–315. London: Tavistock Publications, 1958.

Winnicott, Donald W. (1958a). Psycho-Analysis and the Sense of Guilt. In Donald W. Winnicott, John Bowlby, Ilse Hellman, Marion Milner, Roger Money-Kyrle, Elliott Jaques, and Joan Riviere, *Psycho-Analysis and Contemporary Thought*. John D. Sutherland (Ed.), pp. 15–32. London: Hogarth Press and the Institute of Psycho-Analysis.

Winnicott, Donald W. (1958b). Dr Ambrose Cyril Wilson. *International Journal of Psycho-Analysis, 39,* 617.

Winnicott, Donald W. (1962–1963). The Antisocial Tendency Illustrated by a Case. *A Criança Portuguesa, 21,* 195–209.

Winnicott, Donald W. (1966). A Psychoanalytic View of the Antisocial Tendency. In Ralph Slovenko (Ed.), *Crime, Law and Corrections,* pp. 102–130. Springfield, Illinois: Charles C Thomas, Publisher.

Winnicott, Donald W. (1968). Delinquency as a Sign of Hope. *Prison Service Journal, 7,* Number 27, 2–7.

Winnicott, Donald W. (1969). Letter to Richard Balbernie. 18 March. Box 7. File 10. Donald W. Winnicott Papers. Archives of Psychiatry, The Oskar Diethelm Library, The DeWitt Wallace Institute for the History of Psychiatry, Department of Psychiatry, Joan and Sanford I. Weill Medical College, Cornell University, The New York Presbyterian Hospital, New York, New York.

Winnicott, Donald W. (n.d.). Meet to Be Stolen From. Unpublished Typescript. PP/DWW/A/A/2. Donald Woods Winnicott Collection. Archives and Manuscripts, Rare Materials Room, Wellcome Library, Wellcome Collection, The Wellcome Building, London.

Winnicott, Donald W., and Britton, Clare (1944). The Problem of Homeless Children. *New Era in Home and School, 25,* 155–161.

Winnicott, Donald W., and Britton, Clare (1947). Residential Management as Treatment for Difficult Children: The Evolution of a Wartime Hostels Scheme. *Human Relations, 1,* 87–97.

Wittels, Fritz (1928). *Die Welt ohne Zuchthaus.* Stuttgart: Hippokrates-Verlag.

Wittels, Fritz (1929a). Some Remarks on Kleptomania. *Journal of Nervous and Mental Disease, 69,* 241–251.

Wittels, Fritz (1929b). Große Hasser. *Die psychoanalytische Bewegung, 1,* 329–343.

Wittels, Fritz (1937a). Die libidinöse Struktur des kriminellen Psychopathen. *Internationale Zeitschrift für Psychoanalyse, 23,* 360–375.

Wittels, Fritz (1937b). The Criminal Psychopath in the Psychoanalytic System. *Psychoanalytic Review, 24,* 276–291.

Wittels, Fritz (1938). The Position of the Psychopath in the Psycho-Analytic System. *International Journal of Psycho-Analysis, 19,* 471–488.

Wortis, Joseph (1954). *Fragments of an Analysis with Freud.* New York: Simon and Schuster.

Zilboorg, Gregory (1931). Translator's Note. In Franz Alexander and

Hugo Staub, *The Criminal, the Judge, and the Public: A Psychological Analysis*. Gregory Zilboorg (Transl.), pp. v–x. New York: Macmillan Company.

Zilboorg, Gregory (1954). *The Psychology of the Criminal Act and Punishment*. New York: Harcourt, Brace and Company.

Zilboorg, Gregory (1956). The Contribution of Psycho-Analysis to Forensic Psychiatry. *International Journal of Psycho-Analysis, 37,* 318–324.

Zulliger, Hans (1949). Mental Hygiene of Convicts in Prisons. In Kurt R. Eissler, Susan H. Kubie, and Gertrud M. Kurth (Eds.), *Searchlights on Delinquency: New Psychoanalytic Studies. Dedicated to Professor August Aichhorn, on the Occasion of His Seventieth Birthday. July 27, 1948,* pp. 377–385. New York: International Universities Press.

Zulliger, Hans (1951). Unconscious Motives for Theft. Gerta Balg (Transl.). *British Journal of Delinquency, 1,* 198–204.

PART II

FORENSIC PSYCHOTHERAPY
IN ACTION

The theory and practice of forensic psychotherapy

CHAPTER TWO

True falsehoods:
Estela Welldon's paradoxical insights
in forensic psychotherapy

David Millar

Introduction

If the search for happiness is one of the chief sources of unhappiness, then what fate befalls those whose professional quest leads them into unearthing the meaning of sadness, or despair, or fear, or even . . . perversity? Could the outcome for those who seek the darker truths be an enlightened understanding? Could a close acquaintance with perversion bring a closer insight into decency? Here beginneth my prelude to the work of Estela Welldon, whose most remarkable accomplishment would seem to be the understanding of oppositional states of mind and their paradoxical struggles.

It would be getting rather too close to melodrama to describe her work simply as exploring the "darker side" of human behaviour; but dark and despairing it often is. If you have picked up this book and got as far as this chapter, then you will know an awful lot about Estela Welldon by now. My effort will be to try to describe as best I can what some might regard as the inverted logic in her approach to psychotherapy with criminal offenders and victims of criminal offences. Two significant illustrations may set the scene for what I hope to illustrate further on in this chapter.

Many years ago, while working as a forensic psychiatrist at the Portman Clinic in London, she had a patient who had an affinity for latex rubber in its many guises and uses—not just for doing the washing up, but also for doing what might be called the *dirtying up* as well. In an effort to understand this man's obsessive penchant for using rubber as his go-between in all of his sexual relationships, Estela sought out a shop in London that dealt in "all things rubber" to see if a first-hand experience of the world of latex would help her to understand her patient in more depth. When she told her colleagues what she had done, some of a more orthodox persuasion said that she was "acting out in the countertransference"—in some quarters a strong criticism. Whereas she may have been guilty of a technical *faux pas*, she maintained that it had wholly enlightened her understanding of her patient and his subsequent treatment. The significant point here is that Estela in no way backed down in the face of the clinical criticism of her colleagues. She was not trying to outdo them but to actively undo the complicated mess her patient was in with his never-ending "elastic" relationships involving a degree of excitement but ending in serial failure. Innovation was ever her strong point.

Estela challenged not simply clinical orthodoxy, but also social convention. Perhaps her most abiding contribution to the treatment of perpetrators of crime and victims of crime was to invite some of each to attend the same therapy group. This was considered clinically inappropriate by some professionals, but brave and progressive by others. At the same time, it was felt by the public at large as well as by victim and offender groups that such an approach was doomed to failure at best and potentially dangerous at worst. That Estela ran just such a group, weekly, for a period of over twenty years is the best answer to her critics. As in the first example, the challenge came from Estela, yet the beneficiaries were her patients and the patients of many others who have followed her lead. She was determined not just to court controversy but to *invert* much of what passed as the conventional clinical and social wisdom of the time. If one works to any depth in a psychoanalytic exchange, then it is invariably the paradoxical nature of the human condition that will be revealed. Psychopathology could be said to be the inversion of health, while psychopathy might be construed as the perversion of health. Estela has made it her life's work to expose and, in a sense, to depose these inherent contradictions. She converted accepted wisdom into falsehoods that revealed their paradoxical truth.

All of this will bring me, presently, to "Sanjay".

I first met Estela Welldon at the Portman Clinic in 1982. The Director at the time, Mervin Glasser, was running a weekly lunchtime teaching group for interested professionals in the forensic field; this featured presentations on a variety of topics by all the Portman staff, Estela being prominent among the facilitators. I was, at the time, a trainee child psychotherapist at the Tavistock Clinic (next door to the Portman Clinic and now part of the same National Health Service Trust). I was interested in forensic mental health, having worked for many years prior to my psychotherapy training with "delinquent" adolescents. This thirty-six-week course was my introduction and my conversion to a lifetime interest and practice in forensic clinical work. A few years later, in 1990, when the Portman Clinic offered its first ever accredited training programme in forensic psychotherapy, I applied and was accepted into the first cohort. The course tutor was Estela Welldon. When we graduated the following year, it was Estela's idea and determined effort that resulted in the creation of the International Association for Forensic Psychotherapy, which I joined, and which accorded me the honour of being a founding member.

This is my rather potted history in the forensic field and my introduction to the mind, manner, and might of Dr Welldon.

My first intensive forensic psychotherapy patient after I qualified at the Portman Clinic came to me via a colleague—a psychiatrist—who, knowing of my recent Portman experience, referred this young man, "Sanjay", to me. Thereafter the psychiatrist never enquired into his progress. Curiously—or perhaps not, as those of us in the forensic field have discovered—sometimes highly qualified, experienced, and reputable clinicians find a way to keep forensic work at a distance in much the same way as the public does.

I wrote up my clinical experiences with Sanjay when his treatment had finished—or rather, had ended (see below); this I then presented, at Estela's insistence, at an International Association for Forensic Psychotherapy conference in Boston in 2001. Later the same year, when Estela was retiring from the Portman, she asked me to give this paper at her retirement day. It has never been published until now.

The attractive violator:
when victim and abuser are one—
the analysis of a six-year-old boy twenty-five years on

What do we know about violence? We know that it has a powerful appeal—a magnetic attraction. From a fight in the school playground to the evening news on television, wherever violence is featured you can count on an audience. We teach our children, and try to convince ourselves, that violence does not pay. Yet any schoolboy—and, nowadays, many schoolgirls—will tell you that administering a sound beating to one's enemy solves many problems. In America, there have been many—too many—tales of schoolchildren, some barely teenagers, who have taken guns into a school and have slaughtered their fellow classmates and teachers. To them, a violent end to the lives of their real or imagined "enemies" was the ultimate solution. Some killers will, if the state does not imprison or execute them, take their own lives—because suicide, like homicide, holds out the promise of the ultimate solution to all of life's problems.

We also know that violence sells. Write a book or a screenplay in which violence predominates, and you will be unlucky if you are not lauded as a serious and creative interpreter of our times. Sam Peckinpah used to defend the overt bloodshed in his films by asserting that they promoted anti-violence messages. Quentin Tarantino informs us that his portrayals of brutalising screen cruelty simply reflect the troubled society in which we live. One such popular film of this new millennium was entitled, fittingly, *American Psycho* (2000). Whether you agree or disagree with the premise that life imitates art, the producers, directors, and stars of these films do not have any difficulty in making their mortgage payments. What they have to sell, we wish to buy.

We know, too, that violence is often the currency of political barter. Our presidents and prime ministers, while avowing to eschew "gunboat diplomacy" whenever possible, nonetheless keep the threat of state violence in reserve as the ultimate sanction against violent political transgressors.

Psychoanalysts know that the capacity for aggression and violence resides deep within the psyche of our species and is rarely found in other species. It is rare to meet a patient in psychotherapy, whose presenting problem is violence, without uncovering antecedents or earlier violating experiences. These might range from the manifestly obvious childhood beatings through to more subtle precursors, such as invasive surgery or the complexities of failed or perverted attachments.

Geneticists tell us that aggression and violence can be traced through our DNA to specific genes; and they may well be right. They tell us, further, that identifying, isolating, and then eradicating the gene for violence is only a short time away. Our grandchildren are promised an aggression-free society. A moment's contemplation, however, will tell us that without aggression we may well be left without curiosity or creativity and, probably, civilisation, as we know it. Aggression and its spawn—violence—may, after all, have its evolutionary purpose. As I have suggested, violence will always attract its adherents, its apologists, and its audience.

Sanjay

I would like to relay to you Sanjay's life of violence and violation. In particular, I would like to focus on *psychic intrusion* and its role in the creation of *internal tormentors,* whereby, I believe, one can become one's own abuser. The attraction in this case is not towards that which holds a benign appeal but, paradoxically, towards that which repels. For this tormented young man, repulsion seemed to hold its own perverse attractiveness.

Sanjay thought that life was grand. He had fond memories of a train set that his father had set up for him and his brothers and sister in the loft of their home when he was four. They lived above a parade of shops in a large English city. He could recall vividly the various shops and their owners and customers who made up his neighbourhood—his small corner of the world. His parents had emigrated to England in search of a better life; and for Sanjay, life could not have been much better.

Then, when he was five, his father died unexpectedly of a heart attack. A year later his mother was dead, too, the victim of cancer. Sanjay and his siblings were orphaned, with no extended family in this country to whom they could turn. They were rescued by the intervention of the British welfare system and its agent, the Social Services Department. The four children were kept together and placed with a British family who had previously known the deceased parents, albeit only slightly. Soon afterwards Sanjay had a new and different experience—not one for which his life thus far had prepared him. "Tom", his new foster brother and one of his "rescuers", one night forcibly inserted his penis into Sanjay's anus. Six-year-old Sanjay's body and mind had been forcibly invaded, and life, as he knew it, was never grand again.

Four young children had been delivered into the hands of a perverse and sadistic gang, disguised as a foster family. Sanjay was thrust into a wholly new world, with a new mother and father totally unlike the mother and father who had so recently cared for him. He now had two new foster brothers, one of whom, Tom—ten years his senior—sexually abused not only Sanjay, but also his brothers and his sister and was to become Sanjay's lifelong tormentor.

Sanjay remained imprisoned in this environment for the next nineteen years, until the age of twenty-five. His brothers and sisters left before him, each finding their own time and their own method of leaving. The eldest, "Ravi", left to find work but could never hold down a job for long because of his addiction to alcohol and his aggressive manner with his colleagues. "Sasha", his sister, left at sixteen, heavily pregnant, for a doomed marriage with a partner even more emotionally bereft than she. "Kamray", the brother closest in years and affection to Sanjay, found his own way of leaving, by erecting homemade gallows and exiting this life at the end of a rope, after frequently having informed Sanjay of his intent. Only Sanjay remained in the foster family, too frightened to leave, too unwilling to break the perverse bond that held him there. No one outside the family noticed any of these alarming events in the lives of these four young people. Some brief hope arose when Tom was reported to his parents by the parents of two young girls for whom Tom had been baby-sitting. They were concerned about his inappropriate care of their daughters. Tom's parents responded by saying that they would take him to see a doctor, but nothing further was ever done about it.

Sanjay had his body and his mind violated almost daily for a fateful nineteen years—from the age of six to the age of twenty-five. He could not turn to his foster parents either. While Tom buggered him, "Jill", the foster mother, abused Sanjay emotionally and persecuted him. Sanjay was too intimidated to report his experiences to anyone.

He resisted through the only means at his disposal—in passive terror. He tried not to show any sexual response while being physically abused, and he tried not to show any emotional response to the verbal abuse, both of which he and his siblings had to endure repeatedly. Sanjay, however, seemed to be the "chosen one". His brothers, his sister, and even "Adam", Tom's younger biological brother, were all sexually victimised at different times; but Sanjay remained Tom's favoured target. Tom, no doubt, sensed Sanjay's greater fear and, hence, his greater dependence.

Not surprisingly, Sanjay grew up, failing consistently at school: how could he do otherwise? In ten years of schooling, he never asked or answered a question. He went to a large, underachieving comprehensive school where teachers came and left before they, or he, had a chance to get to know one another. He learned that by remaining silent, no one would ever take an interest in him, so he became an elective mute, totally invisible to an educational system that might otherwise have helped him. At home, social workers visited occasionally but not to speak to him or to his siblings, only to speak to the foster parents, who maintained that all was well. As the social workers never asked any questions, Sanjay never had to answer any, and so they were never to learn of his "prisoner" status. As indicated above, there was a brief moment of hope when Tom was reported by another family for interfering with their two children while he was baby-sitting them, but this was swiftly covered up by the foster family. Sanjay's first and only hope was dashed.

After he left school at sixteen, Sanjay discovered alcohol and thus found a way of creating a buffer of oblivion to combat the psychic reality. It meant, however, that to blur the pain effectively to survive at all he had to become addicted. Survival, for Sanjay, was only a living death in any case. He managed to find menial work such as filling shelves in supermarkets, which was one way, but at least it provided him with a means of leaving the house, and it was the sort of job where he could remain invisible. He changed jobs only when he came to the attention of bosses or managers who, ironically, wanted to reward him for his conscientious endeavours.

Attention and promotion, however, were no reward for Sanjay. In trying to avoid Tom's attention, he avoided *all* attention. Tom tried everything he could to arouse Sanjay, but Sanjay resisted in the only way he knew how, by remaining physically and sexually limp and unresponsive—until, that is, the day when, as Tom buggered him, Sanjay got an erection, the first sign of compliance he had ever shown in the presence of the enemy. His fear was now total. He believed that he was no longer just a forced and passive accomplice but had now become a willing collaborator. Within days he had left the house—his prison for the previous nineteen years—never to return.

In time, Sanjay met an older man, "Paul", a victim like himself, with whom he thought he could share at least some small part of his life. They moved in together; however, by now Sanjay was not only an alcoholic, but also dependent on prescribed antidepressants and sedatives. Paul, the new man in his life, knew little of his past until the day Sanjay tried to take his own life; and then, in a drunken stupor and in a complete state of despair, he revealed his past to Paul, and later, at Paul's insistence, to his doctor. It was soon afterwards that I first met him, as his doctor had referred him for psychiatric help, and his psychiatrist then re-referred him to me for psychotherapy. He was then thirty-one years of age.

The story, so far, has been Sanjay's. I would now like to tell you my story—the story of the therapy.

The therapy

I saw Sanjay in a local Child and Family Mental Health Clinic where I was based, in a town some way—a safe distance, he thought—from Sanjay's previous home. It was also some way from where he had relocated with Paul. The rather bitter irony of our clinical setting was not lost on either of us. He once said that he wanted to spit on the clinic sign as he came; it was, after all, children's services that had let him down so tragically in the past.

I encountered a short, stocky, brown-skinned man whose cherubic expression betrayed years of practised wariness and disarming guile. The six-year-old, terrified orphan could just about be discerned beneath the ingratiating exterior of the thirty-one-year-old embittered addict. Sanjay told me he needed help, and that this was the first time he had ever been able to ask for it. He stammered out the basic outline of his history. There were tears of despair, mixed with rage, in his eyes. I felt what I thought then was a genuine plea for help beneath the cynical defiance. After a second meeting, in which he maintained his imploring demeanour, I offered to see him regularly for therapy. I suggested that we meet three times a week. With patient anguish and ambivalence he accepted my offer, and we agreed to start the following week. When he left, I never expected to see him again, but he returned the following Monday, and we began.

He spoke of his determination to achieve some sort of a life that would be worth living so that he could try to end his lifelong sense of a relentless pull towards death: the death of his parents; the death of his brother; the death of innocence; the death of learning; the death of any experience that could even remotely be called loving; and also the death of hope.

He came to most of his sessions and was always on time—on time to the minute, in fact, because he could not bear to look at or be seen by other people in the waiting room, as he held the rather paranoid belief that they could somehow see into his perverted past. Among a spate of symptoms, Sanjay also suffered from agoraphobia. He could barely go out of the house without Paul accompanying him, and even at home he could never answer the phone or the doorbell. Paul took him out shopping and brought him to his sessions—the pained leading the pained.

In the consulting room, Sanjay managed to speak, but only after long, tortuous silences and with a kind of masochistic effort, as if he had to beat himself up mentally to do so. Mostly, however, he remained silent and passive in my presence, as he had done for most of his life, particularly in the presence of Tom. He experienced me as a kind of Tom, too, I suggested—someone who was trying to convert him to do my bidding. "No! You are nothing like Tom", he protested, as he continued to remain limp and lifeless in my presence in case it seemed that I might want to have my wicked therapeutic way with him. He often came to his sessions reeking of alcohol but with the feigned sobriety of the practised drunkard. Simultaneously appealing to me, Sanjay also flaunted his defiance. He mostly drank homemade wine that Paul had prepared for him. It was Paul's way, it seemed, of both comforting and appeasing him at the same time. Sanjay knew just how to control his friend. Paul was a homosexual, and Sanjay knew just how to sustain his devotion—by *not* submitting to a full sexual relationship with him and by limiting them both instead to only mutual masturbation, which teased Paul with raised hopes and tormented him with unfulfilled expectations. The tables were now turned, and Paul had become, like the six-year-old Sanjay, a frightened but compliant victim. Sanjay, in turn, had become like Tom, with Paul as his obliging plaything.

When I pointed this out to him, adding that he had also recreated a similar scenario in his relationship with me, he was initially stunned and then affronted by my interpretation. His denial of my efforts to understand was invariably followed by a missed session. He found the truth far from palatable. He would then return, obsequious but defiant, pleading forgiveness but scorning my further efforts to help at the same time.

When he could afford it, he would sometimes down a bottle of vodka before a session. Frequently, he came to his sessions after a drinking binge, not having slept for several days. He would haltingly maintain that desperation was the only motivation he had for getting to his sessions, and that drunkenness was his only means of speaking. He was trying as hard as he could, he pleaded. "But not hard enough!", I retorted, abandoning, for the moment, my analytic neutrality, determined as I was to try to utilise his desperation and limit his drunkenness in our sessions.

He spoke, when he could speak, of how he had operated with passive resistance towards Jill, his tyrannical foster mother. In the league of tormentors who populated his inner world, Jill seemed to hold pride of place, supplanting even her buggering son. She seemed to represent the mother who could have rescued him but did not. I, too, was turned into a rescuer who could not rescue, as I experienced the frustration of my hopes being raised and then dashed as he tried to give me a taste of what life must have been like for him. He told me later how, as a young man, he would let other men buy him drinks in the pub. Their hopes were then raised of a sexual return on their investment, but Sanjay never fulfilled their expectations, just as in his therapy he tried to raise, and then thwart, my expectations. We were both now drinking in that same pub, I proffered, only to be met with the most angry and primitive denial. On the contrary, Sanjay retorted in conscious fear, I was his friend, the only one he had ever trusted enough to tell his story to and the only one he believed could help him. I listened to his protestations of innocence and "left the pub" feeling nonetheless unconsciously teased and frustrated.

When he was being more consciously honest, he would fight with me: what could my world do for him, he demanded, a child and family world that purported to help troubled children? But where was I when he was in trouble as a child? It was clear that he came not just to ask for help, but also to make me pay for the help that had not been forthcoming in the past. I had now become the abandoning parent who was not there when he so desperately needed me. I was offering him my help and my understanding, but it was too little, too late; and in his mind, it could be withdrawn at any time.

I, in turn, could feel my own anger, my own frustration, and my own impotence as he made me experience alternately the roles of both victim and persecutor.

Sanjay would sit, squirming in silence, contorting his face, and giving me desperate looks, appealing—so it seemed—for my help. But in fact he was rendering me impotent, and perversely, he was enjoying my inability to get any reaction from him.

I tried to paint for Sanjay the picture of how his hateful outer world had now been recreated internally. He insisted that he lived only to seek his revenge and kill Tom; but Tom, as I tried to help him see, was now an internal figure in his mind, and consequently his contorted efforts at seeking his revenge against him only meant that his efforts were enacted against himself. In wanting to destroy Tom, he was destroying himself, as Tom had now become a perverse part of Sanjay's identity. His double bind was now complete: to accept help from me, he would have to render me impotent. To destroy his tormentors, he would have to destroy himself. To raise hope was to raise fear, and to strive to live was to flirt with death.

As well as drinking, Sanjay also smoked heavily, both cigarettes and cannabis. He burned his body with the lit cigarettes, stuck pins in his eyes, and carved great swathes of his skin with a knife. He showed me the results. On one occasion he came to his session with one eye red and bloodshot. He said that he had stuck a burning cigarette into it to make himself come to his session. I told him that I saw these self-mutilations as attempts to get inside his own body in order to inflict pain and suffering on those internal representations from the past whom he had wanted to kill off and yet still keep alive in order to re-torment, in much the same way that he was kept as the plaything of Tom. He wanted me there to watch, to bear witness to his suffering, so that I could suffer too, for I was no better than Tom, as it was my world that condemned him to his. The burned and bloodied eye was the one that he wanted to give to me.

When I tried to get in touch with what I thought might be the good birth parents somewhere inside him, I learned that in his distorted thinking he believed that his parents had created him solely to abandon him and then die and to pass him into the hands of the evil foster parents. I, too, became part of his paranoid delusion, as it seemed that, like his parents, I existed only to raise his hopes with the near certainty that I, too, would die and leave him.

"Is it normal to want to kill yourself", Sanjay asked me one day. He had told me before that he had thought of killing himself virtually every single day since he was six. "Yes, in your world it is normal", I replied, noting that, "What is not normal to you is meeting someone who wants to stop you from killing yourself." He then asked, "Where do you come from?" I replied, "Do you mean what planet do I come from?" "Yes", he replied, as he struggled to fathom my alien intentions.

I received a phone call one day from Paul, Sanjay's partner, to tell me that Sanjay had taken another overdose. Paul felt that my help was making Sanjay worse, but at the same time he did not want our work to stop, as he felt that this might be Sanjay's last chance. Paul had become caught up in the same double bind as the rest of us.

My efforts to help seemed to be putting Sanjay's life at risk. It was painful for him to challenge his past, as that was where, perversely, he felt most comfortable. To put him in touch with a hopeful present was to stir up the painful prospect of giving up his distorted past, his tortured inner world, for a future that offered some prospect of a life with healthy promise. For Sanjay the certainty of despair was preferable to the cruelty of being teased with tentative hope.

Throughout most of the last century, the city of Chicago had been dumping its waste almost unchecked into Lake Michigan. By the late 1960s it had become so polluted that it could hardly sustain water-borne life. An environmental catastrophe would soon ensue unless major efforts could be made to check the discharge of man-made pollutants. Environmentalists, however, noticed that some species of fish had, nonetheless, survived upon their new diet of toxic waste. These fish seemed to have adapted to a diet of sewage and effluent. The environmentalists saw this as a hopeful and encouraging sign for the continuing survival of that species. Psychoanalysts, of course, would not see this as a good sign. As a metaphor it meant that humans, too, could adapt to, and live off, the unwanted effluent of their fellow humans. This, it seems to me, is what Sanjay did. He learned to adapt to life in the sewer and to feed off of the sewage. My attempts to wean him to fresh water threatened his very existence. He had adapted to his new, blighted environment, and my alternative world posed the most enormous threat to him.

Why, then, did Sanjay continue to see me? In part, I think to prove me wrong, to prove that my world was sicker than his. It was, after all, my world that had polluted his, and he frequently referred to media stories that proved to him how corrupt and perverse it really was. It was Sanjay who, with incredible and cruel irony, brought me the breaking news of the Holocaust of the World Trade Center. He railed against this terrorist world (of mine) and spluttered out his wish to have nothing more to do with it. He needed to remain with the certain comfort of cynicism, hate, and death, rather than learn to tolerate the uncertainty of a world of truth, love, and life. He was dependent on effluent. To accept the "pasteurisation" of hope that I seemed to offer him would be to threaten his whole internal existence.

He once told me that he was afraid to speak to me because he feared that flies would come out of his mouth: that is how filled with shit he thought he was. In the same way that his mouth had become his anus, my words had become, like Tom's penis, a perverse intrusion.

I told him that he preferred to feel worthless, but safe, rather than be tortured with the hope that life could possibly be worthwhile.

Silently, I fear that his life might remain worthless. But some signs of change began to show through. After two years of twice-weekly therapy, Sanjay seemed to be responding to the reality of my being an ever-present advocate for life and a constant interpreter of the perverse manner in which he so desperately clung on to death.

What seemed to perplex him most was my continuing to see him at all. Nobody apart from Paul had ever stayed with him for so long, and Paul was as much a denizen of the sewer as he was. Sanjay kept evacuating his unbearable experiences into me, and he was surprised when I did not attack or flee in response. He once told me that as a child he used to undress in the bathroom and smear himself from head to toe in his own faeces and then climb into the toilet and try to flush himself away. Similarly, he covered me in shit and could not understand why I was not flushed away. He was most perplexed when I said to him, "Thank you for giving me your shit. Now, I can understand you better." No "mother" had ever lovingly changed his dirty nappy or cleaned up his mess before.

It was the suicide of his brother Kamray that, paradoxically, gave Sanjay the will to live and eventually led him to my consulting room. He and Kamray had discussed killing themselves since childhood. Kamray, too, had been sexually abused by Tom, as had Ravi and Sasha. Sanjay illustrated this with a memory of Tom trying to force him and his brothers to fuck their sister while Tom watched.

Sanjay was comfortable with his insane existence, and my sane world represented the worst possible threat to him. He was describing to me one day what death would be like. I said it sounded to me like he was describing Heaven. "Yes", came his reply. This was the destiny he aspired to. On a day-to-day level he could not answer the door or the telephone; he self-mutilated; he could not go out unaccompanied; he could not sleep or stay sober, or have work, or love. And yet, this was the world in which he preferred to remain.

Gradually, after two years of therapy, things began to change in a more integrated manner. Sanjay stopped drinking for a whole day, then two days, and then for a week. He attended his sessions more consistently and actively. He told me things that he had kept secret for many years. He told me how, as a teenager, he would truant from school and be alone in the house. He would go into the bedroom of his foster mother Jill, take down one of her dresses, put it on and stand in front of her full-length mirror, whereupon he would stab himself repeatedly in the back with scissors or a knife in order to try and kill, not himself, but the image of Jill in the mirror.

During this period, at the end of certain sessions he would hesitate while leaving and would make as if to shake my hand or even to embrace me. He told me before a holiday break that he was going to miss me. My world of life, as well as death, seemed to be holding out an appeal to him over his world of a living death only. Occasionally, some humour would slip into a session. He would say, with just enough irony for both of us to appreciate, that *I* was the one who needed help, not him.

I had been trying to take his poisonous projections, detoxify them and return them to him in a manner that he could understand and use. As he struggled to take in more, his mouth, which had previously felt to him like the anus, became the mouth that began searching for the nipple. He was beginning to take in fresh water at last and was trying to give up his reliance on effluent.

One day when I went to collect him from the waiting room, he was alone, on the floor, playing with a toy car, like a six-year-old boy. In that session we talked about toys and playing, and it was then that he told me of the toy train that his father had set up for them in the attic. At last, I felt that we were in touch with the six-year-old part of him that had survived in spite of his life's transgressions.

Then Sanjay announced one day that he had phoned Ravi and Sasha to tell them that they should have nothing more to do with the foster family whom they still visited. No doubt it was with perverse dependency that they still kept in touch in order to assuage their own fear and guilt. Sanjay talked of consulting a solicitor to do something about confronting Tom and his family at last, and he engaged his siblings in the process. He was beginning to feel he could stand up for himself and fight them in the external world and relinquish his internal battle with them. And then, suddenly, with only the briefest of warnings, he left therapy.

It was, paradoxically, as if he had suddenly realised that he had shown me his potency—the "give-away" erect penis that had so frightened him when Tom abused him. He was afraid, I thought, of showing me that I was winning and that he was "in danger" of joining me in my world. He had begun to experience some hope after all, but he quickly turned it into false hope. He had been fighting me all this time, and he suddenly realised that I was winning, not he. Sanjay had, after all, fled from Tom when he had betrayed himself by having an erection, which he experienced as an act of collaboration with the enemy.

Inversely, his world of violence and violation seemed to have won. The violator maintained his attraction, the rescuer his revulsion. At least this is what I thought at the time.

Conclusion

I have tried to illustrate the appeal of the world of violence and perversion through Sanjay's eyes and what I may have learned from working with him.

I learned that, clinically, with such damaged patients, one must be prepared to stand alongside them in their world—by that I mean that one has to position oneself figuratively in tandem with them and not opposite or—as they experience it—in opposition to them. One can then more easily make what John Steiner (1993) has referred to as analyst-centred interpretations, in which the analyst tries to speak from the perspective of the patient. Patrick Gallwey (personal communication, 1982) had advised a similar tactic, wherein the analyst tried to take the view of both the violator and the violated without succumbing to either position. Interestingly, techniques of personal self-defence advocate a similar strategy where one moves to stand bodily alongside the opponent in order to lessen the potential for misunderstanding and confrontation. I certainly find these techniques useful, but I am advocating an approach that is even more pronounced still, which could best be summed up as "learning to swim in the sewer".

The child who is brought up by neglectful, depriving, or abusing parents paradoxically becomes more and more dependent on them. The prisoner, for example, is wholly dependent on the prison guard and, of course, vice versa. We see, pathologically, how the deprived child expects and therefore demands less and less, while the abandoned child identifies with his or her oppressor and becomes the very person whom that child hates the most. The more we love our children, the more we set them free; the more we hate them, the more we enslave them.

Sanjay had become a slave to his own internal world. The more he tried to free himself from his oppressors, the more he collaborated with their oppression, and the more guilt-ridden he became. His guilt turned to revenge, but his vindictiveness made him realise that, in the end, he was just like them. The vicious circle was complete.

I had my own guilt: guilt on behalf of agencies such as my own, which had not done more for him when he was a child; guilt for my own hatred of the foster family; guilt for my anger towards my patient, who would not follow me out of his perverse downward spiral; guilt for not knowing enough, understanding enough, or being good enough to help him.

This is the paradox of guilt. If life is, as it seems, and as the psychoanalysts have always understood it, then we all have a compelling need to relate to one another. If we become transfixed, as Sanjay did, on a terrorising object, then the terror becomes the currency with which we barter all subsequent relationships. But what is the barter of the so-called rescuers? We may sympathise with them or, hopefully, empathise with them, or, if we are weak, take pity upon the victims of terror. What it means is that we both cling to our known relationships in order to understand our world. Babies need their mothers to understand their world, and patients need their analysts, and writers need their readers.

What I learned, mostly, from Sanjay, is that to understand violence and its paradoxical attraction, we need to understand the inherent contrariness of guilt and forgiveness. I am going to suggest that we find forgiveness particularly difficult because, like guilt, it creates a paradox. To forgive is to distance us from all others, to break our ties both with our enemies and our allies, to end, at least for the moment, our need for others. To forgive is to be alone and lonely. Had I been able to forgive Sanjay's family for their apparent evilness, and Sanjay himself for his perverse opposition, and myself for my need to cling to my own omnipotent theories, then his therapy might have taken a different course.

What he needed and what I needed was to be free—free to swim in and out of each other's worlds. Then we might have been able to repair what we felt was wrong with both worlds. But in doing so, we would have been, at least temporarily, on our own. I am making a plea, therefore, for a degree of *professional loneliness*. What we need to do is to be able to put aside our dependency on, and our attachment to, our clinical dogma, our self-protective professional identities, our moral rectitude, our memory, and our desire, all in order to reduce our need to seek altruistic solutions. To understand the deepest dishonesty of the criminal mind and lay bare the most repellent secrets of the pervert, we need to live with the dishonesty in ourselves and bear to bare the secrets of our own perverseness.

Perhaps we need to be a little more like Sanjay, professionally at least—*alone* and *lonely*.

I would like to give the final word to Sanjay. He illustrates the dilemma that I have been trying to focus on better than I can. It was towards the end of his therapy—although I did not realise it at the time—when he suddenly said to me, "I could hug you. You are my dream come true . . . and I could cut your fucking head off!"

Some two years after Sanjay left, I bumped into him and Paul in the street. He told me that some very important things had been happening in his life. He had finally gone to the police and told them the full story of his early life with his foster family. They interviewed Tom, who, surprisingly, admitted it all and was charged with various offences against children. Sanjay said that he could not have gone to the police without my help, and he asked, in his typically somewhat perverse, pleading manner whether he could return to see me. I said that he could. A few days later I received a new referral from his general practitioner. Sanjay returned to therapy. He told me that after all this time away he was "not as happy" as he expected to be, despite the "truth" being out at last. "And maybe during all that time you weren't as worthless as you thought you were, either", I offered.

Tom went to court and pleaded guilty, so that Sanjay did not have to give evidence. He was sentenced to twelve years in prison. The story made the front page of the local newspaper, and the foster family's home was daubed in graffiti.

Sanjay remained in therapy for a further year-and-a-half, leaving by mutual consent when his fragile grasp on hope and life seemed, at last, less fragile.

It takes an unusual and insightful clinician to honour those "perverse" men and women whom most of us dishonour. It takes courage and, paradoxically, it takes great personal vulnerability. This is the main *true falsehood* I have learned from Estela Welldon.

REFERENCE

Steiner, John (1993). *Psychic Retreats: Pathological Organizations in Psychotic, Neurotic and Borderline Patients*. London: Routledge.

CHAPTER THREE

Mothers-in-law:
maternal function and child protection

Gwen Adshead

Introduction

E stela Welldon is justly renowned for her work on mothers and mothering, and how the mothering role can be both idealised and denigrated, with far-reaching effects for children. Her first book, *Mother, Madonna, Whore: The Idealization and Denigration of Motherhood* (Welldon, 1988) explicitly challenged psychoanalytic orthodoxy about perversion by arguing that women could develop perverse psychological structures in mind just as men do; and that they use their bodies, and the bodies of the children, to enact their perverse thoughts and desires. Welldon's work also caused a stir because she claimed to have good clinical evidence that motherhood and mothering is not always a state of bliss for women; but motherhood can be a time when affects of fear, distress, and hatred are experienced and also expressed. She articulated the view (and was perhaps the first person to do so) that those women who abused their children were not monsters but, rather, people who experienced unresolved distress arising from their own adverse experience of being cared for as children; and she suggested that professionals and society could and should take maternal distress and rage more seriously.

In this chapter, I discuss Estela Welldon's work in the light of research that has appeared since the publication of her 1988 book.

This research confirms to my mind the Welldon hypotheses and shows just how far-thinking and clinically accurate Estela has been. I draw on work using an attachment theory paradigm, and I apply this line of thought specifically to women offenders—that is, women who are brought before the courts because they have committed offences involving their children. Like Estela, I have been involved in preparing reports, for both family and criminal courts, that attempt to explain why the woman in question has acted so cruelly towards her child; and I use that experience in this work. In conclusion, I argue that we need more therapeutic services for women who harm their children, and I discuss some existing possibilities.

I want to close this introduction with some personal associations to Estela's work on "mothering" in forensic contexts. It is widely acknowledged that Estela is the "mother" of forensic psychotherapy. She is the Honorary President for Life of the International Association for Forensic Psychotherapy, and her creative maternal function gave rise to the Diploma in Forensic Psychotherapy offered by the Portman Clinic, which helped so many of us to become forensic psychotherapists. The diploma course, in turn, gave rise to the formal training in forensic psychotherapy that is now available to senior trainees in psychiatry. Forensic psychotherapy might have remained an esoteric interest if it had not been for Estela and her efforts to have "intercourse" with forensic psychiatrists and forensic systems, which created potential thinking spaces for therapy with offenders. I know that Estela has been a "mother" to my identity as a forensic psychotherapist in innumerable ways over the last three decades; and it was her professional "mothering" of trainees like me that allowed that identity to grow and develop. I see her as my professional "mother" because like most adult children, I cannot remember when or how I first met her, nor can I imagine what life would have been like without her influence. Her work, her support, and her advice have made my life as a forensic psychotherapist possible, and my debt to her can hardly be set out in words. This chapter is a tiny reflection of the thanks I owe her; and I have referred to her here by her first name, Estela, because that is how she is known all over the world.

Perversion and childhood trauma

In the introduction to *Mother, Madonna, Whore: The Idealization and Denigration of Motherhood*, Estela sets out her main thesis—namely, that the psychoanalytic orthodoxy about perversion focused exclusively on males and male genital structures and did not pay sufficient attention to female sexuality. It is important to note (as Estela does) that the definition of perversion being used here is the psychoanalytic one, wherein perversion is defined as a "dysfunction of the development of the sexual aspect of the personality" (Welldon, 1988, p. 6). This is not synonymous with sexual *deviance*, which usually implies behaviour that is both socially condemned and legally restrained. A woman with a perversion has a psychopathological aspect to her personality structure, which means that she acts out complex and unconscious affective states using a physical body or part of a body, including the body of a child.

This perverse structure in the personality develops during childhood as a result of a highly dysfunctional relationship with the mother. It becomes sexualised, just as other mental structures become sexualised, under the influence of sex hormones during puberty; it also becomes "gendered" during the psychosocial processes of adolescence. The perverse mental structure has both conscious and unconscious aspects to it, which can generate confusion and tension; this is experienced as *sexual* tension and arousal. This tension is generated most often when people with these perverse personality structures experience conscious feelings of intimacy and a wish to be close, which simultaneously give rise to *unconscious* feelings of hatred, fear, and rage. In later work, Estela describes how a vicious cycle can develop of growing tension, arousal, and confusion, acting out of these feelings using the body or body parts, followed by intense feelings of guilt and shame, which have to be defended against by a wish to be close and a search for physical comfort (Welldon, 2011).

Unlike men, who express their perversion using other people's bodies or body parts, women use their own bodies, or the bodies of their children, because in the woman's mind, the baby is not "seen" as separate or as personally distinct. Using Estela's model, repetitive self-harming behaviour is evidence of perversion, as are physical attacks on children's bodies (which may or may not be sexualised). The behaviour has a compulsive and even an addictive quality, and the hostility and rage are consciously disavowed. Only in an ongoing self-reflective process, such as in psychotherapy, can the unconscious negative affects come to consciousness and be accepted and tolerated without acting out (Motz, 2010).

Estela makes a clinical claim, based on her observations in the consulting room, that these women have experienced profound disruptions in their relationships with their mothers: either neglect and rejection, or a type of intrusive smothering attention. In both cases, the child is left without a carer to help them manage their distress and also with associated feelings of hostility and vengefulness towards the carer who has failed them. When they become mothers themselves, the maternal role stimulates unconscious feelings of envy and rage, leading to abuse of children in a variety of forms.

Attachment theory and perversion

Since 1992, there has been a huge expansion in the study of mother–child relationships using empirical paradigms based on attachment theory. As is well known, John Bowlby was a practicing psychoanalyst who developed a theory of how children develop internal working models of their closest relationships (attachments) in childhood. These internal working models of attachment become psychic structures in the mind, with both conscious and unconscious elements that help the child to develop a capacity to regulate anxiety and arousal when distressed, especially in the context of close relationships. "Good-enough" care in childhood—to steal Winnicott's famous phrase—enables the development of "secure" attachments, which, in turn, facilitate the capacity for effective care-giving and care-seeking in adulthood when needed (George and Solomon, 1999). Secure attachment systems in mind also promote the development of the capacity for "mentalizing"—the conscious metacognitive capacity to experience others as having "minds" like one's own.

Bowlby's theories have undergone extensive empirical scrutiny using a variety of research methods. Most famous is the Strange Situation Test devised by Mary Ainsworth (Ainsworth and Bell, 1970), which found that it was possible to classify infant attachment in terms of a child's behaviour upon separation from and reunion with the mother. Children with secure attachments had a recognisable pattern of behaviour that was distinct from children with an *insecure avoidant* attachment and children with an *insecure ambivalent* attachment. Later, another pattern of insecurity was described as *insecure disorganised*; this occurs only in a minority of children.

Ainsworth's work has been replicated extensively and internationally in a variety of cultures (Ainsworth, Blehar, Waters, and Wall, 1978, 2014). From the psychoanalytic point of view, the most interesting work has been the follow-up studies of insecure children (Waters,

Merrick, Treboux, Crowell, and Albersheim, 2000). Not only does insecurity of mind, once established, seem to persist; but different patterns of insecurity are also associated with different patterns of thought and behaviour in adulthood. The Adult Attachment Interview (AAI) (George, Kaplan, and Main, 1996) was devised to capture both the conscious and the unconscious representations of the individual's attachment system; it has been used to assess the attachment security of insecure children when grown up. Unsurprisingly, from a psychoanalytic point of view, children with insecure attachment systems tend to grow up into adults with insecure attachment representations; and insecurity of attachment in adults is associated with a wide variety of psychological problems (Dozier, Stovall-McClough, and Albus, 2008). Not only is insecurity of attachment much more common in clinical populations than in the general community, but disorganised attachment systems are also highly associated with clinical psychiatric syndromes such as psychosis and personality dysfunction (Bakermans-Kranenburg and van IJzendoorn, 2009).

In her introduction to *Mother, Madonna, Whore*, Estela calls for the use of a transgenerational approach to understanding failures in mothering and child care (Welldon, 1988). International research using the AAI in at least three countries has confirmed her clinical suspicion and has validated her suggestion (Fonagy, Steele, and Steele, 1991; van IJzendoorn, 1992). Women who have insecure attachment structures in mind raise children who are not only likely to have insecure attachment systems themselves: they also have insecure attachment patterns that mirror their mothers' attachment style in 80% of cases. Mothers with avoidant attachment styles have babies who are assessed as having avoidant attachment; ambivalent mothers have babies with ambivalent attachment styles. It appears that the unconscious attachment structure in the mother's mind affects her parental sensitivity and, especially, her ability to mentalize her own baby's developing mind (Meins, Fernyhough, Wainwright, Das Gupta, Fradley, and Tuckey, 2002).

When the AAI is used to assess adult attachment, it does so by paying close attention to the words used, to the way that concepts are put together linguistically, and to what is not said or where there are gaps in language (Hesse, 2008). In this sense, the AAI is a close reflection of the psychoanalytic discourse, where the therapist pays attention beyond the manifest content of speech to what is actually being conveyed by the speaker. For example, during an AAI, the speaker may claim to have had a "wonderful" or "perfect" childhood but be unable to recall any memories to illustrate this idea. This would be rated as an idealising stance that defensively helps to keep unresolved distress from conscious experience, which is characteristic of avoidant insecure attachment. If the speaker then later goes on to describe an experience of active maltreatment by the same parent they had early described as "perfect" *and they themselves do not comment on the inconsistency*, then this is not only evidence of active idealising going on in the mind, but also an example of the activity of a mental structure that is likely to be unstable under stress because it is a reality-distorting structure. For example, a crying child may be a powerful conscious challenge to a parent's unstable and unconscious defence against awareness of distress and rage. Attacking a child displaces the tension and distress, just as Estela describes in her cycle of perversion.

Attachment and child maltreatment

So far, I have set out some empirical data that supports Estela's contention that early disruptions in the mother–baby relationship affect how the mother attends to the baby's emotional needs. If a mother neglects or rejects her baby, this may lead to insecure avoidant attachment in the child; if the mother smothers or intrudes into her baby's emotional space, then the baby may develop an insecure ambivalent attachment style. If they are girls, both the insecure avoidant and the insecure ambivalent babies are likely to grow up into adult women with insecure adult attachment systems, which will have a profound effect on how they parent their own child. This effect is manifest at the conscious level and at the unconscious neurobiological level: *consciously*, insecurely attached women may respond with more hostility and distress to their babies' cries than secure women; *unconsciously*, their levels of oxytocin differ from a secure comparison group (Strathearn, Fonagy, Amico, and Montague, 2009).

If the babies grow up to be women with disorganised attachment patterns, then this may be especially problematic for a number of reasons. First, disorganised attachment is more likely to develop after active childhood maltreatment by a carer (Carlson, Cicchetti, Barnett, and Braunwald, 1989) or those in situations where the carer is either frightened or frightening (Schuengel, Bakermans-Kranenburg, and van IJzendoorn, 1999). Thus, babies with disorganised attachment are likely to have been exposed in their early years to high levels of fear from a parent or carer. Follow-up studies of children with disorganised attachment patterns indicate that they are more likely to develop a variety of psychiatric clinical problems in adolescence and thereafter (van IJzendoorn, Schuengel, and Bakermans-Kranenburg, 1999), including dissociative problems. They also develop abnormal interpersonal strategies that involve controlling behaviour towards others: either frankly aggressive behaviour or controlling care-giving behaviour (Solomon, George, and De Jong, 1995). Thus, people with disorganised attachment systems may be more at risk of perpetrating acts of violence (Ogilvie, Newman, Todd, and Peck, 2014).

Karlen Lyons-Ruth and her group in the United States have studied the maternal behaviours of mothers who have grown up with adult disorganised attachment systems as a result of early childhood trauma. She has described how these mothers get into states of mind with respect to their children that are *hostile*, *helpless*, or a *combination of both* (Lyons-Ruth, Yellin, Melnick, and Atwood, 2005). She has shown how mothers who had, as children, experienced abuse and maltreatment grew up to be mothers who are either helpless with their children or hostile to them, or a terrifying mixture of both.

More recent research has found an excess of hostile–helpless states of mind in mothers who physically abuse their children or kill them (Frigerio, Costantino, Ceppi, and Barone, 2013; Barone, Bramante, Lionetti, and Pastore, 2014). There is considerable interest in the relationship between hostile–helpless states of mind and the diagnosis of borderline—or emotionally unstable—personality disorder (Liotti, 2014): an important clinical issue, given the high levels of personality disorder that are diagnosed in maltreating mothers who come before the courts (Adshead, 2015). It is reasonable to speculate that hostile–helpless states of mind are also commonly present in those mothers who repeatedly get pregnant but then fail to care for their children, so that the children are removed from them. They consciously claim to long for a child, but unconsciously they respond to the child's neediness with hostility or indifference.

A common theme in the study of child abuse is the unrealistic expectation that abusers have of children, as if they were older than their years and able to function as adults or even peers (Azar and Rohrbeck, 1986). This represents a significant reality distortion and may, from an attachment disorganisation perspective, indicate that the parent is in a present-tense state of mind that reflects past-tense experience of unresolved childhood distress—that is, the abusing parent actually feels like a child and sees the child as a peer or an adult who is difficult. Bauer and Twentyman (1985) have described how abusive mothers attribute malevolent intentions to their children, and then they use this to justify assaults. These reality-distorting defences are an attempt to make inner anxiety and distress more bearable for the mother, but they make violence more likely and unpredictable.

I vividly remember assessing a young woman who had fractured her child's femur—he was then eighteen months old and only just getting up on his feet. This assault on him would have taken his mother some effort. She told me about having had a difficult childhood, during which her own parents had separated acrimoniously when she was ten years old, and her mother's new partner had sexually abused her. She said that she had told her mother, who had refused to believe her and had subsequently rejected her. This woman then began to act out in adolescence by truanting and self-harming, and then falling pregnant at seventeen years of age. When I asked her about her relationship with her mother, she said, "There's something between us that isn't there." With unconscious poetry, she described an intolerable dilemma for a child about how to access help and comfort from a mother who is there, but also not there. We can only imagine what "absence" or gap in her child's needs for care and love must have activated, and how the breaking of his leg reflected some inner unstable defence that snapped under the strain of being a single parent of an unplanned baby.

Mothers-in-law:
psychodynamic approaches
to expert evidence in the family court

What I hope to have shown is that there is now extensive empirical evidence that supports Estela's original contention that the roots of child maltreatment by women lie in those women's early experiences of maternal care. Women who suffer abuse, neglect, and rejection in their early years are at risk of growing up to be adults with compromised psychological security; they are likely to have significant disorganisation of their social mind, such that they cannot mentalize their own distress or the distress of their children. If they are in stressful situations that activate their attachment systems, such as a bereavement or a dysfunctional relationship, they may be at high risk of treating their own child in exactly the way they had been treated, including neglect, acts of abuse, and failure to protect their own child. Psychoanalytic hypotheses about the intergenerational transmission of trauma have been confirmed by studies such as those conducted by Cathy Spatz Widom (2015) and her colleagues (Widom, Czaja, and DuMont, 2015) and Terence Thornberry and his colleagues (Thornberry, Knight, and Lovegrove, 2012). Different types of abuse have been shown to have different effects on parenting behaviour (Bailey, DeOliveira, Wolfe, Evans, and Hartwick, 2012), which suggests a complex process of conscious and unconscious coming to terms with trauma.

The relevance of this is clear when we consider the social and legal response to mothers who abuse, neglect, or fail to protect their children. In 2014, in England and Wales, some 60,000 children were taken into care, two-thirds on the grounds of abuse and neglect. This would suggest that there are at least 40,000 mothers in the community who either failed to protect their children or who actively neglected or abused them. Nearly 20% of these mothers have had a child removed from their care previously—that is, some 16,000 women somehow failed to learn from their previous experience. Each of these cases was underpinned by a legal process, and in many cases psychiatric evidence will have been called because of concerns about the parent's mental health and the issue of risk to children.

Forensic psychotherapists are ideally placed to assist the family courts with these cases, especially those where there have been previous proceedings. Using Estela's work and the subsequent research that I have described, we can provide for the courts a useful model for understanding how abuse and maltreatment take place and how best to assess the risk. In child protection cases most local authorities already use a Framework of Needs Assessment that is based on attachment evidence, but the focus of the assessment is on the child. This is understandable and necessary, but there must also be a proper assessment of the parent's attachment state of mind and an exploration of whether treatment is possible.

Of course, at this point in the chapter, the forensic psychotherapist will probably be weeping tears of frustration at the lack of psychological therapy services for women who abuse their children. We may compare the lack of services for abusive mothers with the services for dangerous offenders with personality disorder (Joseph and Benefield, 2012) that provide assessment and treatment, and the services for people who commit serious acts of violence while mentally ill. Each of these services costs tens of millions of pounds, and each is tasked with reducing risk and improving the mental health of offenders; but they do not take on mothers who abuse their children. Neither Child and Adolescent Mental Health Services nor perinatal psychiatric services offer therapy to mothers in this situation, even though they may be involved with affected children.

The forensic psychotherapist will therefore have to advise the court that it may not be possible to get the woman the intervention or treatment she needs to make her safer. This is especially frustrating because there is increasing evidence that therapies are available and effective for this group. A very early study by Egeland and colleagues (Egeland, Jacobvitz, and Sroufe, 1988) found that mothers who had been abused as children managed not to abuse their own children if they had support from another adult carer or parent or had *participated in therapy*. There are interventions promoting mentalizing that look promising for people with severe personality disorder, including those with antisocial aspects to their personality (Yakeley, 2014); there are various parenting interventions that address maternal mentalization (Sadler, Slade, and Mayes, 2006; Slade, 2007); and there are places in the United Kingdom that offer these, such as the Anna Freud National Centre for Children and Families and the Tavistock Centre, both in London, as well as the Family and Safeguarding Service in Oxford. But such places are all too few.

Recently, the government of the United Kingdom has provided financial support for a social service project that supports mothers who have had a child removed from their care. This project, called Pause, provides individual weekly support by a social therapist as part of a programme that expressly tries to help these young women to develop more of a sense of self and agency and also to resist using unplanned pregnancy as a way of engaging with the world. Although no expressly psychodynamic therapy is offered, Pause accepts and understands that these women need to make significant psychological shifts in terms of their self-understanding, and the workers are given psychodynamically informed supervision for the work they do. The project has received government funding because it makes sound financial sense to break the cycle of mindless pregnancy, failed care, legal intervention, and loss and distress for both children and mothers in equal measure. Each child removal proceeding costs at least £23,000 just to start proceedings; costs can escalate to ten times that figure.

Conclusion

It took courage for Estela Welldon to publish *Mother, Madonna, Whore* at a time when the idea that mothers might abuse their children was literally unspeakable. The subsequent research I have described has made it clear that not only must we speak about abuse by women of their children, but we must also try to act to prevent it by using our enhanced understanding of how the traumatic effects of abuse and unresolved distress cross the generations to exert pain and harm.

REFERENCES

Adshead, Gwen (2015). Parenting and Personality Disorder: Clinical and Child Protection Implications. *Advances in Psychiatric Treatment, 21*, 15–22.

Ainsworth, Mary D. Salter, and Bell, Silvia M. (1970). Attachment, Exploration, and Separation: Illustrated by the Behavior of One-Year-Olds in a Strange Situation. *Child Development, 41*, 49–67.

Ainsworth, Mary D. Salter; Blehar, Mary C.; Waters, Everett; and Wall, Sally (1978). *Patterns of Attachment: A Psychological Study of the Strange Situation.* Hillsdale, New Jersey: Lawrence Erlbaum Associates.

Ainsworth, Mary D. Salter; Blehar, Mary C.; Waters, Everett, and Wall, Sally (2014). *Patterns of Attachment: A Psychological Study of the Strange Situation.* New York: Psychology Press / Taylor and Francis Group.

Azar, Sandra T., and Rohrbeck, Cynthia A. (1986). Child Abuse and Unrealistic Expectations: Further Validation of the Parent Opinion Questionnaire. *Journal of Consulting and Clinical Psychology, 54*, 867–868.

Bailey, Heidi M.; DeOliveira, Carey Anne; Wolfe, Vicki Veitch; Evans, Elspeth M., and Hartwick, Cailey (2012). The Impact of Childhood Maltreatment History on Parenting: A Comparison of Maltreatment Types and Assessment Methods. *Child Abuse and Neglect, 36*, 236–246.

Bakermans-Kranenburg, Marian J., and van IJzendoorn, Marinus H. (2009). The First 10,000 Adult Attachment Interviews: Distributions of Adult Attachment Representations in Clinical and Non-Clinical Groups. *Attachment and Human Development, 11*, 223–263.

Barone, Lavinia; Bramante, Alessandra; Lionetti, Francesca, and Pastore, Massimiliano (2014). Mothers Who Murdered Their Child: An Attachment-Based Study on Filicide. *Child Abuse and Neglect, 38*, 1468–1477.

Bauer, William D., and Twentyman, Craig T. (1985). Abusing, Neglectful, and Comparison Mothers' Responses to Child-Related and Non-

Child-Related Stressors. *Journal of Consulting and Clinical Psychology*, 53, 335–343.

Carlson, Vicki; Cicchetti, Dante; Barnett, Douglas, and Braunwald, Karen (1989). Disorganized/Disoriented Attachment Relationships in Maltreated Infants. *Developmental Psychology*, 25, 525–531.

Dozier, Mary; Stovall-McClough, K. Chase, and Albus, Kathleen E. (2008). Attachment and Psychopathology in Adulthood. In Jude Cassidy and Philip R. Shaver (Eds.), *Handbook of Attachment: Theory, Research, and Clinical Applications, Second Edition*, pp. 718–744. New York: Guilford Press / Guilford Publications.

Egeland, Byron; Jacobvitz, Deborah, and Sroufe, L. Alan (1988). Breaking the Cycle of Abuse: Relationship Predictors. *Child Development*, 59, 1080–1088.

Fonagy, Peter; Steele, Howard, and Steele, Miriam (1991). Maternal Representations of Attachment During Pregnancy Predict the Organization of Infant–Mother Attachment at One Year of Age. *Child Development*, 62, 891–905.

Frigerio, Alessandra; Costantino, Elisabetta; Ceppi, Elisa, and Barone, Lavinia (2013). Adult Attachment Interviews of Women from Low-Risk, Poverty, and Maltreatment Risk Samples: Comparisons Between the Hostile / Helpless and Traditional AAI Coding Systems. *Attachment and Human Development*, 15, 424–442.

George, Carol; Kaplan, Nancy, and Main, Mary (1996). *Adult Attachment Interview Protocol*. Unpublished Manual. Berkeley, California: Department of Psychology, University of California at Berkeley.

George, Carol, and Solomon, Judith (1999). Attachment and Caregiving: The Caregiving Behavioral System. In Jude Cassidy and Philip R. Shaver (Eds.), *Handbook of Attachment: Theory, Research, and Clinical Applications*, pp. 649–670. New York: Guilford Press / Guilford Publications.

Hesse, Eric (2008). The Adult Attachment Interview: Protocol, Method of Analysis and Empirical Studies. In Jude Cassidy and Philip R. Shaver (Eds.), *Handbook of Attachment: Theory, Research, and Clinical Applications. Second Edition*, pp. 552–598. New York: Guilford Press / Guilford Publications.

Joseph, Nick, and Benefield, Nick (2012). A Joint Offender Personality Disorder Pathway Strategy: An Outline Summary. *Criminal Behaviour and Mental Health*, 22, 210–217.

Liotti, Giovanni (2014). Disorganised Attachment in the Pathogenesis and the Psychotherapy of Borderline Personality Disorder. In Adam N. Danquah and Katherine Berry (Eds.), *Attachment Theory in Adult*

Mental Health: A Guide to Clinical Practice, pp. 113–128. Abingdon, Oxfordshire: Routledge / Taylor and Francis Group.

Lyons-Ruth, Karlen; Yellin, Claudia; Melnick, Sharon, and Atwood, Gwendolyn (2005). Expanding the Concept of Unresolved Mental States: Hostile/Helpless States of Mind on the Adult Attachment Interview are Associated with Disrupted Mother–Infant Communication and Infant Disorganization. *Development and Psychopathology, 17*, 1–23.

Meins, Elizabeth; Fernyhough, Charles; Wainwright, Rachel; Das Gupta, Mani; Fradley, Emma, and Tuckey, Michelle (2002). Maternal Mind-Mindedness and Attachment Security as Predictors of Theory of Mind Understanding. *Child Development, 73*, 1715–1726.

Motz, Anna (2010). Self-Harm as a Sign of Hope. *Psychoanalytic Psychotherapy, 24*, 81–92.

Ogilvie, Claire A.; Newman, Emily; Todd, Lynda, and Peck, David (2014). Attachment and Violent Offending: A Meta-Analysis. *Aggression and Violent Behavior, 19*, 322–339.

Sadler, Lois S.; Slade, Arietta, and Mayes, Linda C. (2006). Minding the Baby: A Mentalization-Based Parenting Program. In Jon G. Allen and Peter Fonagy (Eds.), *Handbook of Mentalization-Based Treatment*, pp. 271–288. Chichester, West Sussex: John Wiley and Sons.

Schuengel, Carlo; Bakermans-Kranenburg, Marian J., and van IJzendoorn, Marinus H. (1999). Frightening Maternal Behavior Linking Unresolved Loss and Disorganized Infant Attachment. *Journal of Consulting and Clinical Psychology, 67*, 54–63.

Slade, Arietta (2007). Reflective Parenting Programs: Theory and Development. *Psychoanalytic Inquiry, 26*, 640–657.

Solomon, Judith; George, Carol, and De Jong, Annemieke (1995). Children Classified as Controlling at Age Six: Evidence of Disorganized Representational Strategies and Aggression at Home and at School. *Development and Psychopathology, 7*, 447–463.

Strathearn, Lane; Fonagy, Peter; Amico, Janet, and Montague, P. Read (2009). Adult Attachment Predicts Maternal Brain and Oxytocin Response to Infant Cues. *Neuropsychopharmacology, 34*, 2655–2666.

Thornberry, Terence P.; Knight, Kelly E., and Lovegrove, Peter J. (2012). Does Maltreatment Beget Maltreatment?: A Systematic Review of the Intergenerational Literature. *Trauma, Violence, and Abuse, 13*, 135–152.

van IJzendoorn, Marinus H. (1992). Intergenerational Transmission of Parenting: A Review of Studies in Nonclinical Populations. *Developmental Review, 12*, 76–99.

van IJzendoorn, Marinus H.; Schuengel, Carlo, and Bakermans-Kranenburg, Marian J. (1999). Disorganized Attachment in Early Childhood: Meta-Analysis of Precursors, Concomitants, and Sequelae. *Development and Psychopathology, 11*, 225–250.

Waters, Everett; Merrick, Susan; Treboux, Dominique; Crowell, Judith, and Albersheim, Leah (2000). Attachment Security in Infancy and Early Adulthood: A Twenty-Year Longitudinal Study. *Child Development, 71*, 684–689.

Welldon, Estela V. (1988). *Mother, Madonna, Whore: The Idealization and Denigration of Motherhood.* London: Free Association Books.

Welldon, Estela V. (2011). *Playing with Dynamite: A Personal Approach to the Psychoanalytic Understanding of Perversions, Violence, and Criminality.* London: Karnac Books.

Widom, Cathy S. (2015). Reflection: Intergenerational Transmission of Child Maltreatment. In Deborah Daro, Anne Cohn Donnelly, Lee Ann Huang, and Byron J. Powell (Eds.), *Advances in Child Abuse Prevention Knowledge: The Perspective of New Leadership*, pp. 83–92. Cham: Springer / Springer International Publishing, Springer Science and Business Media.

Widom, Cathy S.; Czaja, Sally J., and DuMont, Kimberly A. (2015). Intergenerational Transmission of Child Abuse and Neglect: Real or Detection Bias? *Science, 347*, 1480–1485.

Yakeley, Jessica (2014). Mentalization-Based Group Treatment for Antisocial Personality Disorder. In John Woods and Andrew Williams (Eds.), *Forensic Group Psychotherapy: The Portman Clinic Approach*, pp. 151–182. London: Karnac Books.

SECTION TWO

Forensic psychotherapy in hospitals

CHAPTER FOUR

Brain, womb, and will:
a lethal cocktail or a grand affair?

Ronald Doctor

Introduction

I have known Estela Welldon—pretty well, I think—for twenty-five years, and my immediate response after being asked to write a chapter for this book to celebrate her eightieth birthday and to honour her work is that maybe I don't know her. I thought that researching her work and the influence of her creativity for this Festschrift would hopefully give me the opportunity to get to know her.

My earliest memory of her is shockingly intense and vivid. Sitting across an interview table, she asked me this very confrontational question: "What would you do if a perverse patient gave you a gift?" After looking perplexed and dumbfounded, she both gave me the answer and, to my great surprise, the job for which I was being interviewed. She explained that you would neither accept nor reject the patient's offerings but leave the gift on the table for discussion. She told me that I should try to listen to the patient and understand the meaning of the gift and whether this was possibly a seductive collusion or a real offering of gratitude. This incident offers some idea of what it felt like to tumble into the slipstream of Welldon's very considerable personality—a personality that, it turns out, was quite breathlessly maintained throughout her three-decade tenure at the Portman Clinic and beyond. The woman who enlivened any encounter, who addressed her friends and professional colleagues in exactly the same way: at all times affectionate, intellectual, loyal, free-associative, and, at least occasionally, vulnerable. The effect is oddly appealing, and whatever you happen to feel about her work, deeply impressive.

In answer to her question, I was thus introduced to a woman whose intelligence and understanding of human endeavour and malevolence would not only shape the content of this chapter but also inspire a creative and imaginative relationship with Estela for the next quarter-century.

In my mind, Estela's important contribution to psychoanalytic literature is her ability to listen to the patient and to have the courage to think about what this person is saying. It was this talent that allowed her to hear that women were asking for help in the face of their very frightening feelings of both being mothers and also having very perverse thoughts. When she wrote her groundbreaking book *Mother, Madonna, Whore: The Idealization and Denigration of Motherhood*, she put forward the idea that,

> we neglected to acknowledge what really happened with "battered babies"; nobody, even experienced physicians, could believe that those babies' injuries had been caused by their mothers. . . . The failure accurately to diagnose such women came, I believe, partly from society's glorification of motherhood, its refusal to admit that motherhood could have any negative aspects. [Welldon, 1988, p. 10]

The belief system in which motherhood was deified, venerated, and exalted required a certain audacity in order for Welldon to face the reality that women can also be perverse.

Welldon states that female psychophysiology gives a completely different pattern to perversion, and that at the centre of female perversion is the perversion of motherhood. I think that it is her courage in placing motherhood on the agenda for discussion that has had such a profound impact, in order both to help and to support the mother in facing her own sadism and destructiveness. I think it is Welldon's ability to face reality, however unpleasant or distasteful it is, that has put her work at the forefront of psychoanalytic research.

It was Welldon's (2011, p. 140) novel idea that the "psychotherapy involved in forensic psychotherapy is different from other forms precisely because society is, willy-nilly, involved". Forensic psychotherapy has gone beyond the special relationship between patient and psychotherapist. It is a triangular situation: patient, psychotherapist, society. Welldon (2015, p. 212) uses the idea of different triangular situations in working with the forensic patient. Thus, another triangle, besides the society, is the "existence of the triangular process of power dynamics in social roles, such as the bully, the victim, and the bystander (sometimes intervening as rescuer), where the bystander becomes the audience of the bully–victim drama". The bystander role is often an important but unrecognised part of the problem, and psychotherapists can become part of this dynamic.

In this chapter, I describe two patients, a man and a woman, to illustrate the triangular situation of society and power dynamics inherent in forensic psychotherapy. I compare and contrast their differences, with their disordered personalities bordering on psychosis and perversions, with particular emphasis on their sadism and destructiveness and how they deal with their oedipal anxieties by perverse defences. I use clinical material to describe how the patients' sadistic and destructive defences may be difficult to stomach countertransferentially.

It is our countertransference in relation to the personality-disordered and perverse patients that may be hard to tolerate. Symington (1980) states that it is possible to classify the responses aroused by the patient with a personality disorder under three headings: collusion, disbelief, and condemnation, all of which are defences used by of professionals to protect ourselves from very disagreeable feelings. Welldon (2015, p. 212) has stated that there is a third triangular situation of three different "cultures": of blaming, of concern, and of learning. This, I think, compares with Symington's three countertransference feelings. In the treatment of the personality disorder, and in particular in the case of the psychopath or sociopath, the patient will try by every means to get us to do something other than give interpretations.

The patient makes a desperate appeal to us either to collude in order to lend him or her money, or to allow him or her to use our telephone, and so on; or, through projective identification, the patient stirs our own sadism, and this leads to one of two responses: either disbelief or condemnation. The psychopath despises the person who holds onto an illusion that he or she is good; unconsciously, such individuals know that it is a rejection of an important part of the self and will therefore always give a strong clue about the hidden side of their character.

To adhere to the evidence, rather than to disbelieve, requires us to accept our own sadism, which we deny all the more when we are stirred by the psychopath. If we accept what we see in the psychopath, then we have to accept our own sadism. It may be more comfortable to believe that both we and the psychopath are good.

The other reaction is to deny our sadism by projecting it back into the criminal psychopath, who is a particularly suitable scapegoat onto whom we can project our hatred. To relate, with neither disbelief nor condemnation, is extremely difficult, as seen in the response aroused by the psychopath who goes into a psychiatric hospital where he or she is met with disbelief, and in the prison, where he or she is met with condemnation.

Both disbelief and condemnation are products of the same emotional neglect: the failure to accept the psychopath as he or she really is. The psychopath projects inner despair into others and achieves short-term goals in this way. Such patients make others feel what they dare not feel. If the despair comes home to roost, it is catastrophic, and patients have to push it away.

In Welldon's (1998, 2011) seminal work on female perversion, she was able to listen to her patients and to their stories without condemnation or disbelief. She was able to believe in what she was hearing and to introduce the notion of female perversion, describing the narcissistic use of children as an extension of a woman's own maltreatment of her body and as a repetition of an intergenerational pattern of abuse and cruelty. Welldon challenged the assumption that a phallus was an essential prerequisite of perversions.

Estela Welldon introduced startling and unsettling discoveries about the potential for women to use their own bodies and those of their children in the service of perverse and violent activity. For women, as for men, the meaning of the offence is not necessarily accessible to the conscious mind; it becomes clearer throughout the course of analytic forensic psychotherapy, manifested through the relationship with the therapist (cf. Motz, 2014).

It is the enactment on the part of the offender that, I think, defines forensic psychotherapy, and it is the fact that even the most apparently insane violence has a meaning in the mind of the person who commits it. There is a need to be aware of this meaning and to learn from it in an attempt to prevent further violence (Doctor, 2008a, 2008b).

Here I describe the presentations or "gifts"—both conscious and unconscious—that forensic patients bring to the therapy. For women it is the containing body and the narcissistic use of children or the extension of the body in the child in its various forms; and for the men it is the phallic body.

In the first instance I describe a male patient, by whom I was presented with a combined container–phallus. In my mind an image of a bag with a gun inside was placed on the table in my consulting room, which provoked a massive anxiety reaction in me. It is this case that I describe in Vignette 1.

Clinical vignette 1

A forty-four-year-old single man, Mr C, a lab technician, was referred for a psychotherapy assessment outpatient appointment. However, an hour before his appointment I received a telephone call from his general medical practitioner to say that he, the GP, had had a sleepless night, as Mr C had come to his consulting room the previous day to tell him that he had a gun and that he was suicidal. The GP was unsure what to do but urged the patient to keep his appointment with me the following day. Perhaps the GP had succumbed to the bystander effect and had thus unwittingly abandoned the patient. Following the conversation with the GP, my heart was pounding, but I decided that I would keep the appointment. An hour after the telephone call from the GP, Mr C calmly walked into my office. He put a small bag on the table in my consulting room and started the interview: "My problems are complicated. I had a road traffic accident with whiplash injuries and consequent depression, followed by a nervous breakdown due to the incompetence of my solicitors."

This patient had been unable to work for a period of nine months; during those nine months he had attended counselling for six sessions and then the Psychiatric Outpatients Service for management of his depression with medication. Finally, he was referred to the Psychotherapy Service. He said that prior to the aforementioned accident he had been planning to emigrate to the United States, and he used very forceful language to describe his attitude to England. He had clearly been very dissatisfied with his life here for a long time. Another consequence of the accident was that he had been unable to take some examinations that would have enabled him to practise as a lab technician in America; however, in the long term he still planned to emigrate.

He then went on to tell me that his fiancée and her parents were involved in another road traffic accident a few weeks prior to our appointment, and all of them had died from 40% burns! The patient also informed me that in fact he had another friend who had died from an arson attack a couple of years previously. As a result of these four deaths, he now felt very depressed every morning and had been so for the past three weeks, since the death of his fiancée. He said that he had picked up an automatic pistol and pointed it at his head, imagining that he had a bullet in the chamber, and then pulled the trigger. He informed me that he did have bullets in the house but had not yet put them in the chamber of the gun. I blurted out, in shock, at hearing about all these deaths as well as of his impending suicide, that he was playing Russian roulette with himself. He grinned and said that obviously I knew nothing about guns, as one cannot play Russian roulette with an automatic pistol. He went on in a somewhat triumphant way: "You, being a psychiatrist, probably think I am suicidal. I am not suicidal. It is a ritual I am playing. I point the gun at my head and pull the trigger and I play out this ritual every morning for the past three weeks to try to overcome the fear of death." Mr C said to me that he was also moonlighting for a security agency, which had issued him with the firearm, but he could not tell me any more about it, claiming it was a secret.

At this point in the interview I felt very alarmed at what I was hearing, and in my mind fantasised as to what was in the bag on my table. Was it his gun? Was he going to use it? To defuse my terrified mind, I asked Mr C if he could tell me about himself. He went on to inform me that his relationship with a woman came to an end in the middle of the previous year after a four-year very off-and-on relationship. He explained that the woman concerned had often gone abroad without explaining where she was going and then returned to the United Kingdom without telling him she had come back. They then had a period together again, after which she went off once more. Finally, the relationship ended with a telephone conversation in which he discovered that she was living in a different part of the country and was in another relationship. It was not clear whether this was the same woman as his fiancée, who had died in the car accident. He told me that he was upset about this, but more in terms of injured pride, because he felt that he should have ended the relationship rather than be in emotional distress at the loss of the relationship. He said that his parents—both lawyers—had divorced when he was an infant. His father remarried soon after, and Mr C never saw him again, but he knew that his father had died about six years ago. The patient had been brought up by his mother. He also has one sister, now married with children.

Listening to this patient, I could feel myself in a very high state of anxiety, with thoughts of mass murder enacted by this patient going through my mind. I said to Mr C that he had come today to tell me that he had a gun, and that he was letting me know how very serious the situation was, and that he had become very anxious about his situation. I continued to say that by communicating his anxiety, which had now become *my* enormous anxiety, he could remain calm and in control. However, he had come today as he felt his methods of dealing with his anxiety were not working, and he was becoming increasingly frightened as to what he might do.

During a lengthy discussion, characterised by increasing anxiety on my part, I continued to say that he was telling me about his gun and that this was a communication that he wanted me, and us, to think about what we might do about it. I said that we had to take this communication about his gun very seriously. I think that the conversation became quite fixed with the idea in my mind that he had brought his gun into the room, inside the bag on my table. After considering a number of options, including handing the gun back to the security agency that he had mentioned at the beginning of the session, we decided that I would let the police know so that they could contact him to take the gun away. I think at this point I was able to think of Welldon's (2015) triangular situation in relation to this patient and to call on law enforcement to help me with my anxiety. He said that this would complicate matters, but he agreed with the idea that I should contact the police, and I gave him another appointment for two weeks' time.

I subsequently informed the police about this patient who was in possession of a gun; they thought that it was a false alarm—another example of disbelief and doubt that he had a gun. However, the police arrived at his home in a large convoy, and he let them in. After a lengthy search of his house, they found the gun, to their great surprise—but not just one gun. There were over one hundred guns in his possession!

This patient did not commit murder, but he had projected his murderous thoughts into my mind. I think he wanted help in order to contain the enormous anxiety arising from his murderous impulses, as he felt that he was unable to do this. He had probably reached the point where he realised he needed help, initially going to the GP and then coming to the Psychotherapy Service. I never discovered whether he had in reality brought the gun into my consulting room, but in my mind he had brought an image of something very violent into the room, causing *me* great anxiety. Perhaps that was what he wanted: someone to contain his huge anxiety. And at that moment all I could think of was that I needed help as he proved to be more than I could contain.

He was then seen by two psychiatrists who differed in their opinion as to whether or not he was psychotic, but he stood trial for possession of weapons and was convicted and given a custodial sentence. The patient, Mr C, found his home in prison—a place secure enough to contain his murderous anxiety. Perhaps he will be able to look back over his experiences and consider that the professional response he received was appropriate at the time (Binder and McCoy, 1983).

I think that a weak dependent part of the self attempts to make contact with the analyst but is prevented from doing so by an alliance of destructive objects. Rosenfeld (1971) refers to this as the narcissistic organisation, often represented as the unconscious fantasy of a gang—in this case the hundred guns—which can either be idealised or feel very persecutory and thus represent itself as a helper or as a tyrannical persecutor. In fact, it takes over the personality and prevents development and growth. I think that Mr C's collection of guns was initially the idealised gang that protected Mr C from his enormous paranoid anxieties in which the persecutors, projected into the solicitors, ultimately become the whole of the United Kingdom, from which he felt he had to escape. However, with the mounting number of deaths in his life, the gang became the tyrannical persecutor driving him to come for help.

The narcissistic organisation arises when there is a failure of containment in infancy and childhood. Mr C's parents separated in his infancy, and he lost contact with his father. He was brought up by his mother, with whom he was still living, and thus, this failure of containment had probably given rise to an ego-destructive superego. The narcissistic relationship evolves in order to evade the hostile superego, which is either defensive or destructive.

It is usual in contemporary psychoanalytic psychotherapy to assume that in creating meaning for a patient we are engaged in a process of containment. However, there may be more to containment than just meaning. There is clearly going to be a limit to the extent that understanding can provide containment given the severity of the mental illnesses or the level of violence of the patients. They cause distress to other people by the very fact that they break boundaries that defy commonly held expectations about the way people behave in relationships. They find it extremely difficult to set limits on themselves about what they might do, and therefore they are often doing things that are risky, damaging, or dangerous. Equally, they find it very difficult to accept other people setting limits in relationships. Often explosive outbursts will take place when they realise that someone is not going to do something for them when they had assumed that they would. Sometimes containment might mean having to take action or even involve the physical restraint of a patient.

The difficulty might lie in confusion, both in the mind of the patient and that of the professional, about what constitutes an abusive response and what is an appropriate display of care. This difficulty arises in the main out of the dynamic prevalent in these patients' early histories of being brought up by abusive parents or caregivers, where this very distinction between what constitutes care and what is abusive, is absent. This confusion is re-enacted in the relationship between patient and professional who recreate between them the patient's familiar, if destructive, early object relationships. In addition, the patient's projected cruelty and hatred might also resonate with an independent objective hatred that arises out of the professional's own struggle to deal with somebone who so actively attacks any attempts to care for them (Winnicott, 1949). The net result can be an overwhelming desire to attack the patient in return. The intensity of these feelings, which can reach murderous proportions, induces such guilt in the professional that these feelings have to be actively defended.

I think that in my countertransference I know that I did feel guilt for what I had done by calling the police, which is not murderous but may be seen as sadistic by the patient. I also think that he was asking for help with his destructive and murderous feelings, and, rather than ignoring his plea, as the GP had done the day before, I thought that I had to do something that was inherently very unpleasant and objectionable but may, I hope, ultimately have saved lives.

At times, the criminal act is the expression of more severe psychopathology; it is secretive, completely encapsulated, and split from the rest of the patient's personality, which acts as a defence against a psychotic illness (Hopper, 1991). I think Mr C's criminal act—the possession of weapons—was a defence against a hidden psychosis.

Welldon's (2015) important contribution is that she acknowledges that forensic psychotherapy goes beyond the special relationship between patient and psychotherapist. It is a triangular situation: patient, psychotherapist, and society / bystander / culture. This observation was enormously helpful in thinking about what to do about Mr C and his gun, which, in my mind, was lying threateningly on my table.

Mr C presented as a nice but superficial man. However, behind the superficiality of these patients there is a very destructive and sadistic part that patients attempt to hide or cover up. In treatment this emerges, and it has to be recognised as a very real part of the person before any progress can be made. This quality of superficiality and transience is supported and explained in some measure by the original formulations of the as-if personality, characterised by inter-personal relationships that are plastic and artificial, and characterised by "mimicry" (Deutsch, 1942, p. 304) and by a lack of authenticity. The essential characteristic is that, outwardly, patients conduct their lives as if they possessed a complete and sensitive emotional capacity, but eventually the absence of real emotional responsiveness leads to the repeated dissolution of relationships. They neither fly to external reality to escape their frightening minds, nor do they withdraw to an inner world to avoid fears of the outside: instead, they remain terri-fied of internal and external reality. These patients therefore take ref-uge in a state of unreality, which characterises all their relationships.

Freud drew attention to a similar state of mind, which he described as the blindness of the seeing eye where one knows and does not know a thing at the same time. He used the noun "Verleugnung" (Freud, 1927a, p. 374), which was translated as "disavowal" (Freud, 1927b, p. 153), a non-psychotic form of denial, which is central to the perversions and, in particular, to the fetish. Britton (1998) described this phenomenon as the willing suspension of belief, which results in facts being known but not believed. And Steiner (1993, p. 129) used the phrase "turning a blind eye" to describe this defence, relating it to oedipal anxieties in particular. Perversion, as described by Steiner, is not only a sexual deviation but is a turning away from the truth. The patient knows, but also does not know what is right and truthful, but is also led astray or corrupted by an agency working against what is true and right, whereas reality is distorted and misrepresented.

Perhaps Mr C had developed a fetish of guns and had placed his gun (phallus) in the bag, which he brought to the consulting room for me to see, thus attempting to reassure himself that his body—and, in particular, his mind—were still functioning properly. However, Mr C might also have unconsciously wished to communicate that he was in a desperate situation and that he needed help. He had remained calm and superficial as I was experiencing the enormous projected anxiety that he could not bear.

Similarly, Welldon (2011) has described how a woman having a baby gives a unique reassurance to some women that their body container and their reproductive functioning are still intact. Also, having babies may be the only way for some to communicate and express their own emotional needs, which have not previously been properly addressed or recognised in themselves.

Clinical vignette 2

In the case of another patient, Mrs H, superficial social appropriateness was a masquerade that hid a highly disturbed personal relationship. I came to understand that Mrs H's obstacles to contact and to progress and development were related, and that they both arose from the deployment of a particular type of defensive organisation—namely, the narcissistic organisation—and from the triangular process of power dynamics. They are characterised by extremely unyielding defences, namely, projective identification, which functions to help the patient avoid anxiety by avoiding contact with other people and with reality.

Mrs H is a forty-three-year-old married woman with three children who has worked previously as a child minder but who has been unemployed for the last six years. Mrs H's parents had separated when she was very young, and she went into care at the age of nine months. She spent most of her childhood with foster parents, and she was sent to boarding school. Mrs H reported that she had attended a number of schools but had been excluded from all of these institutions for having been "stubborn". She talked of being sexually and physically abused by various members of her family and by her carers. She had only met her father twice, but she was still in contact with her mother, who suffered from mental illness. She was one of twins and had five siblings. Mrs H has been married for six years, but she had known her husband since the age of eighteen. Together, they have produced three children, aged twenty-four, twenty-two, and fourteen years.

Mrs H described frequent arguments in the family and had portrayed herself as "evil", describing her husband as the "solid rock" upon whom she depends. She had used cannabis for twenty years and had also abused alcohol, which often led to violent relationships. She informed me that she had started drinking heavily as a result of being raped for the second time. The first time had been at the age of fourteen, and the second at the age of thirty, when three men thus abused her. She knew one of them and believed the rape was an act of revenge for having become involved in a dispute. No one had been charged, and the three men who had raped her all lived in the neighbourhood. As a result, she felt unable to leave her home. She had resorted to drinking excessively and had started drinking again after one of the rapists had threatened her. She felt that she had become a bit of a recluse, staying at home all the time. Her husband had given up work to look after Mrs H.

To quote the patient in her questionnaire:

> "As you read what I've written you will probably build up an awful picture of me—which is true—because what I have written is true. However, don't be fooled by appearances. I present myself as quite a confident, happy-go-lucky person initially, it's the way I protect myself, just something I have been used to doing all my life."

Mrs H wanted to let me know that there was a very destructive part to her. Indeed, her most recent mental health unit admission had followed her threat to burn down the house with her children in it. She had also threatened to stab her husband.

Mrs H's husband telephoned the day before the first appointment to ask if I could admit his wife into a psychiatric ward. He explained to me that his wife had been drinking excessively for the last two days and had, in fact, been abusing alcohol over the last few weeks. There had been an incident in the house where she had smashed a bottle, and she said that she was going to cut herself with the glass. Her husband took the bottle away from her, but in the process cut himself and required stitches. I explained to him that it would be more beneficial if they could keep their appointment, and that I would see them together the following day. I think it would have been collusion on my part to accept the request for admission, and it would be more helpful to keep to the arrangement and see her the next day.

Mrs H and her husband arrived for their appointment, and Mrs H appeared drunk. She was able to tell me about the incident of the previous day, which involved her daughter, aged fourteen. Mrs H had picked up a knife in a threatening way, and her daughter had said, "Stab me, and then you will see what you have done." I explained to Mrs H that it required her daughter of fourteen to tell her to wake up and look at what she was doing. She was living in a fantasy world, wanting to be knocked out by alcohol or locked up in a ward, rather than awaken and look at what she was doing—namely, killing the vulnerable, dependent child part of her.

Some days later, Mrs H attended her second appointment with her husband. She explained to me that she had become very upset and drunk when she heard that her younger son was having difficulties in Spain and was beaten up by the police. Her son had been drinking excessively, causing chaos. She also said that her older son was prone to taking cocaine, and that her daughter was also drinking to excess. When Mrs H confronted her daughter in a very belligerent way about her excessive drinking, the daughter was able to say to her, "I'm letting you know what it feels like for a member of the family to be drinking." I think that Mrs H's daughter was able to help her mother to think about the abuse of the daughter and to show her mother the projection of her own vulnerability and dependence on alcohol and its destructive influence on the family and on herself.

As one of the consequences of projective identification, Mrs H relates to her daughter not as a separate person with her own characteristics but, rather, as if she is relating to herself. She may ignore aspects of her daughter that do not fit the projection, or she may control, force, and persuade her daughter to enact the role required of her. Therefore, projection leads to a narcissistic type of object relationship—that is, a part of the self, often the unwanted part, becomes split off and projected into an object where it is attributed to that object, and the very fact that it belongs to the self is denied.

The object relationship that results is then not one with a person truly seen as separate but, rather, with the self projected into another person and related to as if it were someone else. This is the position of the mythical Narcissus who fell in love with a strange youth he did not consciously connect to himself. The way I think of all personality disorder is to think of the patient's narcissism, which is usually most obstinately resistant to treatment. In narcissistic object relations, defences against any recognition of separateness between self and object play a dominant part. Awareness of separation would lead to feelings of dependence on an object and therefore to anxiety. Dependence implies love for, and recognition of, the value of the object, which leads to aggression, anxiety, and pain because of the inevitable frustration in relationships and their consequences.

The process of regaining parts of the self lost through projective identification involves facing the reality of what belongs to the object and what belongs to the self, and this is established most clearly through the experience of loss and through the process of mourning when those parts of the self are regained. This achievement may require much working through in therapy.

Conclusion

What I have tried to understand is Mrs H's statement in the questionnaire: "As you read what I've written you will probably build up an awful picture of me—which is true—because what I have written is true, I am evil." To be present to the personality disorder as he or she is becomes the *sine qua non* of successful treatment. These patients will arouse all sorts of feelings, including one's own sadism, in the form of condemnation and disbelief, as they deny, deceive, and evacuate feelings into us in order to escape the reality of their inner and outer worlds. Patients like Mrs H, while being terrified of giving expression to their true selves, are nevertheless keen to affirm their existence. Like an underground subversive moment in a colonised territory, they assert themselves through hidden acts of rebellion and sabotage, often taking the form of anal contrariness to a substantial extent.

These patients often complain of a profound sense of inner emptiness and ignorance of their true identity. It is as if their concealment of their most inner self has been so extensive that they themselves lose contact with it. One of the most substantial tasks of their therapy is the establishment of a secure and solid sense of self. In both these patients, Mr D and Mrs H, there is an attack on their origins and their history, and this creates a void, a lack of narrative, and an emptiness that, as in the case of Mr D, comes to be filled with psychotic debris (guns in this instance), or is, as in the case of Mrs H, expressed through sadomasochistic abuse. This is done in order to encapsulate the anxiety of death and murderous rage. With the emergent fear of death, murderous violence is triggered (Doctor, 2008b).

In these situations, any action or thought that could be considered as resonating with their underlying murderous feelings has to be actively repressed for fear that this will give away the true state of psychic affairs. This renders the treating team impotent, for fear that any potent intervention, such as calling the police, will be more about harming than about helping the patient. It is not uncommon in such scenarios to find that on forensic psychiatric wards the treating team, in desperation, increases the number of nursing staff observing the patient while at the same time making little impact on the actual problematic behaviour. It would seem that the team then becomes involved in the bystander effect, so prevalent in cases of abuse, thus unwittingly ending up abandoning the patient (Darnley, Doctor, Gordon, and Kirtchuk, 2011).

I think that Welldon's (1988, 2011) important contributions to psychoanalysis and forensic psychotherapy are, in particular, her introduction of the notion of the triangular situation with regard to forensic psychotherapy and maternal perversion, and her description of the narcissistic use of children to extend a woman's own maltreatment of her body and to repeat intergenerational patterns of abuse and cruelty. Instead of the collusion or disbelief and condemnation and the ultimate abandonment of patients (triangle of cultures) that would be aroused in terms of women's destructive behaviour, Welldon has challenged the assumption that a phallus is an essential prerequisite for perversion—an observation that shocked clinicians with her startling and unsettling discoveries about the potential for mothers to use their own bodies and those of their children in the service of perverse activity. In her formulation of forensic psychotherapy as a triangular situation, I was able to listen to these patients without condemning them or condoning their actions. Upon considering a triangular situation, I was able to contain my enormous anxieties about death and come to an understanding of the patients' huge struggles with their paranoid anxieties.

Freud (1917) believed that the primary task of psychoanalysis was to fill in the gaps, undo the distortions, and finally arrive at the true narrative of the patient's history. It is important for the patient to be able to arrive at a more complete and better knowledge and understanding of his or her history. Such knowledge can diminish the unconscious pressure for history to repeat itself or to submit to the repetition compulsion and to recreate aspects of the history in the present. In fact, Freud went further and stated that the aim of psychoanalysis is a history of the unconscious, or, rather of its origins, a history of discontinuities in which the moments of burial, concealment, and then resurgence are the most important of all. It is a history of repression in which the subterranean currents are described in as much detail as the manifest character traits.

To come back to my original question: do I know Estela Welldon? Having researched her work in relation to psychoanalysis, am I now any the wiser as to who Estela Welldon really is? I do know that she has been a loyal friend and colleague for the past twenty-five years, and I do know that she has helped me enormously in my work and my life. I am sure that there will be more to learn from her with more potential for growth, and that she will provide further insight into how a brain, a womb, and a will can indeed be both a lethal cocktail and a grand affair.

REFERENCES

Binder, Renée L., and McCoy, Susan M. (1983). A Study of Patients' Attitudes Towards Placement in Seclusion. *Hospital and Community Psychiatry, 34*, 1052–1054.

Britton, Ronald (1998). *Belief and Imagination: Explorations in Psychoanalysis*. London: Routledge / Taylor and Francis Group.

Darnley, Brian; Doctor, Ronald; Gordon, John, and Kirtchuk, Gabriel (2011). Psychotic Processes in Forensic Institutions. *Psychoanalytic Psychotherapy, 25*, 55–68.

Deutsch, Helene (1942). Some Forms of Emotional Disturbance and Their Relationship to Schizophrenia. *Psychoanalytic Quarterly, 11*, 301–321.

Doctor, Ronald (Ed.) (2008a). *Murder: A Psychotherapeutic Investigation*. London: Karnac Books.

Doctor, Ronald (2008b). The History of Murder. In Ronald Doctor (Ed.), *Murder: A Psychotherapeutic Investigation*, pp. 79–91. London: Karnac Books.

Freud, Sigmund (1917). Mourning and Melancholia. Joan Riviere and James Strachey (Transls.). In Sigmund Freud, *The Standard Edition of the Complete Psychological Works of Sigmund Freud: Volume XIV. (1914–1916). On the History of the Psycho-Analytic Movement. Papers on Metapsychology and Other Works*. James Strachey, Anna Freud, Alix Strachey, and Alan Tyson (Eds. and Transls.), pp. 243–258. London: Hogarth Press and the Institute of Psycho-Analysis, 1957.

Freud, Sigmund (1927a). Fetischismus. *Internationale Zeitschrift für Psychoanalyse, 13*, 373–378.

Freud, Sigmund (1927b). Fetishism. Joan Riviere and James Strachey (Transls.). In Sigmund Freud, *The Standard Edition of the Complete Psychological Works of Sigmund Freud: Volume XXI. (1927–1931). The Future of an Illusion. Civilization and its Discontents and Other Works*. James Strachey, Anna Freud, Alix Strachey, and Alan Tyson (Eds. and Transls.), pp. 152–157. London: Hogarth Press and the Institute of Psycho-Analysis, 1961.

Hopper, Earl (1991). Encapsulation as a Defence Against the Fear of Annihilation. *International Journal of Psycho-Analysis, 72*, 608–624.

Rosenfeld, Herbert (1971). A Clinical Approach to the Psychoanalytic Theory of the Life and Death Instincts: An Investigation into the Aggressive Aspects of Narcissism. *International Journal of Psycho-Analysis, 52*, 169–178.

Steiner, John (1993). *Psychic Retreats: Pathological Organizations in Psychotic, Neurotic and Borderline Patients*. London: Routledge.

Symington, Neville (1980). The Response Aroused by the Psychopath. *International Review of Psycho-Analysis, 7*, 291–298.

Welldon, Estela V. (1988). *Mother, Madonna, Whore: The Idealization and Denigration of Motherhood*. London: Free Association Books.

Welldon, Estela V. (2011). *Playing with Dynamite: A Personal Approach to the Psychoanalytic Understanding of Perversions, Violence, and Criminality*. London: Karnac Books.

Welldon, Estela V. (2015). Forensic Psychotherapy. *Psychoanalytic Psychotherapy, 29*, 211–227.

Winnicott, Donald W. (1949). Hate in the Counter-Transference. *International Journal of Psycho-Analysis, 30*, 69–74.

CHAPTER FIVE

Just a normal day: from prodrome to index offence and beyond

Gill McGauley

Introduction

In listening to how patients talk about their index offences, I have been struck by similarities in some of their narrative accounts. A day that culminated in a catastrophic act of interpersonal violence has been described as starting as just a "normal day". Immediately after committing their attack on another person, some individuals report feeling "better" and of experiencing an incredible sense of relief and calmness. What are these patients feeling better from, especially if the day began as just another normal day in the mind of the patient? Within the treatment setting of forensic psychotherapy it emerges that, just as with physical diseases, the offence often has a prodromal period: a time when the disease process has begun, but it is not yet clinically manifest.

In this chapter I discuss how the index offence is conceptualised in forensic psychotherapy and consider the significance of its prodrome with reference to a particular group of forensic patients—namely, those with a diagnosis of personality disorder. I also discuss how one particular mental process, that of mentalization and its failure, relates to the index offence in these patients.

Conceptualising the index offence:
a forensic psychotherapy perspective

Central to predicting future risk of offending is knowledge about previous offences. In other words, what you have done is what you are most likely to do again, as one's criminal record information makes a significant contribution to the prediction of future convictions (Buchanan and Leese, 2006). Consequently, forensic mental health professionals share a common interest in the index offence. Whether we work as forensic psychiatrists, psychotherapists, psychologists, arts therapists, or in other forensic disciplines, we ask our patients to communicate with us about their index offence and then use these narratives to inform our predictions about their future symptoms, behaviour, and risk, and to guide their management.

Depending on our training, discipline, or theoretical framework, elements such as aggression, impulsivity, premeditation, remorse, empathy, a sense of agency, and internal conflict are often highlighted in these accounts, and assumptions are made about their implications for that person's future progress. The forensic psychotherapist pays attention to all these elements but also poses the overarching question: "What can be understood about the internal world of the patient from consideration of the criminal act?" In other words, a key assumption, central to forensic psychotherapy, is that the offence has a meaning to the individual and can be understood in the context of the offender's internal world, mental state, developmental history, and relationships (Cordess and Williams, 1996; Blumenthal, 2010). The offence is considered a symptom that needs to be understood.

Estela Welldon's clinical observations and thinking have been at the forefront of developing this humane approach to conceptualising the offence (e.g., Welldon, 1994): an approach that offers the possibility of insight and therefore hope to the patient that, "he or she may then be able to interpose thought between the urge and the action. In this way a new link is created in order to overcome acting out" (Welldon, 1993, p. 497).

Long before forensic psychotherapy became established as a discipline, psychoanalysts and psychodynamic psychotherapists had applied psychoanalytic concepts to shed light on the meaning of the offence, in order to understand the internal forces that are at play and to offer treatment (Bowlby, 1944a, 1994b; Bromberg, 1951; Zilboorg, 1956). Early psychoanalytic approaches postulated that some criminal acting out was an attempt to assuage an unconscious sense of guilt that preceded the crime and generated a need for punishment (Freud, 1916; Glover, 1960). Welldon has explored several different ways in which the dynamic meaning of the offence can be conceptualised, many of which position the offence as a symptom. At times the offence can be a symptomatic marker of deeper underlying psycho-pathology, which acts as a defence against psychosis or manifests as a chronic depression or as a sexual perversion (Welldon, 2011). Pfäfflin (1992) has described how the patient may need to offend, and, just as with many symptoms, offending cannot be relinquished until it is properly understood.

Indeed, understanding is central, as "A thing which has not been understood inevitably reappears; like an unlaid ghost, it cannot rest until the mystery has been solved and the spell broken" (Freud, 1909, p. 122). It is a characteristic of forensic work that what is forgotten appears, not in ghostly form, but in action (Blumenthal, 2010). The stakes are high for the individual and for society, as a key assumption in forensic psychotherapy is that so many assaults on others are expressions in action of mental states, and if these mental states are not remembered or understood, they might well be enacted in the future (Sohn, 1995). This mental state may comprise unconscious representations of relating to or being related to, often in an abusive and traumatic way, by attachment figures. If the victim or other situational factors in the offence constellation trigger these unconscious representations, then there is a risk of enactment. In this way, the index offence can be understood as a repetition compulsion of previous patterns of interpersonal relationships and traumatic experiences (Yakeley, 2010). The victim fits the need of the attacker's unconscious phantasy, which has, at that moment, been successfully projected into the victim (Sohn, 1999).

What happens when we ask about the index offence?

Interestingly, although as forensic mental health professionals we attach considerable importance to eliciting our patients' descriptions of their index offence, there is no systematic approach to examining and formulating the patient's offence narrative (McGauley, Ferris, Marin-Avellan, and Fonagy, 2013). When we ask our patients, we can often feel confused or despondent, because the narrative around the index offence has either gone missing from the mind of the patient or is recalled in a distorted way.

Consider the following verbatim interview fragment in which an offender talks about his index offence:

> "I don't know. I don't think about it. I don't worry about it. I only think, the only time I think I think about the offence really is when you lot talk to me about it. Apart from that it doesn't really cross my mind. I'm not too worried about the trial."

Or let us examine this vignette:

> A young man who had inflicted a severe and unprovoked violent attack on a stranger told the psychiatrist that a few minutes after his assault he returned to his semi-conscious victim to administer first aid and get help.

Of course it is possible that the first patient in the verbatim fragment may simply be consciously avoiding and resisting thinking about his offence and that the second patient's version of events may be discrepant because he is attempting to "fake good" and to deceive his psychiatrist and himself (Gudjonsson and Moore, 2001). However, it is also possible that these patients cannot access representations of their index offence or that they can do so only in a distorted way. This may be especially pronounced for patients who have a diagnosis of personality disorder. Clinicians postulate that a limitation of the capacity for introspection and perspective-taking is a core symptom of personality disorder and is considered by some clinicians as a diagnostic criterion for the condition (Westen and Shedler, 1999). For example, if a patient with personality disorder sees her friend turn away when she approaches, then it is clear to the patient that her friend is ignoring and excluding her. No other possible explanation can be entertained in her mind. This version of external reality becomes an unalterable fact in her internal world, and thus her affective response to the pain of loss and humiliation she feels drives her response.

For other patients, narratives around their index offence show a marked increase in incoherence (Adshead, 2015), as evidenced by particularly long pauses or gaps in speech, odd associations, or lapses in monitoring discourse when offenders speak about the victims of their murderous attacks as if they are still alive. In attachment terms, these are all seen as markers of unresolved trauma (George, Kaplan, and Main, 1985; Hesse, 2008).

When approached systematically, analysis of index offence narratives using the Index Offence Representational Scales (IORS) predicted the unfolding of both violent and prosocial behaviour in a cohort of violent personality-disordered patients detained in a high secure hospital (McGauley et al., 2013). These scales were designed explicitly to look at the patients' capacity to mentalize their offence. Patients were asked to think about their own mind in relation to their index offence and then the minds of others, including their victim, as well as the impact of their actions on others. The degree to which patients held internal representations of interpersonal violence and malevolence, as measured by the IORS, predicted subsequent violent behaviour. A more empathic victim representation on the IORS predicted better engagement with treatment. In other words, patients who were more able to mentalize the minds of others were more willing to engage in treatment. The IORS might be a promising clinical tool that could help clinicians to maximise the rehabilitation potential of those with sound mentalizing capacities and to identify those patients who need greater therapeutic input.

The prodrome

Whether our patients' lack of accurate awareness of their index offence is accounted for by a failure of introspection or as resulting from a plethora of defensive systems in their minds (i.e., projection, denial, repression, or a combination of these), we are faced with the problem that if neither the patient nor the clinician can access an authentic description of the offence, then the patient's therapeutic progress is impeded in a key task. Indeed, a task that Minne (2003) has described as core to forensic psychotherapy is that of enabling an awareness of the mind and its functions to become available to the owner of that mind—that is, the patient. In particular, patients must have an awareness of what they have done and of the impact of this on their minds and on the minds of others.

If the index offence is conceptualised as a symptom, then of what is it actually a symptom? Has this symptom arisen *de novo*, or has it gradually emerged? For some forensic patients it appears that, just as with physical diseases, the offence has a prodromal period. During the prodrome the individual experiences mounting distress arising from an increase in the level of disturbance in his or her internal world. However, the ubiquitous problem for forensic patients is that they locate the cause of this disturbance externally. Consequently, they embark on ever-increasing attempts at self-cure but, tragically, use maladaptive strategies, such as substance misuse or risk-taking behaviour. Thought about in this way, the index offence occurs as a final doomed attempt at self-treatment to ward off the increasing pressure and distress they feel—like taking an aspirin but, in fact, a toxic aspirin.

Over the years I have met a small number of patients whose offence narratives illustrate this prodromal period. As a group, they share some demographic, forensic, and developmental similarities. The following clinical material is presented to illustrate this prodromal period of the index offence, which was the culminating event in what was far from a normal day and occurred as a result of these individuals failing, maladaptively, to cure themselves of being in a highly disturbed state of mind. The material has been anonymised and drawn from several patients in order to protect confidentiality.

Background and commonalities

In general, these individuals were somewhat atypical of forensic patients in that their early lives were not characterised by high levels of trauma or abuse, although some had experienced parental separations. Their relationship with their parents or remaining parent could best be described as estranged. However, these patients had a loving relationship with at least one other relative—one good object—and with this person they experienced a real sense of also being cared about and loved.

Although capable of learning, these individuals had attacked their capacity to learn while at school. In early adolescence they started to misuse alcohol and drugs, and they quickly developed a liking and need for substances. At school and college they learned little but spent most of their time smoking in the canteen or drinking on the playing field rather than turning up for exams. They replaced learning by risk-taking and rule-breaking behaviour and by taking and dealing drugs, by shoplifting, driving recklessly, and so forth. They appeared to be young men and women who were unable to look after themselves and who had not internalised a caring figure but believed, at some level, that this was normal life. At a surface level, there was an appearance of normality that belied their level of disturbance. These individuals were not destitute. They had homes and families. They had been in relationships and were employed, albeit intermittently in some cases.

Forensically, they had no previous convictions for interpersonal violence; indeed, their previous transgressions had been for driving offences or shoplifting, and they had never been imprisoned. Equally, they had not been admitted to generic mental health units, let alone forensic services. Some had been seen by outpatient mental health services such as child and adolescent and addiction services, but the treatment they had received was either fleeting or had had little effect. In other words, standard risk prediction tools and previous offences would not have picked up their risk; and no one could have seen their future violent offences. At the time of their index offence they were relatively young, which, together with the severely interpersonally violent offences committed by this group made them a high risk with a pressing need for treatment, although how and when they would receive treatment after their convictions and sentencing was a lottery. Some people in this group ended up eventually in secure hospitals only to be transferred to prison; others were to be transferred from prison to secure hospitals.

When in hospital or prison, professionals found it difficult to agree on a diagnosis for individuals in this group, and frequently their diagnoses would change. At various times psychiatrists thought that these patients might have a psychotic illness; certainly they did have periods of paranoid ideation, but on balance they were thought to have a diagnosis of personality disorder—in the main antisocial personality disorder, borderline personality disorder, and psychopathic disorder, or they were described as having psychopathic traits. Many were comorbid, having a diagnosis of substance misuse and, in some cases, substance dependency. However, although these individuals had an intimate relationship with drugs, it is salient that, at the time of the index offence, they were not intoxicated. If they had taken drugs, they had taken only a small amount.

The following details relate to two patients and are given to illustrate the prodrome to the index offence, which began two to three months earlier.

The prodromal escalation

A couple of months prior to his offence, Mr A had broken up with his girlfriend. She had stuck by him, and there was a real sense that they both cared about each other, but his girlfriend had applied for a new job that would advance her career but would mean moving to a different part of the country. Mr A said that their break-up was amicable, and they had stayed in contact in the succeeding months, including the night before his index offence, when she had just sent off her job application. During the months after their break-up, Mr A became increasingly restless and began to experience feeling an incoherent sense of disturbance. To counteract this, he offered himself a variety of self-cures. He would recklessly drive around at speed, smoke excessively, and found himself taking more drugs.

He reported that the day of the index offence started off as a "normal day". He had spent it at a friend's house, and they had watched a movie. He didn't like the movie much, so he drove to a car park, where he took some drugs. He still felt restless and unsettled. Early evening he went back to his house, where he lived with his family; he watched a soft "porno movie" on television, but this did not help him feel better. He then left the house and drove around, in all likelihood driving at speed. Later, he returned home and went to talk to a member of his family to whom he had always felt close, but this did not help either. Later that night he attacked an attachment figure—a person he loved and felt loved by. He then left the house again. He described feeling "better". He wandered around and slept rough. He then woke up thinking that he had had a troublesome dream in which he had attacked someone. The trouble for him was that his waking state was, in fact, his dream, and that this dream was *real*.

Another patient, Ms B, described the day of her offence as a normal day as well. She was a young woman who held down a job and lived with her parents. However, for several years Ms B had a serious and prolonged addiction to alcohol and then drugs. As a child and adolescent her life had been blighted by what sounded like an anxiety disorder that was especially pronounced in social situations. She often felt that she "didn't fit in" and was being picked on and excluded. She had few friends until she had her first drink, when she realised that alcohol, and then drugs, liberated her.

In the weeks leading up to her index offence, Ms B began to feel a sense of increasing pressure. She spent more and more time playing violent video games. She found herself driving more recklessly. She felt that the Highway Code did not apply to her. Indeed, her car was extremely important to her as, in Ms B's world, non-human objects (e.g., cars, animals) did not hurt her and were more reliable than people. Her car was her pride and joy, and she felt safe inside it. She depended on her car both for getting her drugs and as a place where she could take her drugs in peace. Leading up to her index offence, her car had been vandalised by local youths.

The day before her index offence she had felt more unsettled and she decided to go on a trip to the country with her boyfriend. She tried to cure herself by shoplifting, which annoyed her boyfriend, and they had argued. She insisted that they came home, and they then returned to their respective homes, having resolved their argument. Ms B described the morning of her offence as a "normal morning". However, she felt increasingly unsettled and angry. She tried playing some video games, but this did not help. She then decided to "sort out" someone who "had ripped her off" when supplying her with drugs. She went around to this person's house, but he was not in. She then drove to a secluded spot where she would normally go to take drugs, but she did not have any to take. She then attacked a passing stranger. After her attack she described feeling incredibly calm, a feeling that was better than being on heroin.

These vignettes illustrate the offence prodrome during which the individual is engaged in more and more frantic attempts to ward off their increasing sense of internal disturbance that is breaking through. The self-cure attempts they have relied on all fail, and the index offence becomes a desperate final attempt to stabilise the internal world; this happens quite precisely when these self-cure mechanisms fail. The result is catastrophic violence, after which these individuals felt enormously better—one in a dream state, and the other in a state that was felt to be better than being on heroin.

The emergence of the prodrome inside and in treatment

This group of patients has a remarkable relationship with normality that is weird, to say the least. They normalise the abnormal while struggling to tolerate any ordinary feelings of anxiety. Their problem might be described as the fact that they really believe in their self-provided cure. Within the treatment framework of forensic psychotherapy, this difficulty becomes enacted and allows the psychotherapist to link the patient's current state of mind with that in the prodromal period leading up to the offence.

In the early stages of treatment these patients have to cure themselves of any ordinary feeling of anxiety that a person might feel being locked up in a secure institution. Their future reality of how long their incarceration will last cannot be thought about. If the future does intrude into their minds, it is often in a dream-like way in which they imagine the type of car they will be driving or the job they will effortlessly move into when they are released. This psychological distancing means that, as a group, they often appear to settle into the prison or the secure unit quite quickly. They can adopt the role of an auxiliary staff member. Characteristically, these individuals attach considerable importance to their rooms or cells, which are unusual in being both orderly and very cosy or containing an excess of possessions. The markers of temporal reality that the judicial system introduces, such as parole hearings or mental health tribunal hearings, cannot really be thought about, and the patient appears to be going through the motions. Ordinary feelings cannot be borne. Moments of sadness, anxiety, and loss have to be cured quickly—for example, by having a cigarette or by other strategies.

Let us consider another vignette. Mr C starts his session by saying that he was angry yesterday, or perhaps it might have been the day before. He had left his washing in the laundry room and planned to go back later to put it in the dryer, only to find that someone else had loaded it and started the wash cycle at too high a temperature, so a couple of hundred pounds worth of his clothing had been shrunk. "I'm none too pleased", he said, laughing. "I felt like kicking the tumble dryer, but I didn't", he added quickly. "I didn't think it was malicious. I will have to go on a spending spree to buy some new clothes, which is a bit of a pain."

At this moment the patient had shrugged off, with a laugh, his angry and upset reaction to the loss of his clothes. He attempts to reassure his therapist, but in fact he is really reassuring himself that he did not kick the tumble dryer, that he could control his aggressive impulses, and that he has found his solution: he will go on a spending spree, so at that moment he has successfully cured himself. His therapist is then able to try to interest the patient in this phenomenon whereby the minute he has some insight or makes an observation about himself, he has to cure himself. These small events, wherein patients bring a feeling or awareness of their discomfort and their attempts at curing themselves, allow the forensic psychotherapist to link current states of mind to those preceding the offence. In this way, the patient can learn about who they were and what they could not tolerate in the prodrome of their offence.

Secure settings, such as hospitals or prisons, have controlling structures and procedures and regimes that remind these individuals of where they are, and why they are detained. Gradually, through treatment, some awareness and experience of normal feelings such as anxiety about who they were and what they have done can slowly be allowed into consciousness.

Some time further on in treatment, the same patient, "Mr C", arrived at the door and said that he could not come to his session as his room was being searched. And although he had the option not to be there, he needed to be present. He was palpably anxious, but he came and sat down to tell his therapist about this. The search was routine, but this young man was known to have a great deal of stuff in his room. The staff said that he was always pushing the boundaries about what he was allowed, not in terms of prohibited items, but in amount. It was not an ordinary room. In fact, the room was a manifestation of how he denies the reality of being an ordinary patient. He could not bear the fact that the search team would move his possessions around, so he simply had to be in his room and not in therapy.

In the following session, he reported how he felt anxious when a member of staff had moved some valued possessions. He then associated to his anxiety about starting to attend a group programme for violent offenders, and how scared he was at the expectation that he would be asked to talk about his index offence in front of others—in other words, the specificity scared him: "It's your turn, this is what is expected here." His therapist talked to him about how the unforeseen room search had thrown his mind into disarray. He wanted to look after his room, but a part of him wanted to be looked after by having a session. He became symptomatic, and the controlling system in his mind (which nullifies any awareness that he is a patient) had been overridden. The highly controlled event of his room search, during which he had had to stand by and could not control others, had exposed him to being a patient, producing anxiety that was not cured away.

When self-cure fails: the moment of the offence

At the moment of the index offence, the individual's mental infrastructure and the defences that contain cognitions, affects, and impulses have failed. In Peter Fonagy's developmental model of violence (Fonagy, 2003b; Levinson and Fonagy, 2004), the capacity to mentalize is thought to be a crucial inhibitory factor for some interpersonal violence. The moment of the index offence signifies a catastrophic failure of mentalization. One might define mentalization as the process by which we interpret the actions of ourselves and others in terms of underlying intentional states such as personal desires, needs, feelings, beliefs, and reasons (Bateman and Fonagy, 2006). In other words, mentalization is the capacity to think about one's own mental state and the mental states of others (Allen, Fonagy, and Bateman, 2008). It arises within the context of secure early attachment relationships and allows the individual to process experience and to represent and distinguish between mental states of the self and of the other (Fonagy, 2003a; Steele, 2003). It shapes our understanding of others and underpins our interpersonal relationships.

Deficits in mentalization are also seen as core to the psychopathology underlying some personality disorders, particularly borderline personality disorder and antisocial personality disorder. These deficits may be global, so that the individual is generally poor at mentalizing, context-specific, or both. A context-specific situation would involve talking to a particular person such as one's mother, for example, claiming, "She does my head in. I can't think once she starts on me." Indeed, mentalization is prone to fail in states of high emotional arousal, often in the context of attachment relationships.

An individual with a limited capacity to mentalize is unable to tolerate emotional states such as anxiety, anger, shame, and impulses such as the wish to harm others. At these moments the person may become highly aroused and swamped by negative affects. Offenders with personality disorders frequently misread the minds and actions of others, "seeing" rejection, abandonment, slights, insults, and markers of disrespect all too easily. The feelings of shame and humiliation generated are unbearable. Poor mentalization means that these feelings and thoughts cannot be processed and contained by normal mental representational mechanisms; they are experienced concretely as feelings or sensations that need to be expelled through violence (Yakeley and McGauley, 2015). Just as these individuals cannot think about their own mind and emotional states due to a failure of mentalization, so they cannot accurately perceive the minds of their soon-to-be victims. If the person cannot differentiate between his or her own internal experiences and external reality and is thus unable to see the other as having a different mental state from his or her own, then the barriers to violence are reduced and the perpetrator becomes unable to empathise with the suffering that he or she is about to inflict on the other. Indeed, the aggressor may so misidentify the mental state of the other as to be convinced that his victim is as angry and aroused as he is and may, consequently, feel under threat and attack (McGauley, Yakeley, Williams, and Bateman, 2011; Yakeley, 2013).

When conceptualised through the lens of failed mentalization, the index offence can be understood as a final catastrophic attempt at self-cure—the person's last-ditch attempt to stabilise an unbearable internal state. In treatment, it is sometimes impossible to identify with any precision the final trigger and the non-mentalizing way in which the individual experienced and interpreted this. The forensic psychotherapeutic approach can, however, help the patient to gain insight into how he or she is experiencing or mis-experiencing reality. According to the model (Bateman and Fonagy, 1996), the breakdown or suppression of mentalization leads to the emergence of pre-mentalistic modes of experiencing the world, which organise the individual's subjective experience and act as powerful disorganisers of the person's interpersonal relationships.

In the teleological mode of pre-mentalistic thinking, the only way in which the person can work out the intentions of the other is through their physical behaviour and observable actions, as the individual cannot fathom the mind of the other. For example, patients may work out their therapists' thoughts and feelings about them primarily from their actions or absence of them: "If you really cared for me, you would have held my hand; you would have let me phone you; you would have given me a birthday card", and so forth. Self-harm, suicide attempts, and some acts of aggression, often directed towards an attachment figure, are conceptualised as teleological driven attempts to alter the behaviour of the other, as this may be the only way in which the patient can experience being cared about. If the other "steps out of line" or fails to respond in the way the patient expects, this can stimulate intense affect dysregulation and feelings of abandonment. Consequently, patients will evacuate anger in the process.

Vignette

Ms D was aware that "little things" would wind her up. These little things included times when she saw others in attachment relationships—in "happy families". Seeing happy families in the supermarket made her feel abandoned and angry. If her partner was a little late home for dinner, she would text him and then go to the pub to find him. Ms D saw her behaviour as looking after her boyfriend, although he would often chastise her and send her away when she turned up. However, she became aware that she should not text her partner quite so much or check his phone, but she also realised that she felt lonely and empty without him.

Ms D set considerable store by how she looked, and she would spend hours getting ready before going out. When shopping with her boyfriend, she would walk on the inside, so that he would not catch sight of the smart clothes in the shop window. She feared that because she thought that he was handsome, everyone else would fancy him too, especially if he wore fashionable clothing. In a teleological mode of experiencing the world, when her partner did not return her text quickly enough, Ms C knew that he did not love her and must, therefore, be seeing someone else. Later, in their local pub, she saw him cast a glance at the barmaid's cleavage. His action triggered feelings of humiliation and of intense anger. Despite the young man's attempts to say that this did not mean anything, as he loved *her*, she lashed out and attacked him nonetheless. Later, she set a fire in his flat and burned his clothes, so that "if he can't look nice with me, no one else will see him looking nice".

As Bateman and Fonagy (2006) have stressed, in the teleological mode it is not the action itself that carries the most meaning but, rather, the deviation from expected actions that are contingent upon the person's wishes—in other words, not the look in itself, but the fact that, in her mind, his look is a deviation from her view that he should have eyes only for her. Ms D's violence can be conceptualised as an attempt to stabilise the massive affect dysregulation and feelings of abandonment that she then experienced.

Conclusion

Despite the centrality of the index offence and its prodrome, its potential to inform us and help us to answer questions that our patients' disorders prevent them from asking has been underused. Conceptualising the offence and its prodrome as doomed attempts at self-cure can allow us to understand the nature of the disturbance that our patients are trying to treat in themselves.

If the offence signifies a complete breakdown in mentalization (i.e., the mind's capacity to reflect on itself and its functioning), then some of our patients are simply not able to think about their offence to the extent that we may expect. If the patients' non-mentalizing statements about their offence are taken at face value, and if the underlying mechanisms for these deficits are overlooked by professionals, then phrases such as "is unable to think about the index offence" or "shows no remorse" appear in their case reports. These statements, if presented without detailed clinical backup, make it all too easy for health and justice systems to consign these patients to a state of limbo.

For the past thirty years and more, Estela Welldon has developed and championed forensic psychotherapy. Among her many contributions, her energy has allowed her to create forums such as the International Association for Forensic Psychotherapy, an organisation that has, for more than twenty-five years, provided professionals with an opportunity meet and to think about our work and our patients. Forensic psychotherapy offers patients the possibility of seeing their attempts at self-cure as they become accessible to them through treatment and through understanding of how these are precipitated by normal human feelings, such as anxiety and loss, which have to be extruded violently from the mind. Through this process true normality may be reinstated and tolerated, and the prodrome correctly identified as heralding the onset of the abnormal.

REFERENCES

Adshead, Gwen (2015). Safety in Numbers: Group Therapy-Based Index Offence Work in Secure Psychiatric Care. *Psychoanalytic Psychotherapy*, 29, 295–310.

Allen, Jon G.; Fonagy, Peter, and Bateman, Anthony W. (2008). *Mentalizing in Clinical Practice*. Arlington, Virginia: American Psychiatric Publishing.

Bateman, Anthony W., and Fonagy, Peter (2006). *Mentalization-Based Treatment for Borderline Personality Disorder: A Practical Guide*. Oxford: Oxford University Press.

Blumenthal, Stephen (2010). A Psychodynamic Approach to Working with Offenders: An Alternative to Moral Orthopaedics. In Annie Bartlett and Gill McGauley (Eds.), *Forensic Mental Health: Concepts, Systems and Practice*, pp. 151–162. Oxford: Oxford University Press.

Bowlby, John (1944a). Forty-Four Juvenile Thieves: Their Characters and Home-Life. *International Journal of Psycho-Analysis*, 25, 19–53.

Bowlby, John (1944b). Forty-Four Juvenile Thieves: Their Characters and Home-Life (II). *International Journal of Psycho-Analysis*, 25, 107–128.

Bromberg, Walter (1951). A Psychological Study of Murder. *International Journal of Psycho-Analysis*, 32, 117–127.

Buchanan, Alec, and Leese, Morven (2006). Quantifying the Contributions of Three Types of Information to the Prediction of Criminal Conviction Using Received Operated Characteristics. *British Journal of Psychiatry*, 188, 472–478.

Cordess, Christopher, and Williams, Arthur Hyatt (1996). The Criminal Act and Acting Out. In Christopher Cordess and Murray Cox (Eds.), *Forensic Psychotherapy: Crime, Psychodynamics and the Offender Patient. Volume I. Mainly Theory*, pp. 13–21. London: Jessica Kingsley Publishers.

Fonagy, Peter (2003a). The Interpersonal Interpretive Mechanisms: The Confluence of Genetics and Attachment Theory in Development. In Viviane Green (Ed.), *Emotional Development in Psychoanalysis, Attachment and Neuroscience: Creating Connections*, pp. 107–126. London: Karnac Books.

Fonagy, Peter (2003b). Towards a Developmental Understanding of Violence. *British Journal of Psychiatry, 183*, 190–192.

Freud, Sigmund (1909). Analysis of a Phobia in a Five-Year-Old Boy. Alix Strachey and James Strachey (Transls.). In Sigmund Freud, *The Standard Edition of the Complete Psychological Works of Sigmund Freud: Volume X. (1909). Two Case Histories ("Little Hans" and the "Rat Man")*. James Strachey, Anna Freud, Alix Strachey, and Alan Tyson (Eds. and Transls.), pp. 5–147. London: Hogarth Press and the Institute of Psycho-Analysis, 1955.

Freud, Sigmund (1916). Einige Charaktertypen aus der psychoanalytischen Arbeit. *Imago, 4*, 317–336.

George, Carol; Kaplan, Nancy, and Main, Mary (1985). *Adult Attachment Interview Protocol*. Unpublished Manual. Berkeley, California: Department of Psychology, University of California at Berkeley.

Glover, Edward (1960). *Selected Papers on Psycho-Analysis: Volume II. The Roots of Crime*. London: Imago Publishing Company.

Gudjonsson, Gisli H., and Moore, Estelle (2001). Self-Deception and Other-Deception Among Admissions to a Maximum Security Hospital and a Medium Secure Unit. *Psychology, Crime and Law, 7*, 25–31.

Hesse, Eric (2008). The Adult Attachment Interview: Protocol, Method of Analysis and Empirical Studies. In Jude Cassidy and Philip R. Shaver (Eds.), *Handbook of Attachment: Theory, Research, and Clinical Applications. Second Edition*, pp. 552–598. New York: Guilford Press / Guilford Publications.

Levinson, Alice, and Fonagy, Peter (2004). Offending and Attachment: The Relationship Between Interpersonal Awareness and Offending in a Prison Population with Psychiatric Disorder. *Canadian Journal of Psychoanalysis, 12*, 225–251.

McGauley, Gill; Ferris, Scott; Marin-Avellan, Luisa E., and Fonagy, Peter (2013). The Index Offence Representation Scales (IORS); A Predictive

Clinical Tool in the Management of Dangerous, Violent Personality-Disordered Patients? *Criminal Behaviour and Mental Health, 23,* 274–289.

McGauley, Gill; Yakeley, Jessica; Williams, Andrew, and Bateman, Anthony (2011). Attachment, Mentalization and Antisocial Personality Disorder: The Possible Contribution of Mentalization-Based Treatment. *European Journal of Psychotherapy and Counselling, 13,* 371–393.

Minne, Carine (2003). Psychoanalytic Aspects to the Risk Containment of Dangerous Patients Treated in High-Security Hospital. In Ronald Doctor and Sarah Nettleon (Eds.), *Dangerous Patients: A Psychodynamic Approach to Risk Assessment and Management,* pp. 61–78. London: H. Karnac (Books).

Pfäfflin, Friedemann (1992). What is in a Symptom?: A Conservative Approach in the Therapy of Sex Offenders. *Journal of Offender Rehabilitation, 18,* 5–17.

Sohn, Leslie (1995). Unprovoked Assaults: Making Sense of Apparently Random Violence. *International Journal of Psycho-Analysis, 76,* 565–575.

Sohn, Leslie (1999). Psychosis and Violence. In Paul Williams (Ed.), *Psychosis (Madness),* pp. 13–26. London: Institute of Psycho-Analysis.

Steele, Miriam (2003). Attachment, Actual Experience and Mental Representation. In Viviane Green (Ed.), *Emotional Development in Psychoanalysis, Attachment Theory and Neuroscience: Creating Connections,* pp. 86–106. Hove, East Sussex: Brunner-Routledge / Taylor and Francis Group.

Welldon, Estela V. (1993). Forensic Psychotherapy and Group Analysis. *Group Analysis, 26,* 487–502.

Welldon, Estela V. (1994). Forensic Psychotherapy. In Petruska Clarkson and Michael Pokorny (Eds.), *The Handbook of Psychotherapy,* pp. 470–493. London: Routledge.

Welldon, Estela V. (2011). *Playing with Dynamite: A Personal Approach to the Psychoanalytic Understanding of Perversions, Violence, and Criminality.* London: Karnac Books.

Westen, Drew, and Shedler, Jonathan (1999). Revising and Assessing Axis II, Part I: Developing a Clinically and Empirically Valid Assessment Method. *American Journal of Psychiatry, 156,* 258–272.

Yakeley, Jessica (2010). *Working with Violence: A Contemporary Psychoanalytic Approach.* Houndmills, Basingstoke, Hampshire: Palgrave Macmillan.

Yakeley, Jessica (2013). Mentalization-Based Group Treatment for Antisocial Personality Disorder. In John Woods and Andrew Williams

(Eds.), *Forensic Group Psychotherapy: The Portman Clinic Approach*, pp. 151–182. London: Karnac Books.

Yakeley, Jessica, and McGauley, Gill (2015). Treating the Untreatable? *New Associations*, Number *18*, pp. 8–9, 11.

Zilboorg, Gregory (1955). *The Psychology of the Criminal Act and Punishment*. London: Hogarth Press and the Institute of Psycho-Analysis.

Zilboorg, Gregory (1956). The Contribution of Psycho-Analysis to Forensic Psychiatry. *International Journal of Psycho-Analysis*, 37, 318–324.

CHAPTER SIX

The female body as torturer: malignant bonding and its manifestations in perverse partnerships

Anna Motz

Introduction

In her seminal work on female perversion, Welldon (1988) introduced the notion of maternal perversion and described the narcissistic use of children to extend a woman's own maltreatment
of her body, as well as the intergenerational pattern of abuse and
cruelty. She challenged the assumption that a phallus was an essential
prerequisite of perversion and shocked clinicians with her startling
and unsettling discoveries about the potential for mothers to use
their own bodies and those of their children in the service of perverse
activity. Welldon (1988, 2011) offered an extensive description of the
characteristics of female perversion in both her early work and her
later work. As she wrote,

> I believe that a fitting term for my female patients' specific predica-
> ments in relation to their bodies and babies could be "the body as
> the torturer". This would signal the compulsive urges these women
> experience towards their bodies unconsciously making them func-
> tion as the effective torture tool in becoming victimizers to them-
> selves and to their babies. [Welldon, 2011, p. 38]

In this chapter I discuss the lasting impact of Welldon's work and
its relevance to contemporary understanding of violence within inti-

mate relationships, as explored in my own work. Central to this are Welldon's concepts of female perversion and of malignant bonding. The trouble starts with this "malignant" pattern of attachment in early life, which is then repeatedly re-enacted in adolescence and adulthood. The importance of Welldon's insights into traumatic bonding cannot be overestimated, as we can view adult perverse partnerships with this in mind. Welldon's radical and courageous work has offered us a theoretical framework within which we can understand entrenched dynamics that so often characterise violent and sado-masochistic relationships.

I also discuss how Welldon's findings in relation to malignant bonding and female perversion illuminate work with violent and perverse adult couples, both in terms of understanding the dynamics that tie them to one another and to shed light on how certain couples will turn on vulnerable others, including their own children. I refer to Welldon's dramatic and shocking findings in relation to female violence and perversion and the impact of maternal abuse on young minds. I then discuss the disturbed dynamics inherent in perverse adult relationships and domestic violence.

Female violence and intimate relationships: child abuse within a toxic partnership

Using Welldon's insights about perverse women, it is possible to understand female violence in the context of destructive, perverse, and violent partnerships that I refer to as toxic couples (Motz, 2014). I have written extensively about manifestations of toxic couplings elsewhere and have traced the roots of disturbance in both partners to early attachment disorders, often created at the hands of perverse, cruel, or neglectful mothers. As adults, these individuals seek to recreate these relationships, often unconsciously, and find themselves directing their own sexual and aggressive impulses towards one another or towards their own children. This violence can be understood as a reflection of unconscious forces, often in direct contradiction to what is consciously wanted. Although such violence can be dramatically expressed against the woman's partner, her children, or herself, it is often hidden from view, enacted secretly in the private domain of the home, and in unseen places on the bodies or on victims who cannot or will not speak about it. The hidden, clandestine nature is mirrored in the societal response, which is often to deny the fact of such violence altogether, whether in relation to maternal abuse or female aggression within intimate relationships.

Malignant bonding

Welldon (2012, p. 162) describes situations in which children are deliberately killed by a couple as examples of "malignant bonding". A couple unites in their desire for cruel re-enactments, sometimes for sexual excitement, in which children are used as objects to be tortured and violated for the pleasure of adults. She explains how in some cases the children's suffering is recorded for the purpose of homemade pornography. The sadomasochism involved in such sexual torture can be seen as a form of rehearsal for the actual killing; the murder has happened time and time again in fantasy before it is enacted in real life. The children are kept alive in order to be used in sadistic, horrific ways; they are wholly depersonalised and viewed only as a means of gratifying the couple's perverse desires. Welldon (2011) also offers an enlightening definition of perversion in general, describing the following characteristics that are to be found in perverse relationships:

> ⊳ use of sexualisation as a form of manic defence;
> ⊳ fusion of sexualisation and aggression;
> ⊳ defence against anxieties aroused by intimacy: claustro-agoraphobic fears of aggression; anxieties about adequacy;
> ⊳ bestowal of a sense of control and triumph;
> ⊳ sexualised behaviour creating a scenario in which the dreaded situation is often reversed.

For some who engage in these acts of cruelty and degradation, their role as abuser affords an escape from earlier experiences as victim. In this way they can master the trauma (Stoller, 1975) and project unbearable feelings of shame, pain, and humiliation onto others, thus ridding themselves of unacceptable feelings. Stoller has referred to this type of perversion as the erotic form of hatred, in that aggression and cruelty are sexualised. They are enacting the role of their own abuser in order to free themselves (temporarily) from their sense of helplessness and, in this way, to reveal the psychic defence of identification with the aggressor (Freud, 1936). Others who engage in sexual torture and murder of children may not have experienced such abuse themselves, but either become inured to its brutality or become aroused by the sense of power and control it affords. Within such perverse couplings, children are used only as objects and not seen as subjective creatures whose vulnerability needs to be protected and whose autonomy is respected.

In some cases, couples actively kill together, acting as accomplices in murder. The peculiar ingredients that create such a toxic couple can be understood as an unconscious fit between two highly disturbed personalities who, through their partnership, feel validated and enabled to commit horrific crimes. They act as moral arbiter for one another, creating a unique code of ethics that condones violence and murder. When their psychopathologies meet in particular ways, these partners enhance and exacerbate one another's callous disregard for the welfare of others; outside this partnership, neither individual would commit a crime of violence. The perverse world created by this couple is one where children are viewed simply as objects to be used and abused for their gratification. They are treated as poison containers into which the adults pour their own unwanted feelings and hatred (deMause, 1990).

In these toxic couples, the partners have shared violent fantasies that they act on together, excited by the participation of the other. I have encountered this kind of perversion and cruelty in cases where sexual sadism is in operation and the mother has been used as a decoy to elicit the trust of others, allowing the couple to have access to their children. At times, their own children are also abused in this way for the gratification of the adults. Such cases include the highly publicised one of Rosemary and Fred West, in which both parents actively participated in sexually perverse and sadistic acts.

In other partnerships, one partner is apparently the weaker and more easily led, having disavowed her own aggression into her violent partner and then passively seeming to go along with the violence, rather than participating in it in an active way. This is a different dynamic from the "folie à deux" of suspending empathy, compassion, and concern for vulnerable children entrusted to one's care in favour of inflicting brutality—the kind of malignant bonding referred to by Welldon (2012). Nonetheless, the consequences of long-term neglect can also be fatal, and the degree of suffering intense and prolonged. Welldon (2012) uses the concept of malignant bonding to describe how perverse attachment will impact upon the child's mind and how this can lead to a repeated pattern of perverse relationships in later life. She has alerted us to these awful situations that can occur in the most sacred bonding—namely, that between the mother and the child.

Welldon has shown us the power of female violence within abusive relationships, and it is essential for clinicians to remain aware of this when we encounter couples whose attraction is based on malignant forces, often unconscious, but always compelling. These perverse couplings can be highly addictive, and the bond between the pair appears to be based on a shared need to engage in abusive practices (Welldon, 2002). At times, the perverse activity of the couple extends to their own children or those of others, viewed largely as objects to be used for their own gratification. This was graphically illustrated in the following tragic case.

Victoria Climbié

The highly publicised case of Victoria Climbié, who was first systematically tortured and then killed in 2000 at the age of eight years, at the hands of her great-aunt Marie-Therese Kouao and her aunt's boyfriend, Carl John Manning, is a dramatic illustration of these dynamics. Ironically, the great-aunt promised to offer a better life to Victoria, who had come from the Ivory Coast. But in the end, the great-aunt and the boyfriend were convicted for her murder.

The inquiry resulted in a four-hundred-page report produced by Lord Laming (2003). The inquiry report became the catalyst for reviews of child protection systems and for new legislation and policies, consolidated in the most recent Children Act 2004. This revision of the Children Act 1989 highlights the urgent need for inter-agency working in relation to suspected child abuse. The document *Working Together to Safeguard Children: A Guide to Inter-Agency Working to Safeguard and Promote the Welfare of Children* (HM Government, 2006), updated from 1999, underlines the urgent need for inter-agency communication and responsibility to prevent the recurrence of such tragedies, and to tackle the serious problems of neglect and lack of coordination on the part of child protection agencies.

One of the many failings that Lord Laming identified in the case of Victoria Climbié was the lack of communication among professionals, including a member of the medical staff who suspected abuse (though was overruled by his senior, who attributed Victoria's strange marks to scabies) and the social workers involved in the case. Laming lamented the fact that no one had seemed to know or listen to the child herself. I suggest that an additional factor that made it hard for those who came into contact with Kouao to think clearly was that she presented herself as Victoria's mother. Her maternal relationship to Victoria made it almost impossible for professionals to imagine that she would perpetrate sadistic abuse on this defenceless little girl. This tragic case is a clear illustration of society's inability to recognise the range, complexity, and secrecy of female violence and cruelty and demonstrates its typical expression in the domestic arena.

The presence of an apparently strong maternal figure and the conceptual difficulty and emotional pain of attributing acts of systematic cruelty to her were evident in this case. Victoria was not followed up on several occasions, despite injuries that included scalding to her face; nor was Kouao recognised as a sadistic abuser. Nonetheless, various people expressed concern in their notes about bruises on the child and about her apparent fearfulness in Kouao's presence, to the point that on one occasion Victoria wet herself while "standing to attention" (Laming, 2003, p. 40) while, apparently, being told off by her great-aunt. Despite obvious warning signs of abuse, firm conclusions could not be drawn. The truth was too much to bear. It seems that this couple wanted to keep Victoria with them, as she had become an object to be tortured for their gratification. She was completely deprived of her humanity:

> Given that her hands were kept bound with masking tape, she was forced to eat by pushing her face towards the food, like a dog. As well as being forced to spend much of her time in inhuman conditions, Victoria was also beaten on a regular basis by both Kouao and Manning. According to Manning, Kouao used to strike Victoria on a daily basis, sometimes using a variety of weapons. These included a shoe, a hammer, a coat hanger and a wooden cooking spoon. [Laming, 2003, p. 35]

The report of the inquiry informs its readers that, in the last few weeks of her life, Victoria was kept "living and sleeping in a bath in an unheated bathroom, bound hand and foot inside a binbag, lying in her own urine and faeces" (Laming, 2003, p. 1). Here, Lloyd deMause's notion of children as poison containers for their parents' murderous, toxic feelings is graphically and horrifically embodied. As in so many cases of severe child abuse, the child's fear response of incontinence, either urinary or faecal, can further enrage parents or carers, who then mete out even harsher punishment, which in turn exacerbates the situation further. In this case the violence escalated to an almost unimaginable degree in that Victoria was kept inside a bin bag, tied up in an attempt to contain and confine her emotional and bodily outpourings.

The report describes the horror of the abuse, only revealed in full after the child's death:

> At the end, Victoria's lungs, heart and kidneys all failed. Dr Nathaniel Carey, a Home Office pathologist with many years' experience, carried out the post-mortem examination. What stood out from Dr Carey's evidence was the extent of Victoria's injuries and the deliberate way they were inflicted on her. He said: "All non-accidental injuries to children are awful and difficult for everybody to deal with, but in terms of the nature and extent of the injury, and the almost systematic nature of the inflicted injury, I certainly regard this as the worst I have ever dealt with, and it is just about the worst I have ever heard of". [Laming, 2003, p. 2]

The report also stressed that,

> At the post-mortem examination, Dr Carey recorded evidence of no fewer than 128 separate injuries to Victoria's body, saying, "There really is not anywhere that is spared—there is scarring all over the body". [Laming, 2003, p. 2]

Victoria herself may also have been stupefied and too frightened to expose the danger she faced, much as the professionals who suspected abuse could also have felt too frightened to uncover it, as Cooper and Lousada (2005) have suggested. The parallels between the deceived, confused, and frightened workers and the terrified child operate on many levels.

It seems both remarkable and unsurprising that, upon hearing of Victoria's death, Kouao is reported to have said, "This is terrible; I have lost my child" (quoted in Laming, 2003, p. 37), demonstrating in cold blood the sense in which Victoria had become hers—an object to be used and abused—and revealing Kouao's own internal denial of the extreme danger in which she had repeatedly placed her. One can hypothesise that the great-aunt had not intended to secure a child for the purpose of torture, and it may well be that the entire situation escalated out of all control, particularly with the introduction of Manning and the advice given by two different pastors that Victoria was possessed by spirits. Manning's diary entry describes how he was going to go home in order to "release satan [sic] from her bag" (quoted in Laming, 2003, p. 34), conveying the almost psychotic quality of the belief that this distressed and traumatised child was, in fact, considered demonic.

In reading the chronology of events detailed in the inquiry report, it becomes apparent that the abuse intensified after Manning became involved with Kouao, and Victoria appears to have been increasingly tormented for having intruded upon the relationship between the adults. On one occasion documented in the report, Kouao arrived at their home with Victoria and begged her previous child minders—the Camerons—to take her permanently, because of the problems that she caused to her and Manning. It may be that this, also, at some level, was an unconscious attempt to save the child, as well as herself, from an increasingly intolerable situation. Unfortunately, the child minders were not able to take the child into their care, despite their concerns for her, and so, tragically, yet another opportunity to rescue Victoria was lost.

The repeated failure of medical and social services staff to identify the risk to Victoria and to remove her from those who tortured her was all too evident. She is a haunting reminder of the horror of child abuse and the collective responsibility of us all to ensure that children are protected from harm, insofar as we are able to see it and believe what we see. This task is not as straightforward as it might seem.

Rustin (2005) describes how such emotionally painful, frightening situations act as attacks on thinking, and rendering professional workers and others unable to grasp the obvious, despite their awareness that something is quite wrong. Rustin examines the issue of not seeing what is unbearable or, rather, seeing and not seeing, in her exploration of the events and failures of key professionals to protect Victoria. This is all too often the case with female violence, as Welldon has shown us.

The photographic image of Victoria's smiling face as she was when she first arrived in the United Kingdom was frequently reproduced in the newspapers and on the television after her death, in conjunction with reports of her death and her scarred and emaciated body. Her ordinary childish hopefulness and vulnerability were painfully apparent in this portrait. As Lord Laming describes in the inquiry report, Victoria Climbié—and, also, the hope that she represented—was murdered: "In the end she died a slow, lonely death, abandoned, unheard and unnoticed" (Laming, 2003, p. 2). Victoria Climbié's death prompts us to examine the difficulties that mental health, medical, and childcare professionals have in overcoming their own stereotypes, prejudices, and fears related to the cruelty that women, as well as men, are capable of inflicting on those most vulnerable in our society.

Working in child protection

In my twenty-five years of work as a forensic psychotherapist, consultant clinical and forensic psychologist, and independent psychoanalytic psychotherapist, I have often encountered situations in which women were violent and perverse within these destructive partnerships that I have come to refer to as "toxic couples". Like all the professionals involved in the Climbié case, I, too, have found it hard to look unblinklingly at evidence that appears before my eyes, as the impact can be so brutal. This is perhaps most apparent when opening a bundle of court documents prior to preparing a report and finding unsolicited photographs of beaten, burned, and starving children, demonstrating the reality of their parents' and caregivers' neglect and cruelty.

It is at times difficult to bear this visual evidence of injury and equally difficult to hear about and process accounts of the sexual use and abuse of children at the hands of their parents. It is when faced with this emotional overload that we need to turn to a robust theoretical framework to enable us to understand how these parents have come to take these actions or how they can turn away from helpless young children as they are brutalised or left without food, clothing, shelter, or protection from danger, including fire, toxic substances, and weapons. Being able to create and retain such an understanding will, in turn, allow us to identify treatment pathways and to find a compassionate stance, unblinkered by identifications with the children or hatred for the adult perpetrators. This is the stance that Welldon has offered us, with her clear exposition of forensic psychotherapy as the field within which we can encounter both perpetrator and victim in one. Through hearing from these perpetrator parents about the history of their own mothering, we can begin to make sense of their re-enactments, both with each other and with their children.

Toxic couples

Although we often think of domestic violence as perpetrated by one person, usually a male perpetrator, against a victim, often female, I suggest that within a toxic relationship it is the interaction of the two individuals that creates this destructive force, even when one partner is the principal enactor of the violence. Within some such relationships the woman herself is the primary aggressor, using her partner as an object onto which to project her own feelings of disgust, humiliation, and unworthiness. He, in turn, becomes the poison container, filled with shame and a sense of degradation (deMause, 1990). Sometimes women unconsciously locate their own aggressive impulses into their partners, and this frees them temporarily from awareness of their own violent wishes towards others. It is even possible to view as a form of self-harm the attraction of some women to violent partners who abuse them, in that their partners enact their own savage impulses towards themselves.

The development of perversions, including the sadistic use of violence and threats, can be a means of securing a false sense of confidence in one's capacity to manage the threats posed by intimate relationships. The need to control the other is a central feature of per-version and offers the promise that the object will not pose a threat to the psychic integrity of the individual through abandonment or engulfment (Glasser, 1979). Inflicting pain was far safer than facing the risk of receiving it and returning to a place of humiliation and fear.

Viewing domestic violence as simply an expression of the male wish for power and control is both reductive and inaccurate. Some feminist analyses risk this when it is accepted unquestioningly, as Dutton and Nicholls (2005, p. 680) have argued in their review of the literature: "A case is made for a paradigm having developed among family violence activists and researchers that precludes the notion of female violence, trivializes injuries to males and maintains a mono-lithic view of a complex social problem."

The following clinical illustration offers an account of how addic-tive these abusive relationships can be for some women who expect maltreatment, and for whom the intensity and excitement of abuse is a familiar situation to which they return again and again.

Russian roulette:
"Stacey", a woman addicted to violent relationships

"Stacey" was a thirty-three-year-old woman whose elder six children had been removed from her and had been taken into care, and who had recently given birth to a son, "Abraham". I met Stacey at two very different points in her life: first, when she had identified that her violent partners had destroyed her chances of parenting her children and developing her own sense of herself, and had vowed to put her son, "Felix", first; and, second, some five years later, marked by her return to a state of violent abuse, unplanned pregnancies, substance dependence, and neglect of her children.

Stacey had confided in me, and in her older children, about her hope that she could lead a different life, one free from the reign of terror she and her children had endured. Despite a short-lived period of freedom from this state, Stacey had returned to a brutal relationship with a man who had a long history of violence, including a Schedule 1 Offence—an offence against a child—for which he had been convicted. This had been a brutal assault on his own son, who was living with his ex-partner at the time. It was difficult for me to process the shock of her return to her state of self-neglect and her reversion to a violent relationship.

Felix, the baby for whom she had fought so hard when we first met, was now a traumatised little boy, aged six years. He had witnessed scenes of horror and had often been neglected by his mother during these times of crisis and when she was preoccupied with her own wishes and needs. Stacey sometimes forgot about his presence during fights; at other times she had left him in the care of her partner when she went out to the local pub where she worked part-time. She was dependent on alcohol and said she used it to help her manage the stress of daily life. On one occasion when she had left Felix with her violent partner, this man had threatened Felix with a beating with a dog lead and had teased him by locking him in the cupboard for several moments, saying that he would not let him out until he was better behaved.

Felix frequently wet the bed and was socially very anxious, described by his school as "fearful" and as a "loner", despite having been a settled and sociable baby and toddler. He and his mother had been alone together for the first sixteen months of his life, when she had tried to live without the involvement of a partner and had not abused alcohol. Felix was constantly worried about his mother's safety and always wanted to be with her, clearly feeling anxious and afraid whenever he was separated from her. She herself was prone to angry outbursts and freely told me that she would "give as good as I get". It soon became clear that, while she was often badly battered in these incidents, she would retaliate physically, describing it as "helpful to release the stress". Sometimes she would feel so angry with her partner and so suspicious of him, that she would shout at her son and threaten to hurt him. At other times she had picked him up and held him close to her, rather like a human shield. This seemed to be an attempt to stop the physical attacks on her. Stacey felt guilty about this, but she felt that it was the only way of getting the battering to stop. From early in Felix's life, he was literally caught in the crossfire.

Stacey had not undertaken the counselling I had recommended after I had first met her as being essential to enable her to process her previous experiences and to help to provide her with the ego support she required in order to be able to mother her new baby Abraham and to care for herself, as if the most compelling option was to revert to a familiar, if destructive, state of virtual imprisonment within a volatile and dominating relationship. Importantly, she would be violent too, not simply a victim of physical intimidation and brutality but in some ways a willing partner, as she admitted, feeling that she "got a buzz" from the drama. The state of captivity that she had in some ways chosen was one in which she reverted to a way of being and relating that felt enlivening and real rather than difficult and false. The life she was expected to lead, on the other hand, was one where she would engage in counselling, stay in a mother-and-baby unit to learn parenting skills, and then learn how to function as a single parent.

Stacey described herself as "learning-disabled". In a sense, her description was apt in that she did have profound difficulties in learning, but the problem was not a cognitive one per se but, rather, a kind of paralysis in her emotional and imaginative functioning where she could not give up the habitual, destructive pattern of her intimate sexual relationships. She could not necessarily put her thoughts and feelings into words or give vivid accounts of what had happened in her early life, but her behaviour and compulsive attraction to particular types of relationships indicated a sense of relentless, compulsive repetition, as described by Sigmund Freud (1914, p. 150): "We may say that the patient does not remember anything of what he has forgotten and repressed but acts it out. He reproduces it not as a memory but as an action; he repeats it, without, of course, knowing that he is repeating it."

Stacey's own experiences in childhood and adolescence had left her with an impoverished sense of her own inner resources and with a tremendous need to be in a relationship with a man, even one who treated her violently. During our interview she said that her central problem was that, "Mum and Dad aren't here", and so she felt quite lonely at times, and often felt emotionally overwhelmed. It was difficult in this interview, as in my previous assessment, when I got a full history from her, she had described her parents as positive features in her life currently; she said she felt wholly supported by them and spoke of them as being there for her. However, she explained that, while growing up, she had been the "black sheep" who was often farmed out to other relatives and left to get into trouble at school and in the village where she had grown up.

At times of crisis she would go to her parents' house and was pleased that her older children were now in their care. She felt that during hard times she could not focus on the needs of her children, but she assured me that she could learn to manage without being in a relationship with a man (although she acknowledged that this had not been possible for her in the past). She was open about her fear of being alone and her attraction to men whom she saw as strong and protective but who turned out to be violent and abusive. She described a sense of safety within these relationships and a "buzz" that came from the intense emotions she experienced when with her partners and how the whole world seemed to stop and stand still, leaving her all alone with her man. It would feel, she told me, like a dream, like the kind of fairy tale she had loved in childhood. But then the fairy tale would turn nightmarish, her "Prince Charming" would turn into an ogre, and she would go from being the beautiful princess to being the wicked witch, filled with ugly fury and despair.

At times, Stacey also felt overwhelmed by an unmanageable anger, and she knew how bad-tempered she could be with the children, indicating something of her own difficulty in feeling that her strong emotions could be understood and contained. Her history revealed that she had always found interactions with others difficult and had trouble managing her impulses or acting on the advice of others. She identified strongly with her second-youngest child, Felix, seeing him as shy and overly sensitive—much as she had been.

In addition to her psychological difficulty in managing feelings, she was convinced that she could not learn, though formal assessment in my earlier report demonstrated that this did not reach the level of learning disability but fell within the low average range of intelligence. It seemed to have the aspect of a traumatic shutdown of the sort described poignantly by Sinason (1986) in her seminal paper on mental handicap as a secondary consequence of trauma. What could not be expressed or articulated was destined to be acted out and repeated.

Discussion of the case

Stacey seemed to have struggled to learn from experience. She had unmet needs from her early life, as well as a poor capacity to regulate her emotions or delay gratification, and an impulsive aspect to her personality, all of which led her into unsuitable, often abusive relationships. She became somewhat addicted to the excitement and drama that these relationships appear to offer, and she has continued to enter into such relationships without regard for her own safety or that of her children. Once she had entered into such a relationship, she became increasingly less able to see its abusive aspects, as she became desensitised to this. Her view of an independent life, without the apparent excitement of this relationship, was that it was not worth pursuing, and she overlooked those aspects of herself that could eventually offer her the peace of mind and the emotional stability that her children desperately required.

She reported being lonely at night and wanting to contact "Luke", her ex-partner, but she knew this was wrong and that she needed to "be there for the children" and not allow a violent man into their lives. Her apparent awareness of this was, however, strongly at odds with the behaviour she displayed and her real difficulty in staying away from men who had been violent towards her. Stacey's impulsivity was evident during clinical presentations, where she seemed to rush through things and felt anxious to get away; this tendency also seemed present in her decision-making in relation to men. She viewed all partners as potential rescuers who could offer her sanctuary (cf. Craven, 2008).

Working with female perpetrators

When women have enacted violence against children in the context of toxic couples, or when they have been complicit in their abuse, forensic psychotherapists may find themselves in some conflict in relation to their patients. How can the actual violence or tacit acceptance of violence be addressed without a therapist becoming either an accuser or a victim of the perpetrator–patient? The woman may wish to disavow her aggression onto her partner and present herself as another victim—a passive recipient of cruelty. The question of her complicity and any excitement and pleasure that she enjoyed as she turned a blind eye to her child's suffering may feel too much for her to bear. Indeed, the therapist, too, may feel drawn into a split view of the couple, in which all aggression is located in the male partner and the woman is viewed sympathetically, as without agency or voice. This is the model of the traditional paradigm of the patriarchy, and Welldon has wisely drawn our attention to its inaccuracy and simplicity. Attractive as this version of femininity may seem at first glance, it is in fact a caricature that both strips women of moral agency and leaves children at risk of maternal violence.

The issue of avoiding a re-enactment of toxic coupling in the treatment is central. It is all too easy to be pulled into either a punitive or a protective relationship with the patient in therapy who can evoke strong feelings of anger or a powerful wish to rescue. This can be understood as an unconscious projection by the patient of wishes either to be punished in accordance with her own guilt feelings, particularly awakened if she has left or "abandoned" her violent partner, or to be rescued and transformed. The latter is the unconscious wish to be reborn and to receive the protective and loving care of which she had been deprived in early life, and that appeared to be met through the violent relationship that has now broken down.

These conflicting and primitive wishes can be projected directly, and they often resonate with the therapist's own unconscious needs and fantasies. The power of projective identification with these aspects of the patient and her history is intense and offers a rich source of communicative data. The therapist may, at times, become identified with the controlling, punishing partner, who scolds the other for her perceived weakness and reluctance to leave destructive situations. The clinician may feel frustrated and angry, using interpretations as a form of verbal violence. At other moments, the therapist may be in danger of enacting the role of the fantasised saviour who offers endless succour and care. Acting into these wishes is ultimately unhelpful and will not allow the patient to find her own sense of containment and self-efficacy and to express and own the rage that she feels. Rosenfeld (1987) has described the powerful force of such countertransference responses as resulting from the therapist's wish to provide a corrective emotional experience. This must be resisted if the patient is truly to be helped to articulate and process what has previously been unbearable.

The link between homicidal and suicidal urges (Williams, 1998; Motz, 2008) is particularly strong in individuals who have fragile conceptions of self as well as narcissistic ways of relating. Their children are viewed as objects, reflecting aspects of themselves, including hated parts that they disavow. In the case of murderous couples, there is an unconscious contract between the two that enables acts of profound cruelty, deception, and betrayal. This creates the conditions for child abuse and murder, as well as the killing of other third parties who pose a threat to the couple or whose torture and death provide a form of excitement.

This powerful link between homicidal and suicidal feelings is essential for the therapist to bear in mind because, as the woman gains insight into what she has been complicit with, this brings with it the wish to punish oneself. This insight can also be seen when a female accomplice to a killing reclaims her projected aggression and then acknowledges her own murderousness. Once she is no longer able to locate these unacceptable and frightening states of mind in her partner, her psychic equilibrium is jeopardised, and suicidal feelings may then surface with catastrophic intensity. Just as a mother who has actually killed her own child, albeit in a psychotic state, may become seriously destabilised as the psychosis recedes and she recovers insight, so, too, can a woman who has configured herself as a passive, tragic victim in the murder become deeply depressed as she recognises her own active part in the crime. She has also killed off hope, as represented by her child, and this can lead to profound helplessness and depression.

This process of insight is evident when child abusers who have acted as part of a couple or a gang begin to recognise the extent of their own individual culpability and cruelty. Through psychotherapy, they can begin to acknowledge their own responsibility and finally give a thought to the damage they have inflicted, neither of which will have occurred during their immersion in the abusive activity and the partnership that fed on such sadism. Shengold (1989, 1999) has described the impact of child abuse as a form of soul murder, and he has provided rich clinical and mythical material to illustrate this, revealing how the psychological damage in victims becomes manifest in later life. While not inflicting actual physical death, the legacy of severe emotional, psychological, and sexual abuse is so intense and pernicious that the psyche can be considered in some ways to be dead. These kinds of violations are dramatic examples of Shengold's (1979, p. 533) concept of "soul murder", where the very heart of an individual has been so damaged through abuse and neglect that all capacity for life and for joy becomes killed off. Only the most sensitive and intensive psychotherapeutic interventions can address this damage.

Impact on children
of witnessing domestic violence

Unable to process certain traumatic experiences, such as the sight of their parents fighting physically, children often protect themselves against the full psychological impact of this by repressing the sights and sounds through a kind of psychological and physical withdrawal or by finding some internal retreat or sanctuary. There may be a strong wish to protect the injured parent, whose helplessness is unbearable, and one such psychic mechanism is to identify with them, taking on this role themselves or even trying to fight the aggressor and protect their hurt parent. Another equally compelling solution is to adopt the defence of what Anna Freud (1936) referred to as an identification with the aggressor, and to justify the abuse against the injured party and also to find satisfaction and excitement in taking on the powerful role of the violent parent. The gender of the children may contribute to their choice of the parent with whom to identify. As a result male children growing up witnessing the violence of their fathers may feel unconsciously that this way of relating to others represents potency and creates respect; for girls, on the other hand, identification with their mothers may lead to unconscious equations of intimacy with emotional and physical tyranny, and to an increased likelihood that they will find themselves entrenched in abusive relationships in their adulthood. If children of either sex have been neglected and physically abused as part of their upbringing, they will be at increased risk of victimisation in their own intimate partnerships, indicative of a repetition compulsion—that is, a desire to repeat certain familiar patterns of relationships, with the unconscious aim of finding a different solution to a constant psychological problem through its reworking.

In her discussion of the traumatic bonds that develop in these situations, Welldon has reminded us that the roots of this damage unfold within the most intimate and private relationship, that between mother and child, and as such, it will often be a secret—a perverse pleasure—that may not even be expressed in language. A central question for therapists working with adults locked into sadomasochistic relationships, often with brutal and deeply perverse aspects, is how to access the roots of these couplings when the shame of maternal abuse may prevent disclosure and even prohibit the emergence of painful memory. The familiar states of humiliation, powerlessness, and pain are overlaid with sexual pleasure and confused with affection and desire. Infantile sexuality has been hijacked and perverted for the pleasure of the mother, and the abused child has been moulded into the mother's sexual partner—a relationship that they seek to recreate in adulthood. Women who have been so used by their mothers often seek to recreate these relationships with their own children or identify with the aggressor in the sadistic roles they enact in relation to their own adult partners. All of this demonstrates the terrible truth of Welldon's insights.

REFERENCES

Cooper, Andrew, and Lousada, Julian (2005). *Borderline Welfare: Feeling and Fear of Feeling in Modern Welfare*. London: H. Karnac (Books).

Craven, Pat (2008). *Living with the Dominator: A Book About the Freedom Programme*. Knighton, Powys, Radnorshire: Freedom Publishing.

deMause, Lloyd (1990). The History of Child Assault. *Journal of Psychohistory, 18*, 1–29.

Dutton, Donald G., and Nicholls, Tonia L. (2005). The Gender Paradigm in Domestic Violence Research and Theory: Part 1—The Conflict of Theory and Data. *Aggression and Violent Behavior, 10*, 680–714.

Freud, Anna (1936). *Das Ich und die Abwehrmechanismen*. Vienna: Internationaler Psychoanalystischer Verlag.

Freud, Sigmund (1914). Remembering, Repeating and Working-Through: (Further Recommendations on the Technique of Psycho-Analysis. II). Joan Riviere and James Strachey (Transls.). In Sigmund Freud, *The Standard Edition of the Complete Psychological Works of Sigmund Freud: Volume XII. (1911–1913). The Case of Schreber. Papers on Technique and Other Works*. James Strachey, Anna Freud, Alix Strachey, and Alan Tyson (Eds. and Transls.), pp. 147–156. London: Hogarth Press and the Institute of Psycho-Analysis, 1958.

Glasser, Mervin (1979). Some Aspects of the Role of Aggression in the Perversions. In Ismond Rosen (Ed.), *Sexual Deviation: Second Edition*, pp. 278–305. Oxford: Oxford University Press.

HM Government (2006). *Working Together to Safeguard Children: A Guide to Inter-Agency Working to Safeguard and Promote the Welfare of Children*. London: T.S.O. / The Stationery Office.

Laming, Lord [William Herbert Laming] (2003). *The Victoria Climbié Inquiry: Report of an Inquiry*. Norwich, Norfolk: T.S.O. / The Stationery Office.

Motz, Anna (2008). *The Psychology of Female Violence, Second Edition: Crimes Against the Body*. London: Routledge / Taylor and Francis Group, and Hove, East Sussex: Routledge / Taylor and Francis Group.

Motz, Anna (2014). *Toxic Couples: The Psychology of Domestic Violence*. London: Routledge / Taylor and Francis Group, and Hove, East Sussex: Routledge / Taylor and Francis Group.

Rosenfeld, Herbert (1987). *Impasse and Interpretation: Therapeutic and Anti-Therapeutic Factors in the Psychoanalytic Treatment of Psychotic, Borderline, and Neurotic Patients*. London: Tavistock Publications.

Rustin, Margaret (2005). Conceptual Analysis of Critical Moments in Victoria Climbié's Life. *Child and Family Social Work, 10*, 11–19.

Shengold, Leonard L. (1979). Child Abuse and Deprivation: Soul Murder. *Journal of the American Psychoanalytic Association, 27*, 533–559.

Shengold, Leonard (1989). *Soul Murder: The Effects of Childhood Abuse and Deprivation*. New Haven, Connecticut: Yale University Press.

Shengold, Leonard (1999). *Soul Murder Revisited: Thoughts About Therapy, Hate, Love, and Memory*. New Haven, Connecticut: Yale University Press.

Sinason, Valerie (1986). Secondary Handicap and its Relationship to Trauma. *Psychoanalytic Psychotherapy, 2*, 131–154.

Stoller, Robert J. (1975). *Perversion: The Erotic Form of Hatred*. New York: Pantheon Books.

Welldon, Estela V. (1988). *Mother, Madonna, Whore: The Idealization and Denigration of Motherhood*. London: Free Association Books.

Welldon, Estela V. (2002). *Sadomasochism*. Duxford, Cambridge: Icon Books.

Welldon, Estela V. (2011). *Playing with Dynamite: A Personal Approach to the Psychoanalytic Understanding of Perversions, Violence, and Criminality*. London: Karnac Books.

Welldon, Estela (2012). Couples Who Kill: The Malignant Bonding. In John Adlam, Anne Aiyegbusi, Pam Kleinot, Anna Motz, and Christopher Scanlon (Eds.), *The Therapeutic Milieu Under Fire: Security and Insecurity in Forensic Mental Health*, pp. 162–172. London: Jessica Kingsley Publishers.

Williams, Arthur H. (1998). *Cruelty, Violence, and Murder: Understanding the Criminal Mind*. Paul Williams (Ed.). Northvale, New Jersey: Jason Aronson.

Forensic psychotherapy in prisons

CHAPTER SEVEN

Working with gangs and within gang culture: a pilot for changing the game

Carine Minne and Paul Kassman

Introduction

The work described in this chapter is a new project based on the piloting of "Changing the Game", a group therapeutic intervention conceived by Paul Kassman and developed together with Carine Minne, designed specifically for gang members. Despite coming from different professional backgrounds, we came together to trial the project, which adapts therapeutic approaches to address the particular needs and challenges presented by gang members. In this chapter, after a brief overview of the history of gangs, we describe setting up the pilot gangs' group therapy and discuss what emerged from it and what we learned from gang members, as well as think about plans for the future. Dr Estela Welldon would appreciate this unusual combination of a clinician and a sociologist getting "married" and deciding to try to make a therapeutic "baby" in this closed world of gangs, using group therapy principles.

Over the last decade, gangs have increasingly emerged as a more visible issue in English inner cities. Since 2005, gang culture has been attributed as a key factor behind the wave of "postcode" wars and serious gun and knife crimes, which have afflicted inner cities and spilled over into the criminal justice system. In 2008, twenty-eight teenagers were killed in London, with this figure rising to thirty teenage fatalities the following year. Many will remember the regularity of news reports about those teenage victims, as well as the questions that politicians, sociologists, and journalists began to ask about how best to understand this emerging gang culture and how to explain the resulting levels of associated violence. Gangs have remained embedded in the public and political consciousness as well as within the inner-city communities. After the 2011 riots affecting major towns across England that followed the police shooting of Mark Duggan, the political response was to blame gangs and gang culture for public disorder. Indeed, Iain Duncan Smith, at that time Secretary of State for Work and Pensions and head of the Centre for Social Justice, said that, "Gangs are firstly the products of social breakdown, and they are also the drivers of perpetual social breakdown in these communities" (quoted in Wintour and Lewis, 2011). One question raised by this response is whether there is a sense of moral panic, leading to gangs being a useful label for society's ails?

How effectively does society actually understand the concept of gangs and gang culture, which exists in our disenfranchised communities, drawing in a minority of disaffected and often BME (Black and Minority Ethnic) young people into a lifestyle of violence and criminality? In 2008, the Home Office Tackling Gangs Action Programme (TGAP) monitored a data sample of 356 gang members, some 86% of whom were classified as Black Caribbean in ethnicity. More recent Metropolitan Police Trident data identified 90% of gang members as coming from BME communities. And by 2012, the Trident Gang Crime Command was launched, when approximately 3,500 gang members, many from black or ethnic minorities (BME), were identified in London alone by the Metropolitan Police. This was a police unit set up originally to address the problems of gun crime within the black community—in other words, to deal with "black on black" violence—a subject to which we will return. Despite this, there is no mention of ethnicity or diversity in the Home Office report on gang and youth violence—*Ending Gang and Youth Violence: Annual Report 2013. Presented to Parliament by the Secretary of State for the Home Department by Command of Her Majesty* (HM Government, 2013)—as if it was not a relevant factor or, if it was, it could be considered racist to mention this.

How do clinicians understand the gang mentality, and in what way can clinical understanding provide helpful interventions? And is it possible for someone who has no clinical experience with, or any sociological and cultural knowledge of, gangs and the communities in which they are located, to be able to address the chronic and deeply ingrained difficulties of these closed groups, which have socio-political ancestral roots dating back centuries?

Theories of gangs

Gangs have existed throughout the history of humankind. There is an expression used anecdotally in forensic psychiatry: an offender with a mental disorder will often be considered "mad, bad, or sad". There appears to be a similar way for gang members to be considered, except that, in their case, it seems to be more of an assumption of whether they are simply "bad or bad". The idea that one would attempt to understand what leads someone to become a gang member and to soar through the promotions from "younger" to "older", becoming a "don" or an "OG" ("Original Gangster") can be misconstrued as being "soft on crime". The reality that gang members almost all come from marginalised and disenfranchised communities cannot be ignored. However, even this can be twisted into blaming gangs for perpetuating that social breakdown.

Many of the communities in which these individuals have grown up lack not only robust caregivers but also community leaders who can advocate and organise effectively to address local sentiments and priorities. People in such communities then feel left out, left behind, and, paradoxically, dependent on the very sources of those negative cognitions. This leaves them feeling as if they are "other" and not really belonging to mainstream society. This "othering" narrative is particularly noticeable today as different groups of people from various communities, such as migrants and Muslims, to name just two examples in addition to gang members, are left feeling "othered" in society. Gang members are even further "othered" within the secure estate of prisons. If you are marginalised and disenfranchised, you do not have available the hopes and aspirations that the rest of society takes for granted. Even though your grandparents may have come from abroad with such hopes and aspirations, something has gone badly wrong for many of these young men and women. They are faced with insurmountable obstacles in the form of poverty, overcrowding in poor housing areas, dependence on benefits, no jobs, debt, shame, discrimination, and stereotyping. And all of this unfolds within the context of inevitable family breakdown and dysfunction, with consequent mental and emotional difficulties among both children and adults.

Gangs, as we know them, exist within the most deprived communities of our cities. As tempting as it may be to draw comparisons between our urban street gangs and other "gangs" such as the Bullingdon Club, the social and emotional experiences of the members of these two groupings could not be more different. Perhaps the only features these two types of "gangs" have in common is the sense of belonging and loyalty to the gang and also the synergistic effect that gangs can have on behaviours that would never be considered if one were not a gang member but, rather, someone acting alone. There is perhaps an irony that several members of one type of "gang" are in charge of setting up methods to manage the other type of gang—namely, the urban one. It may be that a gang mentality at the centre of politics would need to be addressed before any meaningful plans to deal with the problem of urban gangs are drawn up. Otherwise, there is a high risk of repetition rather than reparation.

To return to Iain Duncan Smith in his former position as Secretary of State for Work and Pensions, he cleverly advocated that the solution to such marginalised communities dependent on benefits would be to stop these benefits and therefore get rid of the dependence on the state in the hope of getting people working. However, we are referring to deeply fractured communities. One would not try to cut costs from the National Health Service by stopping the use of plasters of Paris for orthopaedic fractures by stating that people will no longer therefore be dependent on these. So why cut the metaphorical plasters of Paris from these communities before having healed their fractures? Are these really *symptoms* of communities in which gangs exist or are they *causes*?

From a politico-sociological perspective, one could express concern that if there is an "Americanization" of one social structure (i.e., the loss of the welfare state), then marginalised youth may also "Americanize" their behaviours, often influenced by urban American popular culture, which glamourises the "bling" of conspicuous consumption, higher rates of violence, and the use of guns. It is known that in the United States the urban gang problem exists on a much larger scale than it does in the United Kingdom; consequently, we should try to learn from the American experience.

Sociology of gangs

There have been sociological enquiries into the subject of gangs for almost a century. During the 1920s, the "Chicago School" of sociology advanced a Social Disorganization Theory, focusing on communities in flux around this time, when the now large American metropolises were being built. This urbanisation led to mobile and unsettled communities, in combination with the further impact of mass migration from Europe. Furthermore, those mobile communities were leaving behind what was familiar to them, and they were faced with cultural dislocation. African–American communities from the southern states were also moving to more northern urbanising states, having already suffered traumas of segregation and lynching, bringing the impact of these traumas with them. Robert Park and his colleagues, for example, wrote of the "profound revolution in the psychology of the peasant" (quoted in Hagedorn, 2008, p. 4), as the masses moved from rural to urban situations (e.g., Thomas and Znaniecki, 1918).

Perhaps one way to imagine the experience of these communities one hundred years ago is to consider their equivalent today. For example, we have Somalian and Congolese communities in the United Kingdom who have witnessed or experienced the most unimaginable traumas prior to coming to live here. More currently, we have troubled and traumatised Syrian people trying to flee their war-torn country. When Germany welcomes them, some workers in Germany express astonishment at certain refugees behaving in aggressive and greedy ways. They are then accused of being ungrateful, as if the whole aspect of what they have been through and what they are still facing escapes those trying to care for them. The symptoms of their traumas, expressed behaviourally and interpersonally, are misperceived as "bad" behaviour, not as an indication of being mentally unwell.

So why might some of these issues described above lead to the formation of gangs? Is it that gangs provide a social and emotional anchor for groups of predominantly young men existing in disorganised and unsettled communities? Everyone needs a sense of identity and of belonging. If the experience is of not one having a stable and secure family structure or a stable and secure community, then there will be a need to create stability and security in other ways. One way is to team up with those "others" in similar predicaments and create an alternative family and community. The group of individuals will then form—as is known from group and organisational dynamics—the necessary hierarchical structure, with leaders and followers. Given the amount of trauma already experienced by most of the members, the group dynamics will be fraught with survival difficulties, triggering a need to fend off any threats, real or perceived.

Other similar groupings of what are now gangs become threats in the shape of sources of rivalry. The rivalry gets focused on particular members, the size of the group, income sources, and territory. This might explain the intensity of the violence between gangs, with disregard for any collateral damage. The community where gangs are born now has ingredients similar to a war zone, with angry young people filled with energetic rage, and the source of that rage being located in the rivals, not in the real source, namely, the segregation of the poor still present in society. This is a potentially escalating problem, because some of those refugees of today may turn to gangs in order to be able to survive if they, too, experience feelings of being "done to" or "othered". Saying this is risky, as such a statement could be pounced upon by the anti-migrant "gang" as evidence for not allowing any of these "migrants"—a dehumanising term—into "our" country.

We were amused by the surname of one of the Social Disorganization theorists of a century ago, namely, Frederic Thrasher, as his second name could so easily be a "gang name" as opposed to a "government name"! It is worth quoting Thrasher (1927, p. 253) when he writes, "isolation is common to almost every vocational, religious, or culture group of a large city. Each develops its own sentiments, attitudes, codes, even its own words, which are, at best, only partially intelligible to others." This is so true. For example, when the two authors of this chapter first met our group of young men in prison, there were words and expressions in their narratives that needed to be translated for Carine Minne, whereas Paul Kassman, having grown up in one of these disenfranchised communities, understood them immediately. Furthermore, much of the language of gang members often serves as a shorthand reflecting commonly held beliefs, values, and assumptions.

From a sociological perspective, Émile Durkheim (1897) wrote of the loss of morale leading to the loss of morals in communities where social and cultural structures have been lost, alongside a weakening moral framework of the Church. Such communities are not only physically broken down, but also mentally depressed. His concept of anomie presents the idea of normlessness as an experience of those marginalised groups who are cast adrift by society or othered to fit society's norms.

The sociologist Robert Merton (1949) had described three types of responses that can be triggered by the experience of being marginalised. The first type leads to what he describes as innovators: those who have accepted the American cultural goals of financial success but are alienated from educational opportunities or from the work force and who must, therefore, find alternative, illicit ways of making money. This is the type that could lead to becoming a gang member. The second type leads to the development of rebels who have rejected the goals of success as well as the conventional means of achieving them, becoming drop-outs and leading alternative lifestyles. The third type, known as retreatists, have seen no hope of success whatsoever and simply withdrew from society by becoming, for example, drug addicts. Almost fifty years later, Merton's explanation appears just as relevant in twenty-first-century British society, in which certain communities experience increasing marginalisation, as well as child poverty, as the welfare state retreats. Additionally, the population churn in many inner London boroughs has passed 15% annually, resulting in a huge flux and lack of stability as one in six residents and their families will enter or leave a borough in any given year (Travers, Tunstall, Whitehead, and Pruvot, 2007). Such communities now contain many third-generation immigrants with the experience of something lost, not just that of growing up without fathers within the family unit.

There are also the effects of the broader gang culture and the hype presented to youngsters via contemporary social media and marketing. Furthermore, there is the mainly unspoken and denied or neglected issue of race, given the statistics quoted earlier regarding gang membership and the fact that 90% come from black and ethnic communities. For almost fifty years, enquiries have been conducted into the consistently higher rates of exclusion for black boys from schools. And a continuum can be traced through the perennial issue of stop-and-search, which still sees black males as being seven times more likely to be stopped in the street by police, and more likely to receive harsher decisions from the criminal justice system: criminal charges as opposed to cautions or, even, being on the receiving end of custodial sentences in courts—*The Lammy Review: An Independent Review into the Treatment of, and Outcomes for, Black, Asian and Minority Ethnic Individuals in the Criminal Justice System* (Ministry of Justice, 2017). More recent advances have intensified this narrative. In 2015, the Home Office reported that black men are three times more likely to be tasered by police officers (*Police Use of Taser Statistics, England and Wales: 1 January to 31 December 2015*; HM Government, 2016). Could it be that society's apparent hostility to black men is lived or experienced by the gang members and is responded to angrily? Again, these are issues that are difficult to raise, given that this very hostility within society needs to be defended against or camouflaged by a denial of race being a reflection of who might be affected.

The clinical context

Spelling out what is known widely about poverty and deprivation shaping the landscape for the development of mental health difficulties is beyond the scope of this chapter. However, the following information was made available through unpublished research from the Greater London Authority. A 2010 NHS London and Youth Justice Board Report has identified a high level of clinical need with low levels of engagement for high-risk young offenders. Often, high levels of risk are not recognised as meeting the appropriate threshold of clinical need. For instance, 60% of a sample of 315 high-risk young offenders in seven London boroughs have been assessed by Youth Offending Teams as presenting with emotional or psychological needs through the ASSET risk assessment tool. Only 20% had even any initial engagement with child and adolescent mental health services, suggesting that only a small minority will ever receive any ongoing treatment. Particularly shocking are the following figures from this sample of 315 offenders: 33% had witnessed domestic violence; 30% had experienced bereavement; 30% had experienced abuse (physical, sexual, and/or emotional); 15% had experienced parental mental health issues; 15% had experienced parental drug abuse issues; and 15% had experienced parental alcohol abuse issues (Youth Justice Board and Commissioning Support for London, 2010).

Professor Jeremy Coid and his colleagues examined the prevalence of mental health issues among a nationally representative sample of 4,664 young men, including gang members, and found that the following diagnostic criteria were met in those belonging to gangs: 86% suffered from anxiety disorders (twice the rate found among non-violent men); 29% suffered from psychoses (four times higher than the rate found in non-violent men); and 34% had actually made suicide attempts (thirteen times higher than non-violent men). Interestingly, the only psychiatric diagnosis with lower rates among gang members as compared to non-violent men was depression (Coid, Ullrich, Keers, Bebbington, DeStavola, et al., 2013). But one wonders whether this could be that the depressive symptoms are buried beneath the gang persona. These young people are actually a doubly traumatised cohort: traumatised by their developmental experiences and further traumatised by their gang experiences, with the gang having become their attempt to find some sort of cure for their ailment.

The gang narrative

Probably the most important part of our approach together with these young men was being able to present and demonstrate an understanding of gang culture. This was one of the striking differences in offering a therapeutic approach to other groups of people. Before one could be accepted as having anything to offer, one had to be "issued" with a "hoodpass" in order to be allowed "in". This was something that Carine had not experienced before but was something with which Paul was very familiar. Once "in", then the gang narrative could be voiced and heard safely as the essential starting place in which the emotional troubles of these young men could be aired gradually within that context.

What the gang promotes for these young men is a set of codes, values, expectations, and behaviours in keeping with all of these. There are clearly recognised rules, as well as rewards for following those rules, either through promotion within the ranks or through financial rewards or, indeed, both. There are specific violations and consequent sanctions, often severe, such as having to carry out an atrocity—a stabbing, shooting, beating, or even a killing—in order to prove one's worth. Within the gang there are specific roles arranged along strict hierarchical lines, in keeping with a group that has a formal leader and dependent underlings.

In gangs, the leaders are known as "Olders" or as "Dons", and the underlings are known as "Youngers". And within the gang structure, individuals often assume roles that match the particular skills and attributes that they bring to the group. Some have particular skills in selling drugs or in organising criminal endeavours, while others are "soldiers" or "shooters".

Gangs easily access, and make use of, social media—particularly in recent years—for "marketing" purposes and for propaganda. This, in the shape of YouTube videos and Gangsta Rep, for example, not only normalises the gang experience, but also idealises it. Gangsta Rep was really a hijacking of the original Hip Hop culture, which revolved around break-dancing and D.J.-ing, leading an inner city youth culture into a more ominous and risky direction. Hip Hop and Gangsta Rep portray a gritty, criminalised, deadly urban experience, suffused by violence. The name Gangsta Rep stems, in part, from "Rep", which has a dual meaning both as a noun (i.e., reputation") and as a verb (i.e., "repping" or "representing"). Maintaining one's "rep" and "repping" the gang or the gang's territory becomes the daily goal, and its currency must be protected at all costs. Once having joined a gang, the young person gives up his "government name" and will be given a new identity with a gang name, something akin to a nickname, which will usually be based on some physical, behavioural, or psychological characteristic of this person. For example, a large and muscular person with low impulse control for violent outbursts could end up with a name such as "Merker". Once a man called "Jimmy" becomes known as "Merker", he will have to work hard to maintain his "Rep". This means that he also has to work hard to suppress his "Jimmy-ness". A new identity is born, but it is constantly under threat from external and internal stressors.

Fear, shame, and remorse are forbidden emotions in the gang, and the manufacturing of a "protective psychopathy" is crucial. The young person is then in daily training not to care. This means, for example, that if a gang member should be stabbed or shot, his first, most immediate response must no longer be, "Oh my God I've been shot, I'm going to die" but, rather, something like, "What? That shit had the nerve to shoot me? Doesn't he know who I am?", followed by an immediate plan to repair the now damaged "Rep". We heard in our group from a notorious gang leader who described how shortly after being shot he got back behind the wheel of his car and began to drive, despite the severe pain and haemorrhaging, in order to maintain his visibility and prominence in the local area, sending out the message that he was still fully operational, despite the shooting. If he had not done this, his "Rep" and that of his gang would, possibly, have been damaged irreversibly, and would have resulted in the death of the gang. Alternatively, this man could have lost his "Rep" within his own gang and could have been replaced as leader or "Don".

The social narrative

It is important to refer to social narratives of these young people: those family and community influences in which they had been immersed before entering a gang. Many of them grew up in communities with experiences of immigration only one, two, or three generations previously, meaning that prior to their gang lives they had spent their formative years in dual cultures. Within the home, they experienced the cultural influences of their immigrant parents or grandparents, many having come from the Caribbean or from Africa. These influences relate, for example, not only to food, music, icons, and language, but also to family relationships and expectations in terms of respect and deference to elders or to church members. The second culture for these gang members is a British one, in which they often occupy a marginalised position, often in socially deprived housing complexes. They have grown up confronted repeatedly by racism, one example being the much more frequent "stop and search" by the police of young black men compared to young white men.

We do not refer further in this chapter to all the other blatant racist exposures from football hooliganism to certain political voices with which the reader will most certainly be familiar. It is the more subtle and chronic forms of racism that they all reported having experienced on a daily basis before being in gangs, such as sitting on a bus and noticing the white woman sitting next to them holding on to her bag more tightly and shifting away or, entering a shop and noticing the uniformed security person focusing on them and following them around with the automatic assumption that they were up to no good, simply because they are black. This is reminiscent of what we all think had been long extinguished—namely, the attitude of "No Blacks, No Irish, No Dogs" posted on the doors of landlords with rooms to let. It is essential to take the chronic drip-drip effect of such micro-aggressions into consideration when addressing the narratives of these young people.

These communities are also filled with stories of hopes and of hopes dashed. The case of "Little Jimmy" is a common narrative. Little Jimmy was a very bright child who was at the top of his class. However, despite his evident capabilities, he lacked a bridge that would allow him to envisage himself becoming a success within a professional environment. He and his family lived in poverty on a social housing estate. In his mid-teens, in the absence of sufficient local youth clubs, after-school clubs, or general guidance, the lure of the gang experience became a great temptation. He soon became involved in gang offending and was eventually arrested and sentenced to prison. The local community's response was, "Did you hear about Little Jimmy? What a shame. What a waste." This is a common community narrative. Alas, there are far too many Little Jimmys.

The therapeutic relationship

The best way for us to describe the impact of the pilot therapeutic intervention with the group of ten men is one of a shift from being a gang to being a group. We should point out that these men had already experienced being in prison—HM Prison Grendon, run along therapeutic community lines—for either a few months or a few years. Indeed, it was for this very reason that we chose this prison for the pilot study, and we thank Dr Geraldine Akerman, Wing Psychotherapist, that this was made possible. In our view, we needed to trial this project with individuals already familiar with small and large groups of a therapeutic nature. Afterwards, depending on our findings, we could then think about the necessary adaptations required for running such an intervention on gang members in non-therapeutically run prisons and eventually also in the community.

The men in the prison were told about a specific series of "pilot" group sessions for gang members, and that signing up to it was entirely voluntary. Very soon, ten men decided to join. All ten were serving sentences of between ten and thirty years for extremely serious crimes of violence, including murder. The meetings, which lasted two hours weekly for three weeks, were held in a large private room on one wing of the prison. Men from other wings were escorted to that wing to be able to attend. The space was completely confidential, as no prison officers were allowed, and this was agreed beforehand.

All the men arrived on time for the first session and sat in the circle of chairs. Most of them were dressed in casual prison tracksuits and sweatshirts. Noticeably, they sat mainly in slouching positions and turned away from the two of us. After we introduced ourselves, the first thing they asked us was whether we worked for the government. Once we clarified that we did not work directly for the government (although Carine Minne's salary in the National Health Service is a "government"-paid one), and that we were not reporting to anyone, their postures relaxed. Paul Kassman described in greater detail his own reasons for having developed this intervention and also his knowledge base, both personal and academic. And Carine Minne described her experience of working therapeutically with young violent men. An overview of what we proposed for the three "test" weeks that we would have together with them was introduced, but done in such a way that they were expected to contribute to improving this, based upon their needs and wishes.

Following these short introductions, Paul described having grown up in a community in which gangs and criminality had consigned several of his childhood classmates and peers to prison or to wasted lives. He spoke of having watched subsequent generations of young men repeat the same mistakes with sad predictability. Constricted within the "hype" and scripts presented by gang culture, it seems that many individuals who have fallen victim to the inevitable prison sentence that often follows gang membership lack the space to explore and express how they truly feel about the reality of life in a gang. For example, despite the idealised concept of being backed up and surrounded by a crew whom one would trust to fight, shoot, or kill in order to protect one's status, a parallel reality exists alongside, which involves spending time around a set of violent, severely antisocial men whom one could never trust with one's money, or with one's girlfriend or "baby mother". The conversations started and did not stop for the whole two hours. Many group members complained that their narratives had been rejected as not fitting with the expectations of other therapy groups that they attended. They felt that they were told that they presented with the "wrong type of trauma". Being presented with situations and scenarios that they recognised from their own experiences gave them an opportunity to speak freely within their own narratives and galvanised the conversations. Not needing to explain or translate in terms of the implicit values and reasoning associated with gangs gave the group a sense of being heard.

Everyone attended the following week, and also the week after. The group requested additional sessions, which we negotiated with the prison in order to bring together the themes that had emerged during the three pilot sessions, and this, too, was agreed. A day conference was arranged at the prison to which stakeholders and other interested bodies were invited, as an opportunity to present the findings of the pilot project. Instead of Paul and Carine lecturing to an invited audience, nine out of the ten men stood on the stage and presented their own accounts of having been in a gang, about their index offence, and about what they had gained from the pilot. The tenth member, who was still too shy to present in public, stood, nevertheless, on the stage at the end with the other nine, to be acknowledged at the end of the presentations. We subsequently held a session with that group of men to obtain their feedback of the pilot sessions and of their experience of presenting in public. This was when the idea of preparing a book was born, which this chapter—based on the pilot project—anticipates. The most obvious positive feedback was the 100% attendance throughout the pilot. The most poignant feedback consisted of the men telling us that they had found, for the first time, a safe space in which they could talk about being a gang member, with all its ramifications and, in particular, about what lay behind the "hype". They were able to speak about those suppressed and shameful emotions that hid behind the manu-factured psychopathy. They felt that we genuinely wanted to under-stand with them and learn from them in order to develop a focused and meaningful in-depth therapeutic intervention for them and for others suffering similarly. The term "suffering" was able to emerge in the short course run during the pilot—a word almost anathema to their cultivated "Reps". The third most welcome feedback was their own demand to have the whole ten-week programme made avail-able within the prison system. This was achieved mainly thanks to the men, and it led to the creation of a waiting list!

What did we, as a couple, bring to this group? In our experience, the presence of a "parental" couple, one of whom knew from per-sonal experience the nature of the men's backgrounds and the other, who was experienced in listening and talking to violent young men, was crucial to this group. Nearly all of them had grown up without fathers in the home, and all of them came from deprived and poverty-stricken backgrounds. Some had alcoholic or drug-addicted mothers. Most of them had been emotionally or physically brutalised—or both—in early childhood and had suffered neglect. What was striking was that many of them had been A-grade students at school before their breakdowns into gangs. These were bright young men of whom society was now being deprived.

What were their expectations? Initially, the men were a little curi-ous about who was coming to the group and what they were going to bring, but the expectation was restricted to thinking it was just going to be a "load of crap". This assumption was understandable, given that their gang lives remained closed by their very nature, and they expected us to be coming along arrogantly thinking that we were going to teach them something. They had never before been offered a space specifically only *with* other gang members and only *for* gang members. They had never before experienced someone being interested in accepting, understanding, and hearing their own narratives. Rather than coming along to teach the group how to think or how to reflect prosocial behaviour and values, we were able to ask the right questions, the answers to which allowed us to dismantle the hype that lay behind their gang personas, by using interpretations rendered in a non-judgemental way.

How was the gang experience enacted within the group? At the very start of the first session, during the course of the personal introductions, we noticed that there were further postural shufflings, some men sitting straight and confidently, others sitting more tensely, with their hands wringing. The gang leaders within the group had managed to establish a mini-gang hierarchy, with the others as gang "Youngers". This was pointed out to the group each time we observed it, and by the second meeting the gang had been able to become a group, with only brief moments of gang hierarchical repositionings, which they then caught themselves doing and which they would immediately rectify.

How was a therapeutic group then established? Right from the start, it was crucial for us to help the gang members to frame the conversations they wanted to have. The agenda was theirs, not ours. They swiftly realised, via repeated interpretations, that we did not require or expect them to join, or pretend to join, our "gang"—namely, this group. Indeed, this group and this time was for them as gang members. It was not for gaining a certificate towards parole or for getting brownie points within the prison. It was purely their time to talk about themselves to each other, with us present to frame what they said and to interpret as and when this was therapeutically of benefit. Paul and Carine did have differences in their approaches, Paul's being more psycho-educational or didactic, preparing and bringing handouts, and Carine's being more psychoanalytic and experiential. What was interesting for us was finding ourselves meeting in the middle with the help of the group. Indeed, further feedback they gave us after the pilot was that they did not think the group would have worked with only a Paul or only a Carine. For them, it was the couple, with its differences, that enriched the experience.

Clinical issues

The main aim of our pilot was to provide a group therapy that had an understanding of the specific gang culture and gang issues that arise. After acknowledging and exploring the gang mentality, the aim was to look behind this mentality—tentatively and sensitively—to find the frightened, traumatised young men. Once these could be found behind the "locked door" of the gang persona, then the treatment would have a chance to provide a different kind of solution from the one the gang mentality provided. This is in keeping with Earl Hopper's (1997) fourth Bionic basic assumption of incohesion, especially relevant to people affected by trauma, where mental work is avoided as the suffering could overwhelm.

The main issues addressed were typical of those found in addressing disturbed mental processes in general group therapy, but these could be accessed only via this tailor-made experience for the gang. The issues that arose were, not surprisingly, maladaptive interpersonal relating styles, mainly those along controlling–controlled and threatening–threatened clusters. Impulsivity and affective disturbances were prevalent and related to their difficulties with affect regulation. The whole spectrum of post-traumatic stress disorder symptoms emerged eventually, and we had to remain acutely sensitive to help them to understand that feeling worse meant becoming mentally healthier. Powerful examples of these symptoms being suffered were vividly described. One member, a gang leader, spoke of being in a car full of edgy men, all of whom were carrying guns, and praying secretly for the police to turn up and bring the situation to an end in order to avert an unnecessary shootout. Another remembered becoming incontinent during a gang fight. One member described walking around the high-security prison he had just been remanded to after his arrest for killing and being noticed by another prisoner smiling and humming to himself.

Outcomes

The outcome we hoped for entailed dismantling the hype of the gang persona, which we saw as the gang members' solution to earlier difficulties arising from experiences in their external environments and internal worlds. We hoped to create a safe space where their individual narratives could be heard and emotional honesty cultivated in order for their vulnerabilities to be shown without judgement or loss of face. The remorse when they spoke of the victims—dead or alive—was palpable in the room. They used their victims' first names and imagined what their victims' families and friends must think of them, probably wanting the death penalty for them.

The dismantling, also, of the idealisation of money and the close link between money, exhibition wealth, and self-esteem was vital. This was not easy when, for example, one member would say, "Look, I can get £2,000 in a day flipping "food" (i.e., drugs), and you're telling me I should go to a building site and earn minimum wage." Despite this, they longed to be regular members of society, with jobs and families. Several of them had fathered more than one child and felt deep sadness about not seeing them, becoming absent fathers: a personal and painful experience they all shared, with special despair about the shame their children would feel by having them as a father. They desperately wanted to find ways to make up for this. Most of them had deep regrets about their lack of education. Some had managed to remedy this in prison: one was completing a biochemistry degree, another was reading philosophy. All of them knew of one person from their communities of origin who had become successful in a regular non-criminal way, and this knowledge provided a source not only of envy, but also of hope. All, with the exception of one, wanted to retrieve their government named selves that lay underneath the rubble of their gang personas. The one who did not wish to renounce his gang name had not yet managed to dismantle his gang persona and thus remained attached to the hype. We hope to see him again.

One of the most powerful messages this group of men gave us was that they felt that they had been taken seriously and that we had not turned up only to play football or to do some DJ-ing with them. They wanted to contribute to the development of the project in order to help other youngsters from their broken communities not to get into gangs and thus lose their own lives as well as taking the lives of others. In our view, they were the best but most ignored reference group in those bodies for tackling the problem of the gangs. We look forward to further developments of this project.

REFERENCES

Coid, Jeremy W.; Ullrich, Simone; Keers, Robert; Bebbington, Paul; DeStavola, Bianca L.; Kallis, Constantinos, et al. (2013). Gang Membership, Violence, and Psychiatric Morbidity. *American Journal of Psychiatry, 170,* 985–993.

Durkheim, Émile (1897). *Suicide: A Study in Sociology.* John A. Spaulding and George Simpson (Transls.). Glencoe, Illinois: Free Press, 1951.

Hagedorn, John M. (2008). *A World of Gangs: Armed Young Men and Gangsta Culture.* Minneapolis, Minnesota: University of Minnesota Press.

HM Government (2013). *Ending Gang and Youth Violence: Annual Report 2013. Presented to Parliament by the Secretary of State for the Home Department by Command of Her Majesty.* Norwich, Norfolk: T.S.O. / The Stationery Office.

HM Government (2016). *Police Use of Taser Statistics, England and Wales: 1 January to 31 December 2015* (2016). Available at https://www.gov.uk/government/statistics/police-use-of-taser-statistics-england-and-wales-1-january-to-31-december-2015-data-tables

Hopper, Earl (1997). Traumatic Experience in the Unconscious Life of Groups: A Fourth Basic Assumption. *Group Analysis, 30,* 439–470.

Merton, Robert K. (1949). *Social Theory and Social Structure: Toward the Codification of Theory and Research.* Glencoe, Illinois: Free Press.

Ministry of Justice (2017). *The Lammy Review: An Independent Review into the Treatment of, and Outcomes for, Black, Asian and Minority Ethnic Individuals in the Criminal Justice System.* Available at https://www gov.uk/government/uploads/system/uploads/attachment_data/file/643001/lammy-review-final-report.pdfe

Thomas, William I., and Znaniecki, Florian (1918). *The Polish Peasant in Europe and America: Monograph of an Immigrant Group. Volume I. Primary-Group Organization.* Boston, Massachusetts: Richard G. Badger / Gorham Press.

Thrasher, Frederic M. (1927). *The Gang: A Study of 1,313 Gangs in Chicago.* Chicago, Illinois: University of Chicago Press.

Travers, Tony; Tunstall, Rebecca; Whitehead, Christine, and Pruvot, Segolene (2007). *Population Mobility and Service Provision: A Report for London Councils.* London: LSE London.

Wintour, Patrick, and Lewis, Paul (2011). X Factor Culture Fuelled the UK Riots, Says Iain Duncan Smith: Works and Pensions Secretary Warns Riots Will Reoccur Unless Structural Reforms Are Made to Communities and Families. *The Guardian,* 9 December. Available at https://www.theguardian.com/uk/2011/dec/09/x-factor-culture-fuelled-riots

Youth Justice Board and Commissioning Support for London (2010). Health Needs Assessment for Young People in London with Complex Emotional, Behavioural and Mental Health Problems Who Are or May Be at Risk of Committing a Serious Crime. London: Youth Justice Board / Bwrdd Cyfiawnder Ieuenctid / N.H.S. Available at www.londonhp.nhs.uk/wp-content/uploads/2011/03/The-London-needs-assessment-for-young-people-with-complex-emotional-behavioural-or-mental-health-problems.pdf

Forensic disability psychotherapy

CHAPTER EIGHT

Extraordinary therapy: on splitting, kindness, and handicapping mothers

Alan Corbett

E stela Welldon's influence spreads far beyond the forensic field, and in this chapter, I examine the impact she has had upon the birth and development of a relatively new specialism—namely, psychoanalytic psychotherapy for patients with intellectual disabilities: a body of work known, increasingly, as forensic disability psychotherapy. To apply psychoanalytic understanding not only to the sexual offender, but also to the sexual offender who has an intellectual disability is an audacious act and perhaps one that could only flourish under the remarkable influence of a visionary thinker and practitioner.

The grandparents of psychoanalysis all tend to be extraordinary, to varying degrees. And in trying to make sense of Estela Welldon's role as one of the grandparents of forensic disability psychotherapy, I have found myself wondering whether her unique qualities of clinical bravery and radical thinking, which she personifies, are actually the essential components of being a forensic psychotherapist or, indeed of being a disability psychotherapist.

But is it possible to do this extraordinary work while being ordinary?

Being eighty

In her poem "Old", Anne Sexton (1962b, p. 37) wrote that, "In a dream you are never eighty." It seems to me to be an astonishing paradox that Estela Welldon is now an octogenarian. On the one hand it seems apt. She has the wisdom that comes from decades of work at the clinical frontline, and she has created a new forensic discipline that already has a past, a present, and a future. Her teaching has inspired a new generation of psychotherapists, psychologists, and psychiatrists across the world. These achievements are not those of the young. And yet to think of Estela is to think of the qualities of youth: energy, optimism and, most importantly, a disdain for mindless authority. Despite her love of opera, I tend to see her more through the lens of punk than of classical music: an iconoclast whose theories of female perversion, sadomasochism, and sexual aggression as a defence against intimacy have a shock value that does not detract from their fundamental truth. One does not have to recall the tag-line for the film of Peter Shaffer's *Amadeus* (i.e., "Mozart—the first punk rocker") to appreciate that the shock of the new and the conservatism against which it reacts are as relevant to the world of psychotherapy as they are to the world of music. In considering the impact of Estela's work upon the professions of psychoanalysis, psychotherapy, and counselling, I found it difficult to articulate clearly to myself until I tried to imagine what the forensic world would look like without her voice and vision having shaped it. It would, I am forced to conclude, be a far more split world.

The dangers of splitting

Splitting is a defence against reality that affects the capacity to think. The concept, originated by Freud and then developed by Fairbairn and Klein, is now a central tenet of psychoanalytic theory, it is a defence mechanism that can have a profound and debilitating impact upon both the ego and the object. While by no means found exclusively in forensic patients, splitting lies at the heart of most forensic behaviour, transforming the patient's world into monochrome and organising it into a terrifyingly polarised place. All is experienced as either idealised good or denigrated bad. There is nothing in-between. Others are experienced as part-objects, with the pressures of intimacy and relating subsumed by sexualised aggression. As Welldon (1988,

p. 7) has stated, "perversion involves a deep split between genital sexuality as a living—or loving—force and what appears to be sexual, but actually corresponds to much more primitive stages where pre-genitality pervades the whole picture".

The notion of splitting is key to understanding Estela's work and her influence. Perhaps her most revolutionary idea was to abandon the split between genders and to tear down the prevailing notion that only men abuse and only women are victims. *Mother, Madonna, Whore: The Idealization and Denigration of Motherhood* (Welldon, 1988) shattered the illusion that perversion was solely the province of men. As Juliet Mitchell (1992, p. vi) stated, "Men perverse; women neurotic: Estela Welldon was one of the first—perhaps in her field *the* first—to question the status of this psychosocial truism."

Welldon has also rewritten the rule book about who is suitable for inclusion in group therapy:

> I have felt the need to challenge both my own previous selection criteria for group therapy and those of others, the most obvious being those of Yalom (1970), who advocates group treatment for the Young, Attractive, Verbal, Intelligent, and Successful—so called YAVIS people. In fact, I believe that often the opposite holds true. Those who are considered old, ugly, illiterate, nonvocal, dull and failures can do extremely well in group therapy. [Welldon, 2011, p. 194]

This statement could well serve as a manifesto for disability psycho-therapy. A controversial example of Welldon's tendency to disregard clinical maxims that contradict the evidence of her clinical experience is her refusal to split groups between gender and victim experience. Men are treated alongside women, and victims are treated alongside perpetrators: acts still regarded by some as revolutionary and some-how sacrilegious.

Forensic disability psychotherapy

In considering this question, I find my thoughts going to one of the disciplines that, without her intending or perhaps even knowing, Estela has helped to create, namely, forensic disability psychotherapy, the application of forensic psychotherapy to the treatment of patients with intellectual disabilities. In my description of the development of this specialised discipline (Corbett, 2014), I concluded that it is a modality with two mothers: Dr Estela Welldon as well as Dr Valerie Sinason. More than any other clinician, Sinason is responsible for the creation of disability psychotherapy. Her pioneering theories, such as handicap as a defence against trauma (Sinason, 1986) and the handicapped smile (Sinason, 1992), kicked down the barriers that had banned patients with intellectual disabilities from the consulting room and influenced a generation of therapists able to disregard the misconception that the efficacious use of therapy should depend on the patient's IQ level. This was achieved through a Welldon-like refusal to split. Her most influential book, *Mental Handicap and the Human Condition: New Approaches from the Tavistock* (Sinason, 1992), affords parity between the handicap and the human. The patients she writes about tend to have been abused in the most dreadful ways; and Sinason writes about them as human beings first and foremost. Their disability is, of course, an immensely important component of their sense of self; and she is careful to contextualise this within early infantile (and even prenatal) experiences. The disability is vital to our understanding of our patients, but we are invited to place it alongside their ego, id, and superego, regardless of cognitive impairment. It is difficult to overstate how radical this expression of humanity was in 1992. Sinason dared to foreground the dignity of patients, ignoring almost totally the strange mistake made by most of the rest of the psychotherapeutic world in denying this humanity and in refusing these patients entry into the consulting room.

Estela Welldon has done something similar with forensic patients. All aspects of these individuals are vitally important, but none—especially their gender and their sexual aggression—should be viewed without the rigorous psychoanalytic lens with which we view all our patients. Forensic patients are unique, but not *less than*. Forensic psychotherapy, in the way it has been shaped and defined by Estela, is different but far from "less than". Estela began her working life by teaching children with Down's Syndrome, an experience that helps to explain her lack of hesitation in accepting onto her diploma course in Forensic Psychotherapy at the Portman Clinic a student whose primary clinical experience was with patients with intellectual disabilities. The impact and influence of this course on a generation of clinicians has expanded far beyond the decade in which Estela created and directed the training. She welcomed a wide range of participants: psychotherapists, psychiatrists, probation officers, nurses, clerics, writers, and poets. And she taught them to apply psychoanalytic thinking to their work in consulting rooms, prisons, hospital wards, and in the community.

I recall being interviewed for a place on the course. Having been told by a number of psychoanalytic training institutes that they would not be happy with one of my training patients being someone with a disability, it came as a relief to be told by Estela that, not only would this be no impediment to my joining the course, it would be encouraged! The course seemed able to avoid the splitting exhibited by most trainings that regard disability as a contra-indicator for treatment and learning. At first I wondered whether it was down to the Portman Clinic's primary interest in perversion that my disabled patients were of interest—their perversions being of far greater interest to a forensic clinic than their IQ. This is part of the answer, but once I had joined the course, I came to realise that its interest was actually in the core self of the patient more than in their disability, and actually more than in their perversion. This stemmed from Estela's interest in people: both patients and students alike. She has retained an enviable capacity to monitor and nurture her students even now, more than a quarter of a century since the inception of the course.

Attacks against the pregnant woman's body

Welldon's contribution towards the development of forensic disability psychotherapy is both personal and professional. Her support for the work of Respond, the only clinic in the United Kingdom that provides treatment for victims and perpetrators of sexual crime who have intellectual disabilities, helped to ensure its survival through a time of potentially catastrophic organisational trauma in the 1990s (Corbett, Cottis, and Lloyd, 2011). Her theory-building, particularly concerning the role of the mother in relation to perversion, has helped build the foundations of forensic disability psychotherapy theorising. When interviewed by *The Guardian* newspaper, Estela stated that,

> Perversions are all really, symbolically speaking, attacks against the woman's body. . . . Let's not talk any more about penis envy, envy to the breast, envy to the woman. Envy is towards the pregnant body [because there] is something so appealing about a pregnant woman, but they are also the most vulnerable to attacks, even from their husbands or partners. [quoted in Cochrane, 2011]

All manner of crimes can be understood, symbolically, from this perspective, as she explains: "In any attack against a house, for instance, taking things away from it, or shitting on it, it's always a representation of the mother's body that's being attacked" (quoted in Cochrane, 2011).

This concept has tremendous resonance for all forensic psychotherapists working with patients with intellectual disabilities, for at the root of many of their sexually aggressive, murderous fantasies and attacks lies a complex hybrid of envy, hatred, and loss. The body of the mother represents the site of trauma, the location wherein disability was created. The birth of a baby with disabilities represents a traumatogenic event for both mother and baby. Society privileges intelligence to such an extent that the mother of a disabled baby needs extraordinarily thick skin to withstand all the hate-filled social projections evacuated into her. These projections mix the powerful internal processes instigated by the birth of a baby seen as "less than" by both the external and the internal world.

Winnicott (1952) alerted us to the fact that there is no such thing as a baby—there is always a baby in relation to its mother. When the baby comes with a disability, this dyad is inevitably shaped and coloured by this deficit. There is then no such thing as just a mother and baby: actually, there is the dyad in relation to the baby's disability, and what it does to both mother and baby individually and dyadically. The disabled baby represents the damaged and damaging aspects of the mother, touching on Wolfensberger's (1987) notion of sex leading to the birth of a disabled baby as being death-making rather than life-giving. This collides with society's hatred of disability and its view of the disabled baby as fundamentally and profoundly inferior. This conflation of the mother's fantasy of herself as someone damaging giving birth to someone damaged with society's need to relegate those with disabilities to its margins constitutes an individual and collective trauma that is then projected into the baby. This is both an intrapsychic phenomenon as well as one that is particularly shaped by the social unconscious of the culture into which the disabled baby is born. The social unconscious in relation to disability differs from country to country, being dependent on a mixture of historical, geographical, and religious factors (Corbett and Cottis, 2015).

The twin phantasy

I have previously written about the twin phantasy (Corbett, 2014), a phenomenon I first noticed when conducting treatment groups for male forensic patients with intellectual disabilities. I had already seen in my work with parents of patients with disabilities how some allowed themselves tantalising and agonising fantasies of what their baby would have been like if their brains had not been starved of oxygen, subject to injury, or imbalanced by the wrong ratio of chromosomes. These parents articulated their feelings of loss most vividly when speaking of the child they wished they had given life to—their imaginary baby: a child able to speak and think without any of the obstacles of disability placed in their way. Engaging with what Raphael-Leff (1993, p. 7) has described as "conceived fantasies", during pregnancy they had held in mind a fantasised child—a child that had seemed to die, to be replaced by the feared, disabled child. The death of the imagined baby is an invisible, unwitnessed death for which there are no containing rituals through which mourning can be facilitated. While these narratives were ostensibly of loss, encoded within them were other, darker feelings of murderous rage. To imagine a life without one's disabled child is not just an articulation of sorrow and futility; it is also a connection, albeit unconscious, with feelings of hatred towards the disabled child. This is coloured by feelings of shame fed by their sense that they had done something wrong to ostracise them from the so-called normal world of happy parents with non-disabled babies.

Looking now from the viewpoint of the forensic disability patient, many hold an encapsulated fantasy of the kind of life they would have lived, had their brains not been encumbered by handicap. I was particularly struck by how a member of a forensic group for intellectually disabled paedophiles spoke of having swallowed his twin whole, while both were in the womb. I was taken aback by the detail and certainty of this phantasy, while the other group members tended to concur that this had also happened to them. This group phantasy allowed us to think about these incorporated twins as containing all of the men's potentials. While there was some disagreement as to whether eating up the twin had resulted in the dead twin's intelligence being digested, there was no disagreement that the imagined twin's intelligence was high, and that they personified for the men a version of a life unlived. This twin phantasy co-exists alongside a form of murderous rage towards the mother who had created them.

The handicapping mother

The forensic disability patient tends to conform to Welldon's view of perversion as being linked to the patient's hatred of the pregnant woman's body. Welldon has drawn upon Perelberg's (1999a, 1999b, 1999c) views about such matters. As Welldon wrote,

> violent acts have underlying specific phantasies or unconscious narratives that motivate them . . . Perelberg proposes that in affective or semi-preservative violence, the person's unconscious phantasy of the primal scene is of violence and the relationship to the pre-oedipal mother is engulfing and also violent. These beliefs have developed in the context of a pathological intrusive early symbiotic relationship with the mother . . . The violent act is therefore an attack on the mother's body, the mother being experienced in phantasy as being in possession not only of the child's body but also the child's intellectual and affective experiences. [Welldon, 2011, p. 44]

The murderous rage of the forensic disability patient towards the body of the mother thus motivates much of his or her sexual attacks upon the bodies of others; but crucial to this concept is the presence of hatred stemming from the mother's perceived responsibility for creating the patient's disability. Had it not been for the mother and her imagined death-making sexual appetite, the patient's place in the world would be unencumbered by disability. For the forensic disability patient there is no such thing as just a mother: there is always the handicapping mother. This complicates the already problematic situation of the core complex (Glasser, 1979, p. 278), in which the baby has a deep-seated and pervasive longing for an intense and most intimate closeness to another person, amounting to a "merging", a "state of oneness", "a blissful union"; and yet, at the same time, the person cannot bear the intimacy of what he or she might want. It has to be retreated from or even destroyed. The core of the complex is a fear of intimacy, a need to keep the object of sexual desire at bay, and to treat it sadistically. The forensic patient is saturated with thin-skinned narcissism (Rosenfeld, 1987) stemming from the infantile experience of the mother as being potentially overwhelming and destructive, as well as, in the case of the forensic disability patient, disabling.

These concepts are deeply Welldonian notions and build upon her discovery that, "My patient, like all perverse patients, had used splitting, projective identification and sexualisation as a survival kit in dealing with the outside world" (Welldon, 1988, p. 96). Just as Sinason is the mother of disability psychotherapy, Welldon stands alongside her as the co-parent of forensic disability psychotherapy. Without her capacity to view the internal world of the forensic disability patient with as much compassion, insight, and clarity as she views the internal world of the non-disabled forensic patient, it is doubtful that forensic disability psychotherapy would now be attaining status within the mainstream forensic world. Under Estela's stewardship of the International Association for Forensic Psychotherapy (IAFP), we forensic disability psychotherapists have been provided with invaluable opportunities to share in the birth and development of this discipline on the international stage. Unlike most other clinical institutions, the IAFP has rarely been guilty of splitting off the disability experience or of placing it on the margins.

Welldon has also issued powerful reminders of the dangers inherent within the disability field of it enacting a split-off view of itself:

> In my view, mechanisms of projective identification are used by those professionals working with "fringe" patients, within a "fringe" framework, in a society which operates with splits about "good and evil forces". At times of stress when staff members, in their intense commitment to their work, experience lack of support from those outside, they obtain a sense of solidarity by experiencing the "outside" as failing to understand and threatening—actually as the "bad" ones, for example, ready to close them down. There is also some identification with the patients' anti-authority feelings and rebelliousness. [Welldon, 1996, p. 179]

The disability field is especially vulnerable to operating within a fringe framework, and its practitioners require a particularly forensic form of holding and containing to help guard against the feelings of hopelessness, despair, and rage that come from working with profound disability and damage (Corbett, Cottis, and Lloyd, 2011).

Outside the normal course of events

I have no doubt that other chapters in this book will capture aspects of Estela's personality that can best be described as extraordinary, and that have shaped her particular talent for innovation and inspiration in the forensic field and beyond. What though, does this really mean, particularly in relation to the next generation of forensic psychotherapists? Does one have to be as extraordinary as Estela Welldon in order to create and innovate? The word extraordinary stems from the Latin *extraordinarius*. In fact, *extra ordinem* means outside the normal course of events. Forensic psychotherapy involves engaging with something that is undeniably and profoundly outside the normal course of events. Perversion stems from a psychic catastrophe that is far more profound and unusual than the ordinary vicissitudes of Freud's oedipal conflict, Bowlby's insecure attachment, or Balint's basic fault. As we have seen, Glasser's (1979) core complex is a useful way of understanding that a far more profound annihilatory event propels the infant towards its perverse goals. As Adshead and Van Velsen (1996, p. 361) have added: "Essential to perverse behaviour are defences against thinking (such as dissociation, splitting and projection), compulsive repetition, and the recruitment of the body (or someone else's) as a means of relieving tension and arousal." Some of these intrapsychic phenomena may be seen as existing within the spectrum of normal responses to the incredible drama of early life. What we are talking about when we apply these concepts to the forensic patient is something far more extraordinary—something very far outside the normal course of events.

Does working with the extraordinary require one to be extraordinary? If forensic psychotherapy and forensic disability psychotherapy are to survive in a decreasingly resourced world, are they dependent on extraordinary therapists to keep them alive? If so, what exactly do we mean when we use the word "extraordinary"?

I think that Welldon is extraordinary because at the heart of her clinical approach there is something that is, in the forensic world, both ordinary and rare. For want of a better word, it is kindness. By this I do not mean the brand of sentimentalised and overly empathic approach that tends, in many therapeutic modalities, to replace thought and insight. Kindness on its own has no place in the forensic consulting room. It has to be allied to intelligence, insight, and resilience. Welldon's career has, I think, been posited on the belief that challenge without kindness is not only counterproductive, it is also dangerous, as is kindness without challenge. It colludes with the fissure-like splits that populate the forensic patient's internal world. The forensic approach, if it is to break through the tightly constructed defences of the patient, has to avoid paranoid-schizoid splitting on the part of the therapist. One of our aims is to provide the patient with a relationship in which one can foster the capacity for object constancy, followed, hopefully, by self-constancy. To achieve this goal requires on the part of both therapist and patient the ordinary and often denied skill of abandoning an infantile split view of the world. The monochrome world of the perverse patient has to be countered by the Technicolor world of the therapist. (There is, perhaps, a whole other chapter to be written about the reparative impact upon patients of Estela Welldon's love of extreme colour and beauty in art, music and, most immediately in the consulting room, in her clothes and shoes!)

A plea for a measure of ordinariness

Estela Welldon's clinical career has been built on the avoidance of splitting. She has refused the comfort of splitting between abused and abuser and between male and female in order to work in non-pathologising ways with patients traditionally deemed unsuitable for analysis. This approach has enabled the creation of forensic disability psychotherapy—a discipline that, in addition to not splitting between abused and abuser and, also, male and female, works hard to avoid the split between the disabled and the able. Forensic disability psychotherapy makes use of Welldon's capacity to work with the victim within the victimiser and applies it to working with the able within the disabled as well as the disabled within the able.

Much of this chapter has concerned itself with notions of the extraordinary, and about how one of the legacies of Estela's work has been to enrich the new field of forensic therapy with another extraordinary patient group—people with disabilities.

To end, I wish to paraphrase the late Joyce McDougall's (1980) plea for a measure of ordinariness. Forensic psychotherapy has added an enormous amount to the formation of both disability psychotherapy and to forensic disability psychotherapy. The construction of all three disciplines has been coloured and shaped by Estela's deep under-standing of the dangers of splitting, both within her patients and in the clinicians and institutions that treat them. I believe that all three disciplines are forms of extraordinary therapy that have much to teach the world of ordinary therapy. Perversion, aggression, violence, and hatred are not the sole domain of the forensic world. Without my training as a forensic psychotherapist, and, most importantly, my training under the auspices of Estela, I would be slow to recognise that some of the worried well I treat have pockets of forensic functioning that co-exist with their neurotic symptoms. Being a forensic psychotherapist has made me a better psychotherapist, both with patients with disabilities and those without. The kindness I referred to earlier has to be exercised with Estela's other hallmark quality: an intelligent curiosity that helps inoculate us against an artificial split between the ordinary and the extraordinary.

ACKNOWLEDGEMENT

The brief excerpt from Anne Sexton's (1962b) poem "Old", reprinted from her collection *All My Pretty Ones* (Sexton, 1962a), appears by kind permission of Houghton Mifflin Harcourt Publishing Company. Copyright © 1962 by Anne Sexton. Copyright © renewed 1990 by Linda G. Sexton. All rights reserved.

REFERENCES

Adshead, Gwen, and Van Velsen, Cleo (1996). Psychotherapeutic Work with Victims of Trauma. In Christopher Cordess and Murray Cox (Eds.), *Forensic Psychotherapy: Crime, Psychodynamics and the Offender Patient. Volume II. Mainly Practice*, pp. 355–370. London: Jessica Kingsley Publishers.

Cochrane, Kira (2011). Estela Welldon: "I Speak My Mind. Patients Take That Very Well." *The Guardian*. 17 November. Available at www.theguardian.com/society/2011/nov/17/estela-welldon-speak-mind-patients-psychotherapy

Corbett, Alan (2014). *Disabling Perversions: Forensic Psychotherapy with People with Intellectual Disabilities*. London: Karnac Books.

Corbett, Alan, and Cottis, Tamsin (2015). The Irish Social Unconscious in Relation to Disability. In Earl Hopper and Haim Weinberg (Eds.), *The Social Unconscious in Persons, Groups, and Societies: Volume 2. Mainly Foundation Matrices*, pp. 117–138. London: Karnac Books.

Corbett, Alan; Cottis, Tamsin, and Lloyd, Liz (2011). The Survival and Development of a Traumatised Clinic for Psychotherapy for People with Intellectual Disabilities. In Earl Hopper (Ed.), *Trauma and Organisations*, pp. 111–126. London: Karnac Books.

Glasser, Mervin (1979). Some Aspects of the Role of Aggression in the Perversions. In Ismond Rosen (Ed.), *Sexual Deviation: Second Edition*, pp. 278–305. Oxford: Oxford University Press.

McDougall, Joyce (1980). *A Plea for a Measure of Abnormality*. New York: International Universities Press.

Mitchell, Juliet (1992). Foreword. In Estela V. Welldon, *Mother, Madonna, Whore: The Idealization and Denigration of Motherhood*, pp. iii–iv. New York: Guilford Press / Guilford Publications.

Perelberg, Rosine Jozef (1999a). Introduction. In Rosine Jozef Perelberg (Ed.), *Psychoanalytic Understanding of Violence and Suicide*, pp. 1–15. London: Routledge.

Perelberg, Rosine Jozef (1999b). Psychoanalytic Understanding of Violence and Suicide: A Review of the Literature and Some New Formulations. In Rosine Jozef Perelberg (Ed.), *Psychoanalytic Understanding of Violence and Suicide*, pp. 19–50. London: Routledge.

Perelberg, Rosine Jozef (1999c). A Core Phantasy in Violence. In Rosine Jozef Perelberg (Ed.), *Psychoanalytic Understanding of Violence and Suicide*, pp. 89–108. London: Routledge.

Raphael-Leff, Joan (1993). *Pregnancy: The Inside Story*. London: Sheldon Press.

Rosenfeld, Herbert (1987). *Impasse and Interpretation: Therapeutic and Anti-Therapeutic Factors in the Psychoanalytic Treatment of Psychotic, Borderline, and Neurotic Patients*. London: Tavistock Publications.

Sexton, Anne (1962a). *All My Pretty Ones*. Boston, Massachusetts: Houghton Mifflin Company.

Sexton, Anne (1962b). Old. In *All My Pretty Ones*, p. 37. Boston, Massachusetts: Houghton Mifflin Company.

Sinason, Valerie (1986). Secondary Handicap and its Relationship to Trauma. *Psychoanalytic Psychotherapy*, 2, 131–154.

Sinason, Valerie (1992). *Mental Handicap and the Human Condition: New Approaches from the Tavistock*. London: Free Association Books.

Welldon, Estela V. (1988). *Mother, Madonna, Whore: The Idealization and Denigration of Motherhood*. London: Free Association Books.

Welldon, Estela V. (1996). The Psychotherapist and Clinical Tutor. In Christopher Cordess and Murray Cox (Eds.), *Forensic Psychotherapy: Crime, Psychodynamics and the Offender Patient. Volume II. Mainly Practice*, pp. 177–187. London: Jessica Kingsley Publishers.

Welldon, Estela V. (2011). *Playing with Dynamite: A Personal Approach to the Psychoanalytic Understanding of Perversions, Violence, and Criminality*. London: Karnac Books.

Winnicott, Donald W. (1952). Anxiety Associated with Insecurity. In Donald W. Winnicott, *Collected Papers: Through Paediatrics to Psycho-Analysis*, pp. 97–100. London: Tavistock Publications, 1958.

Wolfensberger, Wolf (1987). *The New Genocide of Handicapped and Afflicted People*. Syracuse, New York: Syracuse University Press.

Yalom, Irvin D. (1970). *The Theory and Practice of Group Psychotherapy*. New York: Basic Books.

CHAPTER NINE

Responses to trauma, enactments of trauma: the psychodynamics of an intellectually disabled family

Richard Curen

Introduction

The forensic field is one that covers a multitude of sins. Due to the structures of the criminal justice and mental health systems, and to the way in which these systems often fail spectacularly to act, the forensic patient with intellectual disabilities rarely fits neatly into the frame. Fortunately, over the last twenty-five years forensic psychotherapy has emerged as a discipline that provides us with critical tools and with profound new ways of understanding perversion, offending, and complex psychopathologies. And under the tutelage and guiding force of Estela Welldon and her pioneering work, the efforts of clinicians engaged at the margins, especially those treating people with intellectual disabilities, have become more possible, and the lives of such patients and their families have, as a result, been vastly improved.

I work at a voluntary sector organisation called Respond. Based in Central London, it provides assessment and treatment for young people and adults with intellectual disabilities or autism who have committed sexual, as well as other, offences. I have worked at Respond since 2002, and my colleagues and I are grateful that Welldon's groundbreaking theories have become a veritable cornerstone in the application and thinking that underpins the organisation's approach to perversion, trauma, and violence.

Welldon served on the Board of Trustees of Respond, and her influence continues to reverberate throughout the organisation. Her compassionate and understanding approach towards the individuals seen at Respond does not shy away from naming and exploring, at a deep level, the enactments that can often shock and repulse. Her measured and thoughtful manner of describing and making sense of complex violent enactments has helped us to develop our own ways of approaching forensic patients with intellectual disabilities or autism in more humane and better informed ways, as I describe below.

Building on Welldon's thinking, I wish to discuss material that throws up challenges facing clinicians, whether or not they work with the intellectually disabled and those with autism. Informed by Welldon's writing on the perversion of motherhood (e.g., Welldon, 1988) and the transgenerational transmission of trauma, this chapter aims to demonstrate the use of her theories in trying to understand the actions, the motivations, and the genesis of the failures in mothering and fathering in some intellectually disabled patients.

Intellectual disability

Historically, no other group of people has had so many different terms used to describe them, ranging from idiot to mental defective, via imbecile, to the current phrase, "intellectually disabled". Over time, a constant feature has been the low status given to this group and the contempt and aggression with which they have had to contend. O'Driscoll (2009) has enlightened this area by providing a historical context to the understanding of intellectual disability and, more specifically, by investigating the early psychoanalytic attempts to understand and treat this often denigrated group of people. The psychoanalytic perspectives provided by clinicians such as Alvarez (1992, 2012), Sinason (1992), and Symington (1992) have opened up possibilities that allow us to think at a deeper level about the impact of intellectual disability on the individual, on their family members, and on society, suggesting that the intellectually disabled become a convenient receptacle for projections of our own disowned fears of disability. By focusing on forensic issues (Corbett, 2014) and on the trauma and loss that is at the heart of people with intellectual disability experiences (Corbett, Cottis, and Morris, 1996; Cottis, 2009; Blackman, 2013), it is possible to view the wide-ranging psychological impact of intellectual disabilities on individuals, families, and society.

A child with intellectual disabilities will probably be far less likely than most other children to navigate developmental stages successfully, especially in regard to the forming of a coherent sense of self. In particular, the two developmental stages of separation and individuation—during latency and then again in adolescence—are key stages in which the intellectually disabled child often struggles due to increased levels of dependency and reliance upon care providers. Winnicott (1965) has written about the baby's need to internalise the good-enough mother, and this relies partly upon the mother's ability, among other things, to contain and process trauma. Corbett (2014, p. 10) has highlighted that without robust levels of support it becomes quite difficult "for the birth of the disabled baby to be anything other than a trauma". The mother who is herself disabled, as described below, feels this much more acutely than others, as the combination of being the fantasised product of someone damaging who creates, in turn, someone damaged, combined with society's hatred of disability, leads to individual and communal trauma being projected into the disabled baby. To counter and make sense of these unconscious phenomena means that a paradigm shift must occur if, as a society, we are to make significant changes in the lives of people with intellectual disabilities.

Most of the patients referred to Respond have been abused, have witnessed domestic violence, or have experienced severely high levels of neglect that have profoundly affected their ability to love and to be loved. These experiences have impacted profoundly and have contributed to significant psychic confusion and to disruptions in the ability to contain primitive thoughts and fantasies of abandonment and engulfment (Glasser, 1979, 1986). Furthermore, the ability to love has often become corrupted and inverted. Welldon (2011, p. 94) has described children who have been exposed to marital violence and who have become utterly confused about the meanings of "love, violence and intimacy"; indeed, those children who have witnessed domestic violence can sometimes end up acting in sadomasochistic ways, as demonstrated below.

Clinical illustration

All of the material I describe has been carefully anonymised in order
to protect confidentiality without losing the essence of the individual's
situation and associated dynamics.

Referral

"Ray" was referred to the clinic at the age of sixteen years. He had
recently been arrested and questioned regarding a number of sexual
assaults. His neighbours had contacted the police after their eight-year-
old son had alleged that Ray had sexually assaulted both him and his
six-year-old brother on numerous occasions over the previous twelve
months. The police had therefore interviewed Ray as well as the neighbours, and a court case ensued.

A local Children with Disabilities Team contacted Respond to
commission a comprehensive risk analysis to help them to understand the level of risk that Ray might pose, and if so, to whom, in
order to provide a consideration of his vulnerabilities. Risk analysis
incorporates both risk assessment and risk management practice
and thinking into a comprehensive, expert opinion with recommendations. Professionals are provided with an in-depth psychoanalytic
report on risk management strategies and treatment plans in order
to reduce or avoid future offending. We undertook such a report on
Ray.

The Children with Disabilities Team had expressed particular concern as to whether Ray might pose a risk to his own siblings. So far,
however, Ray had remained at home with his mother and brother and
sister, and had not, to the best of our knowledge, abused his siblings.

The professionals involved in Ray's case to date had struggled
to make sense of previous failures in caregiving. The professionals
shared a sense that social services had let the family down, and they
hoped this commissioned service from Respond would provide the
professionals with a strategy and a way forward. There was a sense
of "magical thinking" that by bringing in the "experts" matters would
become much easier and that the high levels of anxiety that he had
hitherto engendered in the professionals would fade away. It was
essential for the team at Respond working on the case to provide a
level of containment that would be needed in order to undertake this
work and also be careful not to allow a fantasy to emerge that would
offer a false sense of security.

Weekly sessions with Ray were organised and took place over twelve weeks at the clinic. We also organised two meetings with Ray's mother, "Sherry". The court papers and other documents that were made available painted a picture of a family in meltdown with competing and conflicting needs at every level and on the part of all members of the family. The written material made it clear that there was a long history of family neglect, trauma, and abuse, the details of which were hard to digest. It proved easy to "forget" the deeply affecting details described by this patient of enacted aggression and violence over many years.

Family background

Ray was the eldest of three children. He had an intellectual disability with an IQ of fifty-nine. He also had a diagnosis of autism spectrum disorder. He was living at home with his mother, his nine-year-old brother, and his seven-year-old sister. Ray was developmentally delayed during his early years, slow to sit up, as well as slow to stand and talk. As in similar cases, it proved difficult to tell whether his intellectual disability was due to a genetic disposition or to the inability of his parents to provide an environment in which he could make up for any innate deficiencies. Either way, a combination of factors meant that Ray struggled, due to parental neglect and social deprivation. The family was very isolated, with little or no support from extended family, and Ray grew up in an atmosphere of both threatened and real violence. Social Services became involved from time to time throughout his early years, but Ray's father, "Clive", managed to keep the professionals out of the home through controlling behaviour, insisting that the front door must be opened only by him. Also, the father would not respond to letters; and as Sherry, the mother, could not read, she relied on Clive to correspond and communicate with statutory services.

The mother had a complicated history of her own. Sherry was the eldest of five children, and she, too, had an intellectual disability, with an IQ of sixty-five. Her childhood had been very difficult due to the fact that her parents had both had long-term mental health problems. Sherry's father had sexually abused her from the age of seven until she went into care at twelve years of age. Social services had had concerns about Sherry and her family for many years, but it was only when one of Sherry's younger sisters alleged that the father had sexually abused her that all five children came to be placed into care. Sherry's father died when she was fifteen years old, and she moved back briefly with her mother, with whom she had a very difficult relationship. Sherry would frequently go missing and would be picked up by the police wandering the streets very late at night. A number of times Sherry reported having been raped by various men, but due to her intellectual disability she was considered to be an unreliable witness, and therefore no further action was taken. Sherry struggled at mainstream school, would often play truant and would sometimes "seek out" adult men with whom she would have sex.

Sherry met Ray's father, Clive, when she was sixteen. She became pregnant shortly thereafter. Sherry reported that her mother was very happy when she left home, as she would no longer have to live with her. But Clive was twenty-eight years old and had a history of having relationships with very young women with intellectual disabilities, whom he often dominated and abused. Clive struggled with substance misuse issues and became physically violent to Sherry on a regular basis throughout her pregnancy. He left Sherry when Ray was about six years old, in order to move in with a younger woman, who became pregnant with his child. After Clive left, Sherry started a relationship with another man who had a history of sexual offending against women and who would also be violent and abusive to her from the very start of their relationship. This man, "John", became the father of Ray's younger brother and sister. Shortly after the allegation was made against Ray, Clive—the biological father—disappeared, and Sherry did not know his whereabouts.

Assessment sessions

Ray looked much younger than sixteen, and he often avoided eye contact in the assessment sessions. He was smartly dressed and would spend some of each session untying and tying his laces and then tucking the laces into the sides of his shoes. This had the effect of Ray looking at the floor and avoiding having to look at me. Of note was the way in which Ray spoke: he had a high monotone voice that made him sound prepubescent. This was at odds with his rather large size. Additionally, there was something unusual about the way he walked on the balls of his feet, namely, he did not use his heels. He reminded me of someone who was trying to appear much younger and who was uncomfortable in his growing and developing body.

I started by asking Ray why he thought that he had come. He was clear that it was to do with the boys next door and he started to tell me that he would never do anything like that again, and that this would not be a problem for him any more as the next-door family had recently moved. I wondered about this "solution" to the problem of the boys next door now being absent, and I was struck by Ray's concrete thinking. It was as if he wished his sexual perversion had also "moved away" with the boys. His thinking could be explained partly as an autistic way of thinking about people more as objects or part-objects that come in and out of a person's life; but for me it also highlighted a familiar perverse solution to unbearable levels of anxiety enacted in perverse sexual attacks on others.

The feelings evoked in me in the room ranged from disgust to a frustrating sense of not being able to reach Ray. His way of communicating with me sometimes involved goading me and demanding that I change things that he did not like, such as the broken blinds on the windows. For Ray, the messiness of the blinds was unbearable, and he would want to pull them off the walls. I made a comment about the disorder and mess that I was asking him about, and how he might be wishing that he himself, and his offences, might remain hidden behind a blind so that I could not see inside him. Ray found this interpretation frustrating, as he did most of the things I said. I found myself becoming more and more like a police officer trying to get him to admit to his offences, so that we could both get out of the room. I know from experience that each risk analysis takes on a life of its own and that in almost all cases the conscious and unconscious psychic defences change. The benefit of having twelve sessions is that a therapeutic alliance is usually achievable, which allows for a deeper engagement than possible in only a few meetings.

By the seventh session, the assessment had taken on different qualities, and it felt to me as if Ray was able to trust that I was not going to punish him for what he had done but was, instead, trying to understand with him how his actions had their roots in his experiences as a child. In my explanation I hoped to instil in him a sense of there being a common purpose. It became apparent that both Ray and Sherry, the mother, had great difficulties in understanding the impact on them of the physical and psychological abuse that each of them had experienced at the hands of both of Sherry's partners. Similarly, the consequences of Sherry's experiences of abuse perpetrated by her parents was also out of her awareness, and she spoke about feeling that her father's sexual abuse of her was a way of somehow protecting her mother from her father's violence.

Ray talked about his childhood in a detached way, as he seemed to speak about most things. However, he displayed glimpses of sadness when he brought up his early experiences of being cared for. Ray said that he did not remember much about his early childhood, but he did say that he recalled his father drinking heavily and beating up his mother. On at least one occasion, the father had punched Ray in the face. He also described a time when his mother had left him in the street, and so he went to his father's place of work, although his father became angry at him for that. Ray also remembered throwing his own belongings out of his bedroom window when he was angry and that on one occasion he went to the shops wearing his mother's shoes because he could not find his own. Ray's father heard about the incident with the shoes, and he beat Ray for "dressing like a queer".

I asked Ray if he would tell me about his mother, and he said that he felt he looked after her, especially now that John had left. He wanted to tell me about a time when Sherry was being beaten by his father. Clive was sitting on top of Sherry in the bedroom. Ray said that he was about six years old at the time, and he had heard them arguing, as he often did. He went into the room and saw Clive with his hands around his mother's neck. He jumped onto Clive's back and tried desperately to pull him off his mother. Clive threw Ray across the room, and this gave Sherry a moment to get up and make it out of the flat and across to the neighbours'. Ray said that this was the last straw, and Clive left soon thereafter. Ray also remembered a time when Clive had threatened to burn down the flat with all of them in it. When I asked Ray about his relationship with his father, he looked at me blankly and then asked me what I meant. I explained a little more and Ray said, "He was my dad, but I was the one who was there for my mum."

In another session Ray talked about his mother's relationship with John, who appeared to be less violent than Clive but, actually, more controlling. Ray described numerous occasions when John would take Sherry's phone from her and forbid her to go out of the flat. The threats of violence were often not carried out, but there was not much need, as Sherry, according to Ray, had been "well trained" by Clive. The arrival of Ray's half-siblings brought added tension and turmoil to the family home. John would regularly go off on drug and alcohol binges, returning home when he ran out of money or in order to sleep. In John's absence Ray would sleep in the same bed as Sherry and the siblings; and over time, he reported that he felt that he was the man of the house while John was out. Ray described memories of getting into bed with his mother after Clive or John had been violent towards Sherry. He said that he felt his mother needed to comfort him, although he often ended up comforting her. Ray was very confused, as many children are, by the horror of the violence being perpetrated by father against mother, ending with the child in the same bed as the mother.

This scenario comes up in the clinic on a regular basis in the histories of young men with intellectual disabilities and harmful sexualised behaviours. We know that mothers will sometimes use their children as human shields against further violence and, also, that the children, under the pretext of needing to be soothed, become the soothers for the mothers' emotional and psychological distress. The oedipal confusion of inhabiting his father's and his stepfather's place in the bedroom, together with the intimate security that both Sherry and Ray experienced in bed, left Ray struggling with his disordered and "elevated" position in the home.

When we talked about the allegations by the neighbours, Ray looked anxious. He described that he really liked the boys next door, and what had started as a shared interest in computer games had slowly developed into "mummy and daddy games", in which he would get the boys to examine his body, although not his penis. But he would touch the penises of the boys and would perform oral sex on them. When I asked if anyone had ever done anything like this to him, he said that some of the older boys at school had touched him in this way, but that he had not disliked it and consequently, had not felt any need to tell anyone about it. He also thought that the boys next door liked what they did together, and that he was sad that they had gone to the police. Ray was known to have been bullied at school, but, as with the sexual abuse, he was unable to think about the bullying as having had a bad effect on him.

I also met with Sherry—the mother—on two occasions, and I was struck by her manic state of mind and by the speed at which she communicated. I was struck by the accumulation of saliva in the corners of her mouth, which reminded me of patients with whom I have worked on psychiatric wards dosed with large amounts of antipsychotic medication. Sherry came across as someone desperately in need and utterly unable to access it. During the first assessment sessions she told me that she was pregnant and planned to go ahead with the delivery. The referring professionals had known about this for approximately four weeks but had neglected to inform us, leaving me looking "stupid". Sherry seemed to find some pleasure in being the one to inform me about this, but I was left wondering about the previous systemic failures in caring for this family being repeated with this omission. Sherry's pregnancy added another dimension of urgency to the assessment, as more professionals would become involved in the case. The added scrutiny and concern meant for me that the assessment became even more infused with fantasies of hope and dread.

I was shocked by Sherry's account of her abusive and neglected childhood. She recounted memories of her father raping her while her mother was in the next room. The thought that her mother could have done something to stop her father was not something that had occurred to her consciously. She thought, instead, that she was in some way protecting her mother. I was reminded of Ray's comment about his mother having been "well trained" by his father, but the "training" seemed to have started many years previously, when she was a child. It is not possible to say what was in the minds of Sherry's parents when they decided to have children; sadly, the offspring, especially Sherry, became receptacles of sadistic violence and parental neglect.

When I asked Sherry about her son Ray's alleged abuse of the neighbours' boys, she said that she regretted having let Ray go out as often as he did. She said she knew that he had "sexual problems", as they had often shared a bed over the years, and Sherry knew that this was wrong but thought it would be easier than imagining him all alone in his room.

My contact with Sherry was limited due to Ray being the main focus of the risk analysis, but I made a very strong recommendation that Sherry should have access to psychotherapeutic treatment as soon as possible. Given her history of violent partners, I knew that her personal safety and the future safety of her children relied upon her accessing immediate practical and psychological support.

In the final sessions with Ray, we talked about Sherry's pregnancy. He started playing with the dolls' house in the consulting room, as he had done previously. But on this occasion he demonstrated a part of his chaotic internal world that he had previously not shown to me. He placed all of the human figures into the various rooms, in no apparent order. He then started throwing the animal figures into the rooms in an effort to get the human figures to fly out again. At times he used such force that I worried whether the structure of the doll's house would survive the onslaught. When I vocalised my thoughts about the way the people seemed to be under attack, he smiled broadly and said, "They can all die and go to the bloody hospital." I made a link about his mother needing to go to hospital for the growing baby in her belly as well as for the previous babies she had, including him. Ray ignored my comment and started the process once again of placing the human figures in the room of the doll's house and then throwing the animal figures across the room.

At this point, I became very concerned about Ray's siblings and said that I was thinking about the bloody hospital and who might end up needing it. Ray started to calm down a little and spoke about his wish for a more "normal" childhood. He reminisced about visiting the neighbours' home and wondered about things being so clean and quiet, and how he hated it there, but also wished that he could live as they did. The boys next door "smelt nice", and their parents were so welcoming, and this was what Ray hated and yet wanted to be a part of so badly. I felt very sad on hearing this and asked Ray if he thought that he was a risk to his siblings. He said that while they were all still living together, there was a possibility that he might do something that would get him into more trouble. I said that I would need to inform people about this, whereupon Ray told me that that would be all right.

Summary of the risk analysis

At the end of the process, a comprehensive report was prepared that recommended, among other things, that Ray should attend weekly forensic disability psychotherapy for a minimum of two years. The level of risk was found to be high, given Ray's limited understanding of the impact of his actions and the way he spoke about his lack of impulse control around young boys to whom he felt an attraction. Ray had known from a young age that he was attracted to other boys. He remembered watching his mother changing his brother's nappy when he was seven or eight years old and being fascinated with the intimate care she gave his brother. Ray's autism was a significant feature in his apparent inability to imagine how other people might feel about things. The experience of being mothered in such a violent situation had left him numb to his own experiences of violence and, in turn, numb to the violence acted out on others. In the face of having no opportunities to process what has happened to him, was it any wonder that Ray would not seem to process what he had done?

Following his admission that his stepsiblings could be at risk, Ray was placed in foster care. This happened in spite of the recommendation of the report that he should be placed in a residential therapeutic community for young people with harmful sexual behaviour. Ray

seemed happy to leave home, and he was eventually given a condi-
tional discharge by the judge after having admitted the allegations
against the neighbours.

Discussion of the clinical illustration

Freud's (1914) theory of repetition compulsion, together with Klein's
(1946) theory of projective identification, illuminates the core dynamics
at play in the transgenerational transmission of trauma as described in
the clinical illustration above. Repetition compulsion is an unsatisfac-
tory and damaging way of trying to master early traumatic life experiences. Projective identification is used to describe the process by which
unwanted and unacceptable parts of oneself are projected onto others,
who are then identified with those attributes. These ways of relating
are temporarily satisfactory but are ultimately destructive and often
unavailable to the conscious mind. Rosenfeld (1971) describes the splitting of the mind of the patient involved in the projective identification
of parts of the mind into an object. He differentiates between several
motives for projective identification, such as communication based on
the non-verbal communication between mother and infant: the expul-
sion of unwanted aspects of the self, which can lead to a disavowal
of psychic reality; controlling the mind and body; and getting rid of
awareness of separateness and envy.

Comprehensive risk analysis is not treatment. However, just as in
therapy, the same unconscious ways of communicating and the same
attempts at controlling one's environment are at play. As described
above, the assessment process led to various insights into self-pre-
servative functioning on the part of both Ray and, to a much lesser
extent, Sherry. Ray's perverse acting-out was a temporary solution
to mastering deep feelings of anxiety. Welldon (1996) has described
perversion as having a circular motion with deeply felt anxiety as its
driving force. The id puts pressure on the ego to be temporarily corrupted by its increasing needs as the level of anxiety increases. Acting
out the fantasy provides a momentary release from the hostile sexual
anxiety. The hostility is usually related to feelings of revenge. In Ray's
case this might have been to do with a specific incident, such as the
humiliation he felt from his father when he wore his mother's shoes,
or it could equally be the result of cumulative experience of anxiety
linked to the feared loss of the primary object, namely, his mother.

Welldon has written that,

> Perversion of motherhood is the end product of serial abuse or chronic infantile neglect. This condition involved at least three generations in which faulty and inadequate mothering perpetuates itself in a circular motion, reproducing a cycle of abuse. [Welldon, 2011, p. 70]

Because of Sherry's experiences, Ray became a container for her undigested trauma. Added to this was the intellectual disability on the part of both of them, which was as a response to the neglect and the lack of containing environments in which both of them had grown up, with no hope or encouragement towards the development of thinking and reflecting.

Looking back through the family history, the trauma did not start simply with Sherry's sexual abuse by her father. When attempting to find out more about the older generations, it came to light that Sherry's grandmother, born in 1932, and the grandmother's younger brother, had both been evacuated during the war. They spent three years in a home with an elderly couple who had physically abused her grandmother and her brother. When it was safe to return to London, they went to live with their mother, who was grieving the loss of her husband. Sherry's grandmother struggled with adjusting to life in London, especially as her own mother was depressed and emotionally unavailable. The grandmother had given birth to Sherry's mother at thirty years of age, and Sherry's mother—as described above—developed mental health problems in her adolescence and had met Sherry's father on an acute psychiatric ward where they were both patients.

Welldon (1988) and Motz (2001, 2008) have described that in some cases women are capable of extreme violence, with their primary targets being their bodies and those of the children they treat like narcissistic extensions of themselves. Motz (2014, p. 9) has noted that, "Maternal violence, as well as neglect and abandonment, plays a significant role in the development of childhood disturbance and insecure attachments, alongside exposure to domestic violence and other forms of adversity."

Encouraged by Welldon, many psychoanalytic writers look to the mothering process as the spark that ignites the development of later perversions. What Welldon focuses on is the perversion of motherhood, which then helps us to think in new ways about the reproduction of mothering. Although Sherry was not the main focus of the assessment process, it became apparent that she was unable to think about the needs of her children and her relationship to them. For instance, when asked about how she thought the experience of domestic violence might have affected Ray, she minimised the impact on herself and could therefore not understand how significant it might have been for Ray. The very idea of being able to leave an abusive relationship had never occurred to Sherry. It was all that she had known, and, indeed, it was probably all that was known by her mother as well as by her mother's mother, *ad infinitum*.

Sherry's family history and intellectual disability almost certainly affected the way she thought about herself and her prospects in the search for a partner. In my experience, women with intellectual disabilities are often "targeted" by men without an intellectual disability who wish to dominate them. And if unsupported by family or professionals, these women can become apparently "willing" partners in a sadomasochism-infused relationship. Similarly, in attempting to make sense of the experiences of some learning-disabled mothers, we find that the same applies equally to them, but with the added characteristic of their inability to care, owing to the fact that their own infantile needs sometimes take precedence over those of any children and, also, that they may be on the receiving end of societal projections of hatred for being a drain on the limited resources of the state.

Sherry was the receptacle of her father's sexual abuse and of her mother's neglect and, also, of the neglect of her mother's mother. Sherry's sadomasochistic relationships, first with Clive and then with John, came to represent her self-hatred of her own body. As Welldon (2011) has shown, this perpetuates and reiterates the original abuse. Through a process of identification with her aggressors, Sherry became the victimiser of her own children through neglect or through apparent indifference to their continued suffering.

Conclusion

Society tends to devalue the unintelligent and the disabled and, by association, their families. Some families and individuals have the resources within them and around them with which to counter this attack; but they are the exception rather than the rule. People in need of help and support can often be left to fend for themselves, and when they ask for help, they can be made to feel like a drain on already overstretched resources. Society has a need to maintain the illusion of homeostasis, with the intellectually disabled becoming the receptacles for disavowed feelings of inferiority and of the fear of becoming disabled. Examples can be seen in enactments of disability hate crime and disability-related harassment, which, in extreme examples, leaves individuals treated as despised pets, tortured, and occasionally murdered (Quarmby, 2011). In a chapter of this nature it is important to hold in mind the pathological tendencies for intolerance and aggression that coexist in both the individual and in society as a whole.

The intersection of intellectual disability and perversion is one that continues to throw up new ways in which individuals try to gain mastery over unconscious processes that provide respite from unbearable feelings of anxiety. Welldon's theories provide us with an essential framework for understanding the unconscious motivations and fantasies of people like Ray and his mother. Welldon's highly significant additions to psychoanalysis and her theories on motherhood continue to influence and aid clinicians at Respond to uncover and make sense of perverse enactments. Thus armed, it is the job of clinicians—specifically forensic disability psychotherapists—to better understand this patient group and to attempt to contain and metabolise what is often designed to push people away.

REFERENCES

Alvarez, Anne (1992). *Live Company: Psychoanalytic Psychotherapy with Autistic, Borderline, Deprived and Abused Children*. London: Routledge.

Alvarez, Anne (2012). *The Thinking Heart: Three Levels of Psychoanalytic Therapy with Disturbed Children*. Hove, East Sussex: Routledge / Taylor and Francis Group.

Blackman, Noelle (2013). *The Use of Psychotherapy in Supporting People with Intellectual Disabilities Who Have Experienced Bereavement*. PhD Dissertation. University of Hertfordshire, Hatfield, Hertfordshire.

Corbett, Alan (2014). *Disabling Perversions: Forensic Psychotherapy with People with Intellectual Disabilities*. London: Karnac Books.

Corbett, Alan; Cottis, Tamsin, and Morris, Stephen (1996). *Witnessing Nurturing Protesting: Therapeutic Responses to Sexual Abuse of People with Learning Disabilities*. London: David Fulton Publishers.

Cottis, Tamsin (Ed.) (2009). *Intellectual Disability, Trauma and Psychotherapy*. London: Routledge / Taylor and Francis Group, and Hove, East Sussex: Routledge / Taylor and Francis Group.

Freud, Sigmund (1914). Weitere Ratschläge zur Technik der Psychoanalyse: II. Erinnern, Wiederholen und Durcharbeiten. *Internationale Zeitschrift für ärztliche Psychoanalyse, 2,* 485–491.

Freud, Sigmund (1914). Weitere Ratschläge zur Technik der Psychoanalyse: II. Erinnern, Wiederholen und Durcharbeiten. *Internationale Zeitschrift für ärztliche Psychoanalyse, 2,* 485–491.

Glasser, Mervin (1979). Some Aspects of the Role of Aggression in the Perversions. In Ismond Rosen (Ed.), *Sexual Deviation: Second Edition,* pp. 278–305. Oxford: Oxford University Press.

Glasser, Mervin (1986). Identification and its Vicissitudes as Observed in the Perversions. *International Journal of Psycho-Analysis, 67,* 9–17.

Klein, Melanie (1946). Notes on Some Schizoid Mechanisms. *International Journal of Psycho-Analysis, 27,* 99–110.

Motz, Anna (2001). *The Psychology of Female Violence: Crimes Against the Body.* Hove, East Sussex: Brunner-Routledge.

Motz, Anna (2008). *The Psychology of Female Violence, Second Edition: Crimes Against the Body.* London: Routledge / Taylor and Francis Group, and Hove, East Sussex: Routledge / Taylor and Francis Group.

Motz, Anna (2014). *Toxic Couples: The Psychology of Domestic Violence.* London: Routledge / Taylor and Francis Group, and Hove, East Sussex: Routledge / Taylor and Francis Group.

O'Driscoll, David (2009). Psychotherapy and Intellectual Disability: A Historical View. In Tamsin Cottis (Ed.), *Intellectual Disability, Trauma and Psychotherapy,* pp. 9–28. London: Routledge / Taylor and Francis Group, and Hove, East Sussex: Routledge / Taylor and Francis Group.

Quarmby, Katharine (2011). *Scapegoat: How We Are Failing Disabled People.* London: Portobello Books.

Rosenfeld, Herbert (1971). A Clinical Approach to the Psychoanalytic Theory of the Life and Death Instincts: An Investigation into the Aggressive Aspects of Narcissism. *International Journal of Psycho-Analysis, 52,* 169–178.

Sinason, Valerie (1992). *Mental Handicap and the Human Condition: New Approaches from the Tavistock.* London: Free Association Books.

Symington, Neville (1992). Countertransference with Mentally Handicapped Clients. In Alexis Waitman and Suzanne Conboy-Hill (Eds.), *Psychotherapy and Mental Handicap,* pp. 132–138. London: Sage Publications.

Welldon, Estela V. (1988). *Mother, Madonna, Whore: The Idealization and Denigration of Motherhood.* London: Free Association Books.

Welldon, Estela V. (1996). Contrasts in Male and Female Sexual Perversions. In Christopher Cordess and Murray Cox (Eds.), *Forensic Psychotherapy: Crime, Psychodynamics and the Offender Patient. Volume II. Mainly Practice,* pp. 273–289. London: Jessica Kingsley Publishers.

Welldon, Estela V. (2011). *Playing with Dynamite: A Personal Approach to the Psychoanalytic Understanding of Perversions, Violence, and Criminality.* London: Karnac Books.
Winnicott, Donald W. (1965). *The Maturational Processes and the Facilitating Environment: Studies in the Theory of Emotional Development.* London: Hogarth Press and the Institute of Psycho-Analysis.

Forensic psychotherapy in the community

Committing crimes without breaking the law: unconscious sadism in the "non-forensic" patient

Brett Kahr

The sub-clinical forensic perpetrator

In 1969, Peter Sutcliffe, a twenty-three-year-old sometime grave-digger from the market town of Bingley in the West Riding of Yorkshire, attacked a female prostitute by hitting her on the head with a stone wrapped in a sock. The victim did not press charges; consequently, Sutcliffe remained at liberty. In 1975, some six years later, Sutcliffe attacked another woman, assaulting her with a ham-mer and slashing her stomach with a knife. Over the next five years, Sutcliffe perpetrated many more offences, which became increas-ingly violent in nature and resulted in the murder of many innocent women, whom he bludgeoned with hammers and skewered with screwdrivers (Burn, 1984). Regrettably, this extremely dangerous man would not be apprehended until 1981, more than a decade after his first detected offence; and eventually, having served several years in Her Majesty's Prison Parkhurst on the Isle of Wight, he would in 1984 be transferred to the high-security Broadmoor Hospital, where he remains to this day.

When Peter Sutcliffe—reviled in the press as the "Yorkshire Rip-per"—stood trial, the court psychiatrists debated the appropriate diagnosis of this multiple murderer. But although those who assessed Sutcliffe clinically may have struggled as to whether they should classify him as suffering from paranoid schizophrenia or from a personality disorder, everyone would have agreed that he merited the designation of "forensic patient": someone whose substantial psychological illness contributes to the enactment of violent crime consisting either of the destruction of property or of attacks on the body of another person or persons, or, indeed, upon oneself.

When forensic mental health professionals and members of the public alike encounter multiple murderers, career paedophiles, serial arsonists, and marital rapists, few, if any of us, doubt that these offenders have crossed a very dangerous line. Consequently, forensic patients will require special treatment, which invariably consists of confinement in an institutional setting and, wherever possible, psychological care as well, perhaps even the opportunity to undertake dynamically orientated psychotherapy.

Thankfully, most people who attend for psychotherapy have never perpetrated acts of gross forensic criminality and do not suffer from an overtly diagnosable mental illness. Most psychotherapy patients conduct their lives with considerable honour and dignity, and most will "contain" their violent impulses with a reasonable degree of success. We might refer to such individuals as "non-forensic" patients.

But although these predominantly law-abiding patients never commit murder, arson, or rape and never physically attack small children, many of our otherwise "normal" patients have, nevertheless, perpetrated acts of violence, even criminality, which have often remained undetected. From time to time, those of us who work as clinical psychotherapists may find ourselves in the truly uncomfortable and morally agonising position of being the only people privy to confessions of such acts of destruction.

Of course, every human being—whether a forensic psychiatric patient or an upstanding member of the community—has the capacity to harbour violent thoughts and fantasies. In 2007, I published a large-scale study of the sexual fantasies of more than 19,000 British adults (Kahr, 2007). Fully 29% of Britons admitted that they have experienced sexual fantasies of "playing a dominant or aggressive role during sex" (Kahr, 2007, p. 588), while 7% had fantasised about "using a whip or paddle or cane or slipper or strap" (Kahr, 2007, p. 588) on someone. Likewise, 23% of British adults have engaged in coital or masturbatory fantasies about "tying someone up" (Kahr, 2007, p. 588), and 4% have enjoyed "gagging someone else" (Kahr, 2007, p. 589); 1% of the respondents in my study admitted to having fantasised about "sex with a child" (Kahr, 2007, p. 589). While the figure of 1% may seem mercifully small, one must remember that 1% of the adult British population represents, nevertheless, nearly half a million individuals.

In 2008, I obtained comparable data about the pervasiveness of aggression and cruelty in the sexual fantasies of ordinary American men and women aged eighteen and older (Kahr, 2008). Clearly, we readily encounter sadism quite widely in the so-called normal population.

One might assume that my data, though carefully collected through the use of an anonymised and highly respected computer polling research network, might, in fact, have provided only a very conservative estimate of the true state of affairs. After all, many respondents may not have wished to confess their more violent fantasies to a team of investigators. But those who did admit to masturbating about forensic activities did so without restraint. One of the participants in my survey, a man called "Yannis", revealed that he fantasises about, "taking all my enemies, anyone who's ever been cruel to me, and fucking them until they bleed to death" (quoted in Kahr, 2007, p. 336).

My own findings on the prevalence of violent sexual fantasies underscores the work published two years earlier by Professor David Buss (2005), an American psychologist, whose large-scale investigation had confirmed that as many as 91% of American men and 84% of American women have experienced vivid, detailed fantasies of committing murder.

Obviously, masturbating while fantasising about murder or rape in no way guarantees that one will actually perpetrate murder or rape in the forensic sense. But where does one draw the line? And to what extent do violent fantasies place a person at risk of an ultimate forensic enactment at some point in the future?

Over the course of several decades, I have become increasingly aware that many patients undergoing psychotherapy have, often quite unconsciously, progressed beyond the realm of masturbatory or coital fantasy and have committed acts of violence or have even broken the law. None of these patients has ever, to the best of my knowledge, perpetrated such grotesque acts of murder as the Yorkshire Ripper had done, and none has ever attracted the attention of the police or the courts or the forensic psychiatrists. But in certain cases, ordinary, seemingly "normal" or "neurotic" men and women have engaged in violence that has, from time to time, even resulted in the death of another human being.

I have come to think of such individuals as "sub-clinical" forensic patients, whose sadism—often deeply unconscious—has remained undetected for long periods of time.

In the pages that follow, I endeavour to explore the psychodynamics of the so-called "sub-clinical" non-forensic patient, concentrating on how and why such individuals function in this quasi-forensic fashion. I also consider what impact this unconscious "criminality" might have upon these patients, upon their intimates, and, also upon the independent psychotherapist, working in a private office, who has undertaken to provide treatment.

In my experience few, if any, practitioners of psychotherapy would deny that a capacity for violence lies at the very core of the human mind. Each of us has the potentiality to fantasise about murder, but most of us develop the capacity to harness and encapsulate such fantasies and to neutralise their toxicity through an investment in loving attachments and in creative sublimations.

And yet, in spite of the fact that most of us find it very easy to refrain from setting buildings on fire or from assaulting our colleagues with hammers and knives, every single one of us has, at one time or another, committed a crime.

I shall never forget that, nearly thirty years ago, during my very first seminar as a young student at the Portman Clinic, Dr Mervin Glasser, then Medical Director at this specialist institution for the treatment of forensic patients, pontificated to my cohort of trainees that one need not be a murderer or a paedophile in order to be a criminal. As Glasser warned us, anyone who had ever taken a paper clip from his or her clinic office and used it to attach any *personal* papers, as opposed to *clinic* papers, has, in point of fact, committed an act of theft. As Dr Glasser spoke, a shame-filled hush descended over all the students in this seminar on the psychology of violence, as each one of us recalled instances of having rung our spouses from the clinic telephone, having nicked a pencil from the storeroom cupboard, or, worst of all, having used a stapler for private purposes. Technically, we had all engaged in enactments of thievery. But did such activities really qualify us as forensic patients? When I confessed to my own training analyst later that day that I had, over the years, purloined a paper clip here and there, he merely chuckled. After all, he had treated *real* murderers and rapists in his time, and he simply analysed my guilt as a vestige of early childhood fears of having murdered my siblings in my mind: a criminal from a sense of unconscious guilt (Freud, 1916).

But . . . sometimes acts of cruelty and violence among the non-forensic population can be much more extreme, and over the years I have encountered numerous instances of such "acting-out" among the seemingly normal ambulatory patients with whom I have had the privilege of working in a private practice setting in a comfortable part of London.

Clinical case material

Mrs A arrived at my consulting room for a session in a state of fury. Her mother-in-law, whom she hated, had become frail and incapacitated after having broken a hip. Mrs A's husband had hoped that he and his wife might be able to offer his mother a bedroom in their large house, but Mrs A told me how she had adamantly refused to do so, because the presence of a mother-in-law would unduly restrict her own social life. Mrs A admitted that, although her mother-in-law had never done anything untoward, my patient simply and honestly did not wish to extend herself in this way.

I reminded Mrs A that she and I had devoted many previous sessions of psychotherapy to an exploration of her fantasy of being an "unwanted" child, in view of the fact that she had arrived some ten years after all her other siblings. Consequently, Mrs A had come to think of herself as a "mistake" and carried a great deal of rage in her heart at all times.

I wondered whether Mrs A's attack on her fragile mother-in-law might well constitute a displaced attack on *her* mother of infancy. Perhaps by denying shelter to her husband's mother, Mrs A had succeeded in gratifying an unconscious wish to attack her own mother.

Mrs A then spurted out, "Why should I give my mother-in-law a room? I had to sleep on the staircase as a child!"

I enquired further and soon discovered that, during Mrs A's very early childhood, her father had lost his job, and that, consequently, the family had to move to a much smaller house, with fewer bedrooms. And for a period of time Mrs A did, indeed, have to sleep on a mattress placed, unceremoniously, in the stairwell. In view of this, how on earth could Mrs A have developed sufficient generosity of spirit to have created a bedroom for her sick mother-in-law decades later?

In spite of my valiant efforts to explore and to interpret the interconnection between Mrs A's early childhood experience and her adult state of mind, she refused to alter her position with regard to her mother-in-law and explained with steely resolution, "I simply refuse to look after that woman. It's not my responsibility." Mrs A spoke with such ferocity that I came to regard her decision not as a lifestyle choice or as the assertion of her autonomy but, rather, as an expression of historical cruelty.

But does the refusal to allow one's mother-in-law to sleep in the spare room constitute a forensic enactment? After all, Mrs A broke no laws. But might she have committed a crime? In many respects, I would argue that for Mrs A to have made such a verbal pronouncement, prohibiting her mother-in-law from occupying the spare bedroom, does indeed qualify as a type of forensic gesture.

It saddens me to report that Mrs A eventually sent her mother-in-law to a care home, attended by a nurse; six months later, the aged woman suffered a heart attack after falling in the bath, whereupon she died instantly.

Let us also consider the case of Mr B, a generally calm, quiet, creative gentleman who works long hours in a respectable profession and who pays all of his bills on time, yet who harbours strong anti-Semitic sentiments. During the course of a lengthy analysis, Mr B wondered on many occasions whether I might be of Jewish origin. Although I never answered him directly, I always explored what possible meaning or meanings such a preoccupation could serve. Mr B, a Labour Party supporter who read *The Guardian* newspaper, knew only too well that his hatred of Jews had no rational basis. He even had Jewish friends. And yet, secretly, while lying on the couch, he enjoyed indulging in fantasies of Jew-killing.

When, after several years of treatment, I resolved to raise my sessional fee by a relatively tiny amount, Mr B, a wealthy man, exploded. He simply could not believe that after four years of work I would dare to do something so seemingly cruel, and he then explained that my ostensible outrageousness provided him with proof-positive that I *must* be Jewish. He began to rant with a fury that I had never before encountered in clinical practice, and he delighted in telling me that if he had worked in Auschwitz during the Second World War, he would have escorted me and my entire family personally to the gas chambers and would have poured the Zyklon-B poisonous pellets into the pipes himself, rejoicing in our agonising deaths.

It pleases me to report that Mr B's abusiveness has not resulted in my death. In this respect, he has not committed a forensic enactment as such. But the quality of cruelty that he displayed in the transference very much mirrored the sadism experienced by his wife, whom he had often insulted viciously and whom he had occasionally struck with his bare hands, causing tremendous marital distress, threats of divorce, and legal consultations. Does Mr B qualify, therefore, as a sub-clinical forensic patient? Should we agree to expand our definition of what constitutes the forensic state of mind, then Mr B might very well meet the criteria.

Ms C, a highly seductive and flirtatious person, had no difficulty enticing numerous men into her bed. Physically very beautiful and very superficially charismatic, she often identified herself with the siren "Lorelei" who lured sailors unsuspectingly to their doom. For three years, immediately *prior* to the commencement of her psychotherapy, Ms C had had a long and passionate affair with Mr D, a man who had hoped to marry her; but Ms C grew tired of this gentleman and she dumped him unceremoniously. Distraught, Mr D retreated to a pub and drank himself senseless in order to relieve his unbearable anguish. In a state of great inebriation, Mr D tripped, plunged down a flight of stairs, and injured his neck, becoming partially paralysed. In spite of numerous pleas from Mr D for a visit, Ms C refused to oblige.

Should we consider Ms C to be a forensic patient? Once again, she broke no laws and perpetrated no crimes that would excite a lawyer or a police officer or a court. In fact, she had remained at home with her three flatmates, in Highgate in North London, on the evening that Mr D became crippled at a pub in Clapham in South London. From a legal perspective, she had a perfect alibi. And yet, she had nevertheless unleashed a terrific degree of sadism upon her lover and, one might argue, had stimulated his deep pain and his consequent act of alcoholic self-harm, which resulted in the tragic damage to his spinal cord.

Marital couples, in particular, have a huge capacity to become violent in a sub-clinical manner. Often each member of the couple will comport himself or herself in life with great compassion and great dignity, but when the two partners interact as a couple, the sadistic underbelly of each spouse becomes infinitely more visible.

Mr E and Mrs E, a long-standing marital couple, had come to consult with me in a state of anguish. Mrs E explained that her husband, who had recently turned forty, had begun to drink excessively; and Mrs E attributed this sudden increase in her husband's alcohol consumption to a "mid-life crisis". One evening, Mr E returned from the pub after having consumed twelve pints of lager—four pints more than his ordinary intake. Feeling sexually aroused, he began to make love to Mrs E, but in the middle of intercourse he vomited all over her face.

How does one conceptualise this act in classificatory terms? To the best of my knowledge, one cannot be convicted of a criminal offence for vomiting on one's spouse as a result of inebriation. Indeed, to the best of my knowledge, no one has ever identified the phenomenon of "forensic vomiting". And yet, Mrs E felt attacked, humiliated, and despoiled. Does such an interchange qualify as a sub-clinical forensic enactment? As Mrs E exclaimed in the course of one of our marital psychotherapy sessions, "My husband is a thief. He stole my sense of safety!" Certainly, this woman experienced her husband's *vomitus* in criminal terms.

Mr F and Mrs F presented for couple psychotherapy after Mrs F, riddled with ovarian cancer, had discovered that her husband had recently slept with Mrs F's own sister. In fact, Mrs F, while trawling through her husband's trouser pockets, had found a receipt for a hotel room just around the corner from the hospital, which Mr F had used for his incestuous rendezvous. Damningly, the time of check-in and check-out—printed on the receipt—confirmed that Mr F had hired this hotel room during one of Mrs F's chemotherapy treatment sessions. Mr F attempted to exculpate himself by claiming that he experienced his wife's ovarian cancer as so unbearably painful that he simply *had* to sleep with his sister-in-law in a desperate attempt to find some respite from the prospect of losing his wife.

Needless to say, this explanation did not satisfy Mrs F, who felt viciously betrayed and profoundly murderous as a result. Mrs F stopped speaking to her sister in consequence, and she eventually kicked her husband out of the house. Two years later, in spite of her valiant struggle against cancer, Mrs F passed away. One cannot help but wonder whether Mr F considered himself a widower or a murderer.

Over the years of working in private practice, I have encountered the most enormous array of acts of cruelty—both conscious and unconscious—committed by otherwise law-abiding and reasonably mentally healthy men and women. Some of these sadistic activities could, one suspects, be subject to prosecution if a member of the law enforcement community should ever come to know about them. Mrs G, for instance, told me that her ex-husband, whom I had never met and whom I certainly never treated, would, when angry, pour a tiny number of drops of acid into shampoo bottles in the bathrooms of his friends' homes whenever he attended a dinner party. When Mrs G discovered her husband's "sub-clinical" treachery, she knew that she would have to divorce him, and eventually she did so.

Mr H threw a kitchen knife and a fork at his wife during a horribly heated marital row. Fortunately, Mr H missed Mrs H, albeit only by a few inches. Nevertheless, one wonders what would have occurred if he had had better aim, and whether this action should be considered forensic in nature, and if so, to what extent.

And Mrs I, yet another patient, told me that she had discovered that her fourteen-year-old son had obtained a forged identity card and that he had used this card to purchase alcohol. When I expressed concern, Mrs I told me that she proposed to do absolutely nothing about this, explaining that most of her son's friends snorted cocaine and other dangerous drugs; therefore, her son's drinking did not concern her in the least. In fact, she hoped that, by turning a blind eye to this, her son might not progress beyond bourbon and vodka.

These aforementioned clinical vignettes—all taken from moments of private psychotherapy practice—raise the most enormous number of deeply disturbing questions. For instance, what might be, or, indeed, *should* be, the responsibility of the mental health clinician when confronted with such data? Do we simply listen to these recitations of cruelty in a "neutral" manner? Do we interpret the unconscious sadism vigorously and risk, potentially, becoming policemen or policewomen in the transference? Do we turn a blind eye ourselves? Or do we step out of our roles as private practitioners and speak to social services or to law enforcement agencies?

I shall never forget that as a very young student at the Portman Clinic, nearly thirty years ago, one of my colleagues presented the case of a man who had perpetrated various sexual crimes against children. The trainee psychotherapist became understandably agitated, unsure of what her professional obligation might be. The seminar leader—a deeply compassionate and highly experienced psychoanalyst—spoke with resolution. He explained, "You have one responsibility and one responsibility only. You must persevere with the psychoanalytic work, and you must do nothing else. If you telephone the authorities, you will cause the patient to flee from treatment, and if that should transpire, then you will never have a chance to work through the patient's paedophilic tendencies."

This remark made a great deal of sense to me and to my fellow students at the time and allowed us to experience some psychological relief, knowing that we would not have to "turn in" our patients to the police. But in the intervening decades, British law has changed dramatically, and different professional bodies have now come to adopt newer rules and regulations about mandatory reporting. It will therefore come as no surprise that most mental health professionals struggle to know whether they can, could, should, or must report their patients for criminal activities, even though psychotherapy offers—at least in theory—the pledge of complete confidentiality (Bollas and Sundelson, 1995).

Such matters become infinitely more complex, particularly as many psychotherapists and counsellors might have completed a prior training in medicine, in social work, in education, or in psychology—disciplines that do require its members to report suspected cases of child abuse and other crimes.

The case of Mr J

Sometimes the private practitioner will be confronted by a particularly complex and challenging case of sub-clinical forensic enactments.

Many years ago, a local general medical practitioner rang me and explained that she had given my telephone number to a prospective psychotherapy patient in great need of help. She told me his name— Mr J—and she explained that in view of the urgency of the situation, this gentleman would ring for an appointment forthwith.

The patient did, indeed, telephone . . . *two years later!*

In spite of the very long delay between the referral and the first telephone contact, I had indeed remembered Mr J's name from my earlier conversation with his doctor, and I agreed to offer him an appointment for the following week.

I saw Mr J for a first consultation in the month of January, on a cold and blustery day. To my surprise, he arrived wearing only a T-shirt and jeans, revealing an overly developed muscular chest, which he displayed prominently. Within minutes, he told me that he had suffered from a deep depression for as long as he could remember. Mr J also reported that he had lived with the HIV virus for more than ten years.

Having already undergone psychotherapy many years previously, Mr J had no difficulty providing me with a full recitation of his early childhood, during the course of which he had endured many traumata.

Towards the end of our first consultation, I asked Mr J whether he might find it useful to return for a second consultation. He told me that he had very much enjoyed our conversation and that he would, indeed, like to see me again, but that he had left his diary at home and that, therefore, he would call me later in the day to discuss his availability.

Mr J did, indeed, ring, as promised, but *not* that January afternoon. Instead, he next telephoned me the following October—some *nine months later*—and requested a second consultation.

Naturally, I devoted most of my interpretative efforts to an understanding of the meaning of Mr J's reluctance to engage in human contact and to his profound fear of doing so, as evidenced by the fact that he took two years to call me for his first appointment, and then nine months for his second appointment. Privately, I thought to myself that if we continued at this rate, I might not be alive to see his treatment through to a successful conclusion: no doubt a pertinent countertransferential response, stimulated by the patient's own anxieties about living in the shadow of a potentially deadly illness.

Mr J told me without hesitation that he had delayed for nine months before ringing me back because he had experienced me as extremely frightening, and he thought that I looked like a monster. He explained that he had found my physical appearance—especially my eyes—very, very scary indeed; but he also knew that I had come highly recommended, and so, in desperation, he thought that he would attempt a second consultation. He then stood up from the chair and moved to the far side of the room, near the door, and told me that he would prefer to sit on the floor some nine or ten feet away from me, as he felt very much safer.

I risked a transference interpretation at this point, and I wondered whether he had *really* experienced me as frightening and scary and thus needed to protect himself from me, or whether, perhaps, he actually wanted to protect *me* from *him*.

The patient had certainly not expected such a frank comment, and it had rather startled him. In fact, he did not know what to say, and he simply sat on the floor, staring at me with discomfort: quite a change from his otherwise free and easy revelatory style.

As the second consultation neared its conclusion, I knew that we would have to address the possibility of a third consultation, and I experienced considerable trepidation, knowing that Mr J would find this both desirable and dreadful at the same time. Once again, he promised that he would ring me. I asked him how many months he would take to do so; Mr J laughed and promised to call me later that day.

He then telephoned for his third appointment in March of the following year, only five months after his second appointment. I took some small sense of satisfaction that the gap between our sessions had begun to narrow and that perhaps Mr J could, bit by bit, tolerate an increasing amount of human contact.

Eventually, Mr J and I began to develop a deeper rapport, and he confessed that he no longer thought that I resembled a monster but, rather, merely a greedy Hampstead psychotherapist who charges high fees.

Although I suspected that Mr J would benefit from extensive multi-frequency psychoanalytic treatment, I thought it quite unlikely that he would ever consider such an arrangement, and so, upon discussion, we agreed to embark upon once-weekly psychotherapy. I felt quite prepared to fail utterly with Mr J, knowing the extent of his psychopathology. I appreciated that the enforced intimacy of psychotherapy might seem rather like a prison sentence to this very frightened individual who had had thousands of one-night stands with strangers. But I also appreciated that, in spite of the extremely long gaps between our appointments thus far, Mr J also wanted to reach out for help and, to his credit, had refused to kill me off entirely.

To my surprise and delight, Mr J did engage with our weekly appointments, but he invariably arrived late. Unlike other patients who occasionally ring the doorbell two or three minutes tardy, after having rushed through traffic, this man always pressed the buzzer at exactly twenty-five minutes—halfway through the session. I interpreted to Mr J that he really wanted me to know that fifty percent of him wanted to engage and that the other fifty percent continued to find both me and this process rather scary. Mr J still sat on the floor, explaining that he regarded the patient's chair—some six feet away from mine—as far too intimate.

After one year of late arrivals, cancelled sessions, and "forgotten" appointments, Mr J finally began to attend on time, and he did, eventually, return to the chair, which I came to regard as a huge achievement. Moreover, he could now confess two hugely important experiences of biography.

In our very first meeting, Mr J had revealed to me that during his eighth year, his mother had suffered a cerebral aneurysm, which resulted in her immediate death. I knew that such a trauma had left Mr J alone and isolated, cared for only by a very bereaved and often absent "macho" father, who hated his feminised son. After his mother's death, Mr J used to dress up in his dead mother's clothes in a desperate attempt to bring her back to life. He and I had, of course, talked about the impact of this early, horrific trauma in virtually every session. But on this occasion, Mr J confessed some further, previously unknown, facts about his mother's death.

I knew already that the mother had died in the family home one afternoon at 4.00 p.m., shortly after the eight-year-old Mr J had returned from school. But I did not know what had happened in the few moments immediately *prior* to the mother's death.

Apparently, Mr J had asked his mother if she could teach him how to bake a cake, but she refused, explaining that she felt unwell. Mr J pleaded but to no avail, and in a state of protest, he stormed out of the kitchen and began to play in the room next door. Shortly afterwards, he heard an anguished gurgling sound coming from the kitchen. With no one else in the house, Mr J knew that this strangulating noise must have come from his mother's mouth, but little Mr J, feeling angry and stubborn, did not return to the kitchen to investigate. Approximately one hour later, he did seek out his mother's company, and when he walked into the kitchen, he found her collapsed on the kitchen floor. Unable to rouse her, he ran next door to the home of a neighbour, who called an ambulance, but, alas, the paramedics pronounced her dead.

Mr J related this story with a look of horror upon his face and then confessed that, through his negligence, he had killed his mother and had sentenced himself to a life of misery with a father who hated him and whom he reviled in return.

Shortly after having told me this deeply painful and highly important story about his mother's death, he also revealed that he had yet another secret to tell me—namely, that he had a tattoo on his back. Before I could respond in any way, Mr J ripped off his T-shirt, exposing a full-length tattoo of a very terrifying sea monster, with gnashing teeth, blood-red claws, and fuming smoke, which extended from Mr J's shoulder blades to the very top of his buttocks. As Mr J stood before me in a state of semi-nakedness, he smiled, as if taking pride in having shocked me, which he had indeed done, and then he quickly pulled his T-shirt back on over his head and torso.

I commented on the importance of his revelation about his mother's death, and, with sympathy in my voice, I expressed deep concern and sadness, aware that as an eight-year-old boy he had had an unbearable shock. I then paused and interpreted further that by having just whipped off his T-shirt so abruptly, he might have hoped that he could shock me by revealing the monster that he had carried inside himself all this time.

Mr J listened carefully to my words but did not reply in a direct way. Instead, he sat silently, pensively, almost dreamily, listening to my comments. The silence continued. I then made one more remark: I reminded him of how monstrous he had found me when he had first stepped into my office more than a year earlier. I interpreted that by having carried the guilt of killing his mother—by not having rushed to her side immediately upon hearing her gurgle—he had suffered all of his life under the weight of being a murderous monster. And I underscored that by finding his own scariness unbearable he took secret comfort in locating this frightening feeling into other people.

Mr J burst into tears and then told me that he had, in fact, killed not *one* person, but *two*.

Through his sobs, Mr J explained that he held himself responsible not only for the death of his mother, but also for the incipient death of a former male lover, whom he had infected with HIV.

The patient reported to me that, ten years previously, not long after he became diagnosed as HIV-positive, his boyfriend at the time, for whom he cared deeply, pleaded with Mr J to have unprotected anal intercourse. Mr J refused to comply with this dangerous request, but the boyfriend kept insisting again . . . and again . . . and again. Eventually, Mr J succumbed and consented to his partner's pleas for unsafe sex. Some months later, the boyfriend, too, received a similar positive diagnosis and, subsequently, became very seriously ill on many occasions.

Although the boyfriend remains alive to this day, Mr J carries a terrific sense of guilt that he has, in fact, killed this man by having sentenced him to a life afflicted by a serious disease, albeit one that can now be survived due to the heroic advances in modern pharmacology.

I shall refrain from commenting upon the ethics of the increasingly common practice of HIV-negative adults actively seeking to become infected by HIV-positive adults—a phenomenon known as "pozzing" or as "poz-chasing". Some people may well regard such an activity as perfectly justifiable, assuming that the "poz chaser" will have offered "informed consent". But others among us might well regard this behaviour as an unadulterated example of suicidality or as the enactment of unconscious traumatic experiences. Never having met Mr J's boyfriend, I do not know the meaning of his wish to be infected, but I did come to learn more and more about the awful psychological burden on Mr J for having agreed to the plan.

In subsequent psychotherapy sessions we devoted considerable attention to the possible interconnections between the death of Mr J's mother and the "pozzing" of Mr J's boyfriend. I came to hypothesise that by infecting his boyfriend in the 1990s, at a time when effective medication had become more widely available, Mr J had succeeded in both killing off his boyfriend by infecting him with a life-threatening illness and, at the same time, in bringing him back to life by paying for the boyfriend's private medical care—something that he could not have done, alas, for his dead mother.

Although we could devote infinitely more thought to the case of Mr J, and although I could describe the subsequent unfolding of his psychotherapy in much greater detail, I have chosen to discuss him in this context primarily as an illustration of the fact that one can be a murderer without having committed any crimes and without in any way having broken the law. Indeed, by having participated in consensual, adult sex with his age-appropriate boyfriend, he broke no laws, in spite of having already known about his diagnosis of HIV. And yet, in view of Mr J's traumatic history and his fear that he had killed his own mother, he lived with the burden of having committed not one murder . . . but two.

The private forensic practitioner

Thus far, I have presented a series of vignettes to demonstrate that the community-based independent psychotherapy practitioner will often encounter very seriously violent individuals who have a capacity for great cruelty. But I have not, as yet, offered any indication as to the specificities of providing treatment in such a context.

How, then, does one work with the sub-clinical forensic patient in psychotherapy?

In order to consider the practicalities of psychotherapy for such individuals, we would require a much more extended discussion. But we can, however, consider a small number of key observations and recommendations.

First and foremost, unlike our colleagues who work in secure or semi-secure forensic institutions, supported by large multi-disciplinary teams of psychiatrists, psychologists, psychiatric nurses, social workers, and creative arts therapists, the independent psychotherapist functions in virtually complete isolation and must, therefore, consider his or her own physical safety. When Miss K, a staggeringly beautiful fashion model dressed in a mini-skirt with stiletto heels, arrived in my office and explained to me that her boyfriend suffers from pathological jealousy and has, on many occasions, threatened to kill any man with whom she spends any time, I listened to her cordially, engaged her in discussion, questioned her as to the authenticity of her boyfriend's threats, and then promptly referred her to a Consultant Forensic Psychiatrist who works in a secure institution. The community-based forensic psychotherapist must always be courteous and professional but need not be unnecessarily heroic and certainly must not be masochistic.

The private practitioner must not only consider his or her own safety but must also maintain very rigorous clinical boundaries in an effort to provide structure and containment for potentially violent patients. For instance, if an ordinary, reliable neurotic patient with a good track record of attendance asked me in a thoughtful and appreciative manner to reschedule a particular session in order to attend her daughter's play at school, I would not hesitate to be helpful. But if a sub-clinical forensic patient did likewise, I would, in most instances, politely decline to do so and adhere stringently to the original appointment time. As the psychoanalyst Dr Hanna Segal (1973) observed, when working with patients who struggle with timekeeping—a metaphor for their state of disorientation—the clinician must become the reliable clock. In this way, the psychotherapy can begin to serve as something of a secure base (Bowlby, 1988). Whenever the aforementioned Mr J, the man who had infected his boyfriend with HIV, asked for changes of appointment time, I invariably declined; I found that by my doing so, his attendance record at sessions actually began to improve.

In addition to the insistence upon physical safety and the maintenance of regularity and reliability—essential characteristics of *all* psychotherapeutic work, but of special importance for the forensic psychotherapist—one must also avail oneself, quite classically, of the rich opportunities for analysis of the transference.

Mr L, a homosexual man, worked in a perfectly respectable profession by day, but in order to make extra money, he established a pornographic video business by night, in which he convinced handsome heterosexual men to masturbate on camera and then posted these amateur films on-line. As Mr L described to me the ways in which he would entice these ostensibly consenting adult males to perform sexual acts for him, I became rather concerned as to whether the men in question really understood the ultimate fate of their sex videos, and whether Mr L had truly offered them the opportunity to provide informed consent. Although Mr L had committed no obvious crime— as any consenting adult male may agree to be filmed—this patient certainly flirted with sexual exploitation. As the treatment unfolded, I endeavoured to maintain my analytically neutral position but also continued to express vigilance and concern about Mr L's after-hours business venture.

During the course of a psychotherapy session in which Mr L spoke quite painfully about his extremely difficult relationship with his emotionally distant parents, he began to cry as he recalled certain childhood memories. He told me that although he appreciated having thrice-weekly psychotherapy with me, he found the "exposure" of his mind, while free-associating on the couch, very difficult indeed. I interpreted that perhaps he harboured a wish to sit in the analytic chair himself and to place me on the couch instead, so that he could locate the feeling of being exposed into me, just as he did each night when filming these exposed heterosexual men who volunteered to participate in his pornographic videos. My comment rather surprised Mr L, who began to cry further and who, some months later, acquired a much better understanding of the potential violence of his film activities. Soon thereafter, the patient shut down his production company.

Mr M, a successful businessman, also taught me a great deal about the value of interpreting any signs of "criminality" that might creep into the transference as a creative and effective means of examining the ways in which patients might project their forensic aspects onto or into the psychotherapist. Each month I would present Mr M with a bill, and each month he would pay me with a wad of cash, sealed in an envelope. When I tried to analyse his motivations for settling his account in this fashion, wondering why a businessman of his stature would not pay by cheque, he sloughed me off each time, explaining that he had a bit of spare cash lying around at home and that he needed to use it.

Extraordinarily, on many occasions Mr M would overpay me by £50. Consequently, I would then have to return this money to him at the beginning of the next session. This enactment between us occurred for many months, until I interpreted to Mr M that perhaps he wanted me to know something about his own anxieties surrounding his business dealings, and that perhaps he struggled from a fear of some kind of criminality, which he tried to project into me, secretly hopeful that I might pocket the extra £50 in an unethical manner. This interpretation provoked much useful discussion about Mr M's fears of being robbed of money—a metaphor for his memories of being robbed of love by his mentally ill mother decades previously—and of his wish to entrap somebody else and to shame them, as he had felt shamed throughout his childhood.

The notion of the sub-clinical forensic psychotherapy patient can hardly be described as a novel idea. Since the very inception of psychoanalysis, practitioners have encountered men and women who have expressed deeply violent conflicts while reclining on the consulting room couch. As early as 1907, Professor Sigmund Freud treated a gentleman called Ernst Lanzer, better known to us as "Der Rattenmann" [The Rat Man], described by a friend as "ein tadelloser Mensch" (Freud, 1909a, p. 360) ["a man of irreproachable conduct" (Freud, 1909b, p. 159)], yet who considered himself to be a "Verbrecher" (Freud, 1909a, p. 360) ["criminal" (Freud, 1909b, p. 159)], tormented by "ein verbrecherischer Impuls" (Freud, 1909a, p. 360) ["some criminal impulse" (Freud, 1909b, p. 159)], owing to his violent and obsessive murderous thoughts.

Dr Donald Winnicott also encountered sub-clinical forensic enactments on a regular basis in his private practice in Central London. For instance, Winnicott's patient Dr Margaret Little, a qualified psychoanalyst but also a very troubled, tormented woman, committed an act of violence at the very outset of her treatment. As Little recalled,

> In one early session with D.W. I felt in utter despair of ever getting him to understand anything. I wandered round his room trying to find a way. I contemplated throwing myself out of the window, but felt that he would stop me. Then I thought of throwing out all his books, but finally I attacked and smashed a large vase filled with white lilac, and trampled on it. In a flash he was gone from the room, but he came back just before the end of the hour. Finding me clearing up the mess, he said, "I might have expected you to do that [clear up? or smash?], but later." Next day an exact replica had replaced the vase and the lilac, and a few days later he explained that I had destroyed something that he valued. [Little, 1985, p. 20]

Winnicott tolerated the destruction of objects in the consulting room with grace and equanimity. In fact, during the 1960s, his niece, Miss

Celia Britton, and her boyfriend took tea and cucumber sandwiches with Winnicott at the end of a working day, and while there, in his home, the elderly psychoanalyst pointed to a potted plant with a missing leaf. He explained to his niece and to her partner, "that plant saved my life. My last patient this evening tore it apart rather than me" (Jeremy Holmes, personal communication, 26 September 2015).

Not only did Donald Winnicott and his fellow psychoanalysts engage with patients of the sub-forensic variety, but even non-psychoanalytic psychologists have come to appreciate the widespread prevalence of so-called "ambulatory psychopathy" or "subcriminal psychopathy". Helpfully, the distinguished American psychopathologist Professor Cathy Spatz Widom (1977) had, as a young researcher, first examined the phenomenon of violence among the non-institutionalised population, inaugurating a programme of study into subclinical psychopathy.

Thus, mental health professionals have a long familiarity with the challenge of dealing with violent thoughts and enactments among ordinary psychotherapy patients undergoing treatment in warmly furnished consulting rooms situated in pleasant parts of town!

What, then, might we reasonably conclude from this brief examination of the sub-clinical forensic psychotherapy patient?

First and foremost, we may take great comfort in the knowledge that most human beings manage to contain their most violent impulses quite substantially, and that most psychotherapy patients do not enact their destructive, murderous fantasies in a deadly manner. Happily, the vast majority of men and women undergoing psychotherapy would be refused a bed at Broadmoor Hospital or at any other forensic institution.

And yet, many non-forensic patients, by virtue of being humans who have suffered from impingements, misattunements, and even traumata during infancy and early childhood, carry within their bosoms a smouldering rage, which often provokes aggressive fantasies, and which erupts, from time to time, in sub-clinical forensic enactments. Therefore, every psychotherapist must become increasingly vigilant about the possibility of meeting a sub-clinical forensic patient at one or more points during the course of a clinical career.

Sub-clinical forensic enactments vary in depth, scope, and intensity. While Donald Winnicott had no difficulty surviving the destruction of one of the leaves of the potted plant in his Belgravia consulting room, other practitioners—myself included—have struggled greatly with the complexity and with the ethicality of possessing knowledge about individuals who lace shampoo bottles with acid and who willingly infect their sexual partners with the human immunodeficiency virus. Consequently, ordinary psychotherapeutic practitioners working in the community must come to acquire a strong forensic spine and a sharply focused diagnostic radar. In view of the fact that one will, from time to time, encounter scantily-clad women who claim to have Mafiosi boyfriends, or businessmen who try to entrap one in an act of dishonesty through overpayment in cash, the private psychotherapy practitioner must endeavour at all times to remain within the bounds of professionalism in a rigorous and thoughtful manner and must find a way to create a medium secure unit of sorts in Hampstead or Harley Street or in Crouch End or Kensington, without the aid of locked wards, teams of doctors and nurses, psychotropic medications, or the protections provided by the Mental Health Act 2007.

The jobbing psychotherapist must seek appropriate clinical supervision from an experienced forensic practitioner when confronted with unexpectedly violent or potentially violent patients and must, if at all possible, avoid the sin of being too naïve. Even the most loyal, honourable, and decent of patients can surprise us with acts of criminality, either symbolic or real.

In summary, I wish to propose that we must begin to think about creative ways in which we might helpfully expand the definition of the forensic patient. Obviously, our community-based patients do not pose a threat to our society in the way that Peter Sutcliffe—the Yorkshire Ripper—had done. No one need fear walking the streets of Hampstead and of being assaulted by an accountant leaving my consulting room. But by internalising a forensic lens, the independent practitioner of psychotherapy will have the opportunity to become more sensitive to, and increasingly savvy about, the possible range and meaning of various enactments within daily clinical practice, owing to the fact that our caseloads may contain many more sub-clinically forensic patients than we might, at first, have fully appreciated.

As an independent psychotherapist who, years previously, had worked in forensic settings and who undertook training in forensic psychotherapy at the Portman Clinic, I confess that I have found such experiences deeply invaluable for my work with more ordinary patients. My immersion in the forensic world, and my continued association with forensic colleagues, has allowed me to become, I trust, more observant and even more suspicious about the potential

sadistic underbelly of human behaviour. Such contact with the forensic world has, I believe, helped me to develop a greater awareness
of the disturbing fact that every forensic patient had begun life as
a "sub-forensic" or, indeed, "pre-forensic" or, even, "non-forensic"
patient, prior to committing acts of violence. The community-based
independent psychotherapy practitioner might, therefore, find himself or herself in a valuable position to help identify and treat those
patients who have not *yet* exploded and who have not *yet* become full-
fledged forensic individuals. The traditional, classical, independent
mental health professional working in private practice might, therefore, perform an increasingly important role in terms of prevention.

With greater exposure to forensic psychotherapeutic thinking,
every mental health practitioner of whatever core professional background or theoretical orientation will have the opportunity to become
increasingly sensitised to the nature and scope of violence in its many
shapes and forms. Additionally, psychotherapeutic practitioners will
develop an improved understanding of the fact that most, if not all,
of our forensic and sub-clinical forensic patients have experienced
a welter of traumata during the earliest years of life, which will
have contributed hugely to the development of violent fantasies and
behaviours in years to come.

Psychotherapists must begin to discuss our more frightening cases
more fully, more regularly, and more honestly, so that we may all help
one another to navigate complex ethical problems and also to verbal-
ise our own countertransferential hatred (Winnicott, 1949; Kahr, 2011,
2015, 2017) towards these patients. By doing so, we will become more
proficient at facilitating the psychotherapeutic process.

How many of us have ever wondered what might have happened
if the young, impecunious Adolf Hitler, during his years as a struggling artist in Vienna, had stumbled into Sigmund Freud's consulting room for treatment? Many dramatists have, in fact, written plays
about such an imaginary encounter, such as the 2007 radio play, *Dr
Freud Will See You Now Mr Hitler*, penned by Laurence Marks and
Maurice Gran. Although one suspects that Freud might well have
failed to treat Hitler successfully, we must remember that even the son
of Alois Schicklgruber and Klara Pölzl Schicklgruber had begun life
as a non-forensic baby who then became a sub-clinical forensic man,
prior to his eruption as a full-fledged proto-forensic mass murderer.
If we intervene early in our community-based settings, we might,
perhaps, be able to contain even just a little bit of the violence that
surrounds us all too chillingly.

REFERENCES

Bollas, Christopher, and Sundelson, David (1995). *The New Informants: The Betrayal of Confidentiality in Psychoanalysis and Psychotherapy*. London: H. Karnac (Books).

Bowlby, John (1988). *A Secure Base: Clinical Applications of Attachment Theory*. London: Routledge.

Burn, Gordon (1984). *". . . somebody's husband, somebody's son": The Story of Peter Sutcliffe*. London: Heinemann / William Heinemann.

Buss, David M. (2005). *The Murderer Next Door: Why the Mind is Designed to Kill*. New York: Penguin Press / Penguin Group, Penguin Group (USA).

Freud, Sigmund (1909a). Bemerkungen über einen Fall von Zwangsneurose. *Jahrbuch für psychoanalytische und psychopathologische Forschungen, 1*, 357–421.

Freud, Sigmund (1909b). Notes Upon a Case of Obsessional Neurosis. Alix Strachey and James Strachey (Transls.). In Sigmund Freud, *The Standard Edition of the Complete Psychological Works of Sigmund Freud: Volume X. (1909). Two Case Histories ("Little Hans" and the "Rat Man")*. James Strachey, Anna Freud, Alix Strachey, and Alan Tyson (Eds. and Transls.), pp. 155–249. London: Hogarth Press and the Institute of Psycho-Analysis, 1955.

Freud, Sigmund (1916). Einige Charaktertypen aus der psychoanalytischen Arbeit. *Imago, 4*, 317–336.

Kahr, Brett (2007). *Sex and the Psyche*. London: Allen Lane / Penguin Books, Penguin Group.

Kahr, Brett (2008). *Who's Been Sleeping in Your Head?: The Secret World of Sexual Fantasies*. New York: Basic Books / Perseus Books Group.

Kahr, Brett (2011). Winnicott's *"Anni Horribiles"*: The Biographical Roots of "Hate in the Counter-Transference". *American Imago, 68*, 173–211.

Kahr, Brett (2015). Winnicott's *Anni Horribiles*: The Biographical Roots of "Hate in the Counter-Transference". In Margaret Boyle Spelman and Frances Thomson-Salo (Eds.), *The Winnicott Tradition: Lines of Development—Evolution of Theory and Practice Over the Decades*, pp. 69–84. London: Karnac Books.

Kahr, Brett (2017). *Winnicott's Anni Horribiles: The Creation of "Hate in the Counter-Transference"*. London: Karnac Books, in press.

Little, Margaret I. (1985). Winnicott Working in Areas Where Psychotic Anxieties Predominate: A Personal Record. *Free Associations*, Number 3, 9–42.

Segal, Hanna (1973). *Introduction to the Work of Melanie Klein: New, Enlarged Edition*. London: Hogarth Press and the Institute of Psycho-Analysis.

Widom, Cathy Spatz (1977). A Methodology for Studying Noninstitutionalized Psychopaths. *Journal of Consulting and Clinical Psychology, 45,* 674–683.

Winnicott, Donald W. (1949). Hate in the Counter-Transference. *International Journal of Psycho-Analysis, 30,* 69–74.

INDEX

Roots of Crime: Psychoanalytic Studies
(Franz Alexander and William
Healy), 35
Rorschach inkblot, 24
Rosen, Ismond, 56
Rosenfeld, Herbert, 134, 176, 230
Royal Commission on Capital
Punishment, United Kingdom,
49
Royal Opera House, London, 2
Rustin, Margaret, 169

Sachs, Hanns, 8, 28, 36
Sadism, 17, 23, 28, 37, 241, 245, 259
Sadomasochism, 140, 164, 178, 221,
232
Sadomasochism (Estela V. Welldon), 13
Sadomasochism in Art and Politics
(Estela V. Welldon), 13
Sanatorium Schloß Tegel, Tegel,
Berlin, Germany, 35, 59
San Quentin, California, USA, 37
Sarkar, Sarasil, 38
Sayers, Dorothy L., 25
Scannell, Timothy, 5
Schicklgruber, Alois, 259
Schicklgruber, Klara Pölzl, 259
Schmideberg, Melitta, 46, 52–53
Schutzstaffel, 51
Schwarz, Hedwig, 45
Second World War, *see* World War II
*Secrets of a Soul, see Geheimnisse einer
Seele*
Section on Forensic Psychiatry,
American Psychiatric
Association, USA, 52
Secure attachment, 113
Secure hospital, 150
Segal, Hanna, 254
Self-harm, 112, 156, 245
Selznick, David O., 54
Separation, 149
Sex Now Talk Later (Estela V. Welldon),
13
Sexton, Anne, 206
Sexual deviance, 112
Sexual deviations, *see* Perversions
Sexual fantasies, 240–241

Sexual offences, xii
Sexual perversions, *see* Perversions
Shaffer, Peter, 206
Shakespeare, William, 19, 21
Sheehan-Dare, Helen, 46
Shengold, Leonard, 177
"Shooters", 191
Shoplifting, 149
Simmel, Ernst, 35, 59
Sinason, Valerie, 11, 174, 208, 213
Smith, Iain Duncan, 184, 186
Smith, Maurice Hamblin, 41
Social Disorganization Theory, 187,
188
Social Services, 223
Social unconscious, 210
Sociopathy, 129
"Soldiers", 191
"Some Character-Types Met with
in Psycho-Analytic Work"
(Sigmund Freud), *see* "Einige
Charaktertypen aus der
psychoanalytischen Arbeit"
(Sigmund Freud)
Somerset, England, 18
Soul murder, 177
South America, 37, 38
South London, London, 245
Special Hospital for Officers,
Kensington Palace Green,
Kensington, London, 45
Spellbound, 54
Spirit-possession, 38
Splitting, 206–207, 209, 213, 214, 215
S.S., *see* Schutzstaffel
State Society of Judges and
Barristers, Budapest, Hungary,
see Reichsverein der Richter
und Staatsanwälte, Budapest,
Hungary
Staub, Hugo, 33–35, 36
St. Bartholomew's Hospital, London,
4, 5
Stealing, *see* Theft
Steiner, John, 107, 136
Stekel, Wilhelm, 29
St. Elizabeth's Hospital, Washington,
DC, USA, 52

For Product Safety Concerns and Information please contact our EU
representative GPSR@taylorandfrancis.com
Taylor & Francis Verlag GmbH, Kaufingerstraße 24, 80331 München, Germany

www.ingramcontent.com/pod-product-compliance
Lightning Source LLC
Chambersburg PA
CBHW050701280326
41926CB00088B/2415

9 781782 205050